Sir Brian Unwin studied at the universities of Oxford and Yale. After a career in the Civil Service he became President of the European Investment Bank. He has a long-standing interest in European History and is the author of *Terrible Exile: The Last Days of Napoleon on St Helena* (I.B.Tauris), which was shortlisted for the Fondation Napoléon History Prize.

'Paris and London, during the tumultuous years of the late 18th and early 19th centuries, are the background for a linked biography of two remarkable diarists, Fanny Burney and Adèle de Boigne. Both were caught up in the French Revolution and the Napoleonic wars, Adèle de Boigne escaping to England from revolutionary Paris, Fanny Burney trapped in France with her French husband after the Peace of Amiens. Brian Unwin skilfully interweaves their stories, drawing on their journals to give a fascinating picture, not only of their private dramas, but of many of the leading figures of the age.'

– Linda Kelly, author of *Holland House*

A Tale in Two Cities

Fanny Burney and Adèle, Comtesse de Boigne

Brian Unwin

I.B. TAURIS
LONDON · NEW YORK

Published in 2014 by I.B.Tauris & Co Ltd
6 Salem Road, London W2 4BU
175 Fifth Avenue, New York NY 10010
www.ibtauris.com

Distributed in the United States and Canada
Exclusively by Palgrave Macmillan
175 Fifth Avenue, New York NY 10010

ISBN: 978 1 78076 784 0

A full CIP record for this book is available from the British Library
A full CIP record is available from the Library of Congress

Library of Congress Catalog Card Number: available

Set in Arno Pro by Tetragon, London

Printed and bound in Sweden by ScandBook AB

CONTENTS

LIST OF ILLUSTRATIONS

COLOUR PLATES

BLACK AND WHITE PLATES

To my wife, Diana

PREFACE

I owe the inspiration of this book to my friend and former banking colleague Rembert von Lowis, who unexpectedly presented me one day with a copy of the *Mémoires de la Comtesse de Boigne,* with a brief 'I think these will interest you'. As I ploughed slowly through them, I became totally fascinated, both by the personality of this extraordinary woman and by the amazing range of memories she had recorded of leading events and personalities, both French and English, of the late eighteenth and early nineteenth centuries – from the 1789 Revolution to the fall of Louis-Philippe in 1848. I wondered why I had not read about her before and why she seemed to be ignored or unnoticed by most historians, and I felt a compulsion to write about her myself.

Since her memoirs covered her life in both France and England, in Paris and London, I thought that writing about her should be complemented by finding an equal and opposite English author of similar experience. I first set my cap on the indomitable Fanny Trollope, the mother of the more illustrious Anthony, who lived in Paris in the 1830s, and wrote extensively about her experiences there. But my wife Diana wisely pointed me in the direction of another Fanny, Fanny Burney, who not only was a great novelist but also left voluminous letters and diaries covering her life in London and Paris during the same era and who had a number of eminent friends in common with Adèle. To add to the attraction of writing about her, I discovered that the most crucial meeting of her life, that with her French husband-to-be Alexandre d'Arblay, occurred only a short distance from my home in Surrey, at Juniper Hall, which acted as a place of refuge to a group of distinguished French refugees from the Revolution in early 1793.

I sought, therefore, not to compose a structured chronological account of this dramatic period of European history, but to present glimpses of many of the events and personalities of that time through their eyes. I have accordingly made extensive use of quotations from their own works, in order better to convey the vividness and immediacy of their recollections and experiences. In Fanny's case, I have transcribed these quotations exactly as she wrote them, which occasionally gives rise to somewhat curious punctuation, grammar and syntax, to say the least. In the case of Adèle, I have quoted her in French throughout but have added an English translation in deference to non-francophone readers, and I hope this will not prove distracting. I thought it important to use Adèle's own words whenever possible.

Thus it is that through their own accounts we find ourselves at Versailles in 1789, with the sans-culottes storming the gates, at dinner with the fashionable Mrs Thrale, while Samuel Johnson holds forth, in Kew gardens with the 'mad' King George III, chasing after Fanny, on the Tuileries parade ground as Napoleon reviews his troops, and at Talleyrand's death bed as the old intriguer negotiates with the Pope, almost to the last breath, his readmission to the Catholic Church. I hope that readers will enjoy these accounts as much as I have done in selecting and writing about them, and also that they will particularly welcome being introduced to the less-well-known Adèle.

As well as putting me on to Fanny, I am deeply grateful to Diana for letting me monopolize our home computer unreasonably over many months and for reading through each chapter as it emerged, checking the proofs and making many valuable corrections and suggestions. As with my previous book on Napoleon, the Reform Club librarian Simon Blundell generously helped me by producing and allowing me the long lease of crucial texts. I am also grateful to the Director of the Juniper Hall Field Centre, Dr Clive Bramhall, who gave me the full run of his archives and produced some splendid pictures of Juniper Hall itself and nearby Mickleham church; to Gérard Legrain, whose timely last-minute gift of a beautiful commemorative Ville de Chambéry publication about General de Boigne enabled me to include fresh material about him in my book; and to Isabelle Janvrin, who introduced me to the delightful memoirs of the Marquise de La Tour du Pin. My warm gratitude also goes to my son Mike, a talented and very busy author and illustrator himself, for his professional advice and for again producing the chapter heading illustrations that adorn the book. Finally, I am grateful to I.B.Tauris for their support, not least from the history editor Jo Godfrey, who encouraged me in this project from the start, and to Amy Himsworth, Alex Billington and Bryan Karetnyk, each of whom added their professional skills to the production of this book. Needless to say, any errors of fact or judgement are entirely mine.

DICTIONARY OF PRINCIPAL CHARACTERS

Adélaïde, Mme (1732–1800): Daughter of Louis XV, she greatly admired Adèle's mother, who became her lady-in-waiting at Versailles. She was especially fond of Adèle as a child and fled to Italy at the onset of the Revolution.

Alexander I, Tsar (1777–1825): Emperor of Russia. Signed the Treaty of Tilsit with Napoleon in 1807 but, after Napoleon's invasion of Russia in 1812, joined the allied coalition against him and occupied Paris in 1814 and 1815. He was much admired by Adèle.

Arblay, Alexandre d' (1748–1818): French artillery officer who had been adjutant-general to La Fayette and formed part of the group of French aristocrat refugees who sought refuge at Juniper Hall in Surrey in 1793. He married Fanny Burney on 31 July 1793 and took her to live in Paris from 1802 to 1812. He was made a count and promoted to the rank of lieutenant general by Louis XVIII.

Artois, Charles, Comte d' (see Charles X)

Berry, Charles-Ferdinand, Duc de (1778–1820): Second son of the Comte d'Artois, the future Charles X, and thus in line to the throne. He held extreme conservative views and was dramatically assassinated at the Paris opera in 1820.

Berry, Marie-Caroline, Duchesse de (1798–1870): Daughter of the King of Naples, she had two children by the Duc de Berry and followed Charles X into exile in Prague. Her unsuccessful attempt to incite a royalist insurrection in the Vendée in 1832 is brilliantly described by Adèle in her memoirs.

Boigne, Benoît Leborgne, General, Comte de (1751–1830): A career soldier who made his fortune by the successful commanding of large armies in central India. On his return to Europe he married Adèle, who was then only seventeen, in June 1798, and although she made it clear that she could have no affection for him, he provided generously for her and her parents for the rest of his life. He was revered as a benefactor in his native Chambéry.

Burke, Edmund (1729–97): A friend of Dr Burney's and a leading English conservative political philosopher and politician. He campaigned against corruption in the East India Company and played a leading part in the impeachment of Warren Hastings. His best-known work, *Reflections on the Revolution in France*, condemned the events in France.

Burney, Charles, Dr (1726–1814): The father of Fanny, respected musicologist and minor composer. He was a friend of Dr Johnson's, David Garrick's, Sir Joshua Reynolds's and other literary and artistic celebrities of the day, and attracted many of them to his home, where Fanny met them. He wrote a major history of music as well as accounts of his travels on the Continent, collecting material for it. He had enormous influence over Fanny, who for many years worked as his amanuensis.

Burney, Susanna (1755–1800): Fanny's favourite sister, to whom many of her letters were addressed. She married an officer in the Royal Marines, Captain Molesworth Phillips, and lived in the village of Mickleham in Surrey, close to Juniper Hall, where she introduced Fanny to a group of exiled French aristocrats, including her husband-to-be, Alexandre d'Arblay.

Caroline, Queen (1768–1821): She married the Prince of Wales, the future George IV, who later refused to have anything to do with her and did not allow her near her child. After scandalous behaviour on the Continent, she returned to London on his accession to the throne in 1820, but he initiated a bill to dissolve the marriage and refused her admission to his coronation in Westminster Abbey.

Castlereagh, Robert Stewart, Viscount (1769–1822): English statesman, who was foreign secretary from 1812 to 1822. He played an important role at the Congress of Vienna but was subsequently unpopular in domestic politics and committed suicide in 1822, possibly as a result of hereditary dementia.

Charles X, King (1757–1836): The third son of Louis XV, who fled France during the Revolution and on return became leader of the Ultra-Royalist party. He succeeded his brother Louis XVIII as king in 1824, but was replaced in the July 1830 Revolution by Louis-Philippe, the Duc d'Orléans, and went into exile in Prague.

Charlotte, Queen (1744–1818): The wife of King George III, who was kind to Fanny when she served as her Second Lady of the Robes from 1786 to 1791; she awarded Fanny an annual pension of £100 from her private purse.

Chateaubriand, François-René, Vicomte de (1768–1848): An important figure in French literature, although he always aspired to a great political career. He admired Napoleon, but was unafraid to criticize him (as in his most famous work, *Mémoires d'outre-tombe*) and served as ambassador to London and then foreign minister for Louis XVIII from 1822 to 1824.

Constant, Benjamin (1767–1838): French novelist and political writer. Under the influence of his would-be lover, Madame de Staël, he supported the new regime in 1794, and in 1814 wrote a satirical pamphlet on Napoleon before, to his surprise and relief, being asked by him to draft a new constitution in 1815.

Crisp, Samuel (1707–83): A cultured English art connoisseur and collector as well as a close friend of the Burneys'. Known as Daddy Crisp, he maintained an influential correspondence with Fanny in her earlier years, when she often visited his Chessington home for rest and an opportunity to get on with her writing.

Delaney, Mary (1700–88): A friend of Dr Burney's and favourite of King George III and Queen Charlotte, who made available to her a grace-and-favour house at Windsor. She introduced Fanny to the king and queen there, which led to Fanny's being offered and reluctant accepance of the post of Second Lady of the Robes to Queen Charlotte.

Digby, Stephen, Colonel (1742–1800): Vice-Chamberlain to Queen Charlotte, he paid court to Fanny at Windsor, leading her to believe that he intended to propose marriage, but his surprise decision to marry a maid of honour to the Queen caused her great distress.

Dillon, Fanny (1785–1836): Daughter of General Arthur Dillon, whose second wife was a cousin of the Empress Josephine's, and one of Adèle's best friends. She was compelled by Napoleon to marry the grand marshal of his court, General Bertrand, and under protest accompanied him with Napoleon into captivity on St Helena.

Garrick, David (1717–79): English actor, playwright, producer and theatre manager. A pupil of Dr Johnson's at Lichfield and a close friend of the Burneys', his most famous role was Shakespeare's Richard III, and as manager for 29 years he made Drury Lane one of the most famous theatres in Europe.

George III, King (1738–1820): King of Great Britain and Ireland from 1760 to 1820, he is best remembered for his loss of the American colonies, his patronage of the arts, and his suffering from periods of the metabolic disease porphyria, which in the end left him permanently insane and confined from 1811 until his death.

George IV, King (1752–1830): King of the United Kingdom and Hanover, succeeding his father George III, for whom he acted as Regent from 1811 to 1820. In 1785 he secretly married a Roman Catholic, Mrs Fitzherbert, but the marriage was declared invalid and in 1795 he married Caroline of Brunswick. He repudiated her in the following year and refused thereafter to associate with her, excluding her from his coronation in 1820. As Prince Regent he was notorious for his extravagance and dissipation.

Hastings, Warren (1732–1818): British colonial administrator, who, as governor general of Bengal, laid the foundations for future British imperial rule in India. Unpopular with many of his colleagues, he was impeached for corruption before the House of Lords in 1778, but was finally acquitted, though at substantial personal financial cost. Fanny attended part of his trial and described it in detail in her journal.

Johnson, Samuel, Dr (1709–84): Celebrated British poet, critic, conversationalist and lexicographer, who almost single-handedly produced the great *A Dictionary of the English Language* in 1755. Among his other major works were a novel, *History of Rasselas, Prince of Abissinia*, an edition of Shakespeare's plays and *The Lives of the Poets*. His wide circle of celebrated friends included Dr Burney, David Garrick, Sir Joshua Reynolds, James Boswell (his biographer), Edmund Burke and Mr and Mrs Thrale, at whose house in Streatham he became almost a permanent guest until Mr Thrale's death and Mrs Thrale's marriage to Gabriel Piozzi in 1784. He was very fond of Fanny and particularly admired her first novel, *Evelina*.

Joséphine, Empress (1763–1814): First married to Alexandre de Beauharnais, by whom she had two children (Eugène and Hortense), she married Napoleon Bonaparte in 1795 and became Empress of the French when he was crowned Emperor in 1804. Unable to give him an heir, she was divorced by Napoleon in 1809, but remained on good terms with him.

Larrey, Dominique-Jean, Baron (1766–1842): Surgeon-in-chief to Napoleon's armies from 1797 to Waterloo in 1815, he introduced many improvements in military medical provision, including flying ambulances. Highly regarded by Napoleon, he carried out the mastectomy on Fanny Burney in Paris in 1811.

Lock, Frederica (1750–1832): Wife of William Lock, and god-daughter of Frederick the Great, she was a lifelong patron, friend and correspondent of Fanny's.

Lock, William (1732–1810): Wealthy art connoisseur, collector and country gentleman who built Norbury Park in Surrey, near Box Hill, and acted as friend and patron to Fanny and her sister Susanna. With Susanna he introduced Fanny to the Juniper Hall set in 1793 and paid their rent on the house. He later made available the land on his estate on which Fanny and her husband built their home, Camilla Cottage.

Louis XVI, King (1754–93): King of France from 1774 to 1791, he was overwhelmed by the Revolution and arrested at Varennes in June 1791 while attempting to flee from the Tuileries Palace to the country. Imprisoned in the Temple with his wife and family, and subsequently tried for treason, he was condemned to death and guillotined on 21 January 1793.

Louis XVIII, King (1755–1824): Brother of Louis XVI, he was King of France in name from 1795, following the death of his nephew, Louis XVII, but remained in exile until Napoleon abdicated and went to Elba in May 1814. After a brief restoration, he again fled into Belgium during the Hundred Days but was restored for a second time after Waterloo in July 1815. Suffering from gout and obesity, his well-meaning attempts to reign as a moderate constitutional monarch were frustrated by the Ultra-Royalists.

Louis-Philippe, Duc d'Orléans (1773–1850): Roi des Français (King of the French) from 1830 to 1848, he was known as the Bourgeois King. After initially supporting the Revolution, he lived abroad until 1814, and on return to France supported the liberal opposition to Louis XVIII and Charles X. He came to the throne in 1830 as a result of the July Revolution, but his initial moderation turned to repression in the face of popular discontent, and he was forced to abdicate during the Revolution of 1848. A close friend of Adèle's, he retired to exile in England at Claremont House in Surrey.

Marie-Amélie, Duchesse d'Orléans (1782–1866): Daughter of Ferdinand IV, King of Naples, and Marie-Caroline, the elder sister of Marie-Antoinette, she was Queen of the French from 1830 to 1848 and a very close friend of Adèle's.

Marie-Antoinette, Archduchess of Austria (1755–93): Queen of France, she was the daughter of Francis I of Austria and Maria Theresa, and married the Dauphin of France, Louis, in 1770. Her extravagance and alleged immorality contributed to the unpopularity of the throne. She died under the guillotine in October 1793.

Napoleon I (1769–1821): Emperor of the French from 1804 to 1815, he was born on Corsica, educated at military schools in France and rose to prominence as a young artillery officer. After a succession of outstanding victories, and promotion to the rank of general, he became first consul in November 1799, consul for life in 1802 and emperor in 1804, crowning himself in Notre-Dame in the presence of the Pope Pius VII. After the disastrous Russian campaign of 1812 and the defeat at Leipzig in 1813, he abdicated and was sent to Elba, but returned to France in February 1815 and was defeated by Wellington and Blücher at Waterloo on 18 June 1815. He was sent by the British to St Helena and died there from stomach cancer in May 1821; his body was exhumed in October 1840 and returned to Paris for burial in Les Invalides.

Narbonne, Louis, Comte de (1755–1813): French soldier and aristocrat, close friend of Alexandre d'Arblay and supporter of a constitutional monarchy, he met Fanny when he formed part of the Juniper Hall set in early 1793. He was briefly minister of war to Louis XVI in 1791–2 and after returning to France from exile in 1801 he served Napoleon in a series of high military and diplomatic posts, distinguishing himself particularly in the 1812 Russian campaign.

Ney, Michel (1769–1815): One of the original eighteen marshals created by Napoleon, and later made Prince de la Moscowa, he was nicknamed the 'Bravest of the Brave' for his outstanding courage on the retreat from Moscow in 1812. He abandoned Napoleon in 1813 but returned to fight for him at Waterloo, where he was blamed by Napoleon for destroying his best cavalry. On the restoration of Louis XVIII, he was tried for treason and executed by firing squad on 7 December 1815. Adèle blamed the Duke of Wellington for not obtaining a pardon for him.

Osmond, René-Eustache, Marquis d' (1751–1838): Adèle's father, descended from an ancient Norman family. After an early military career, he joined Louis XVI's diplomatic service but went into exile in Italy and England during the Revolution and the immediately succeeding years. He refused to serve Napoleon and was rewarded by Louis XVIII by being appointed ambassador in Turin and later in London, where Adèle, over whom he had a great influence, accompanied him.

Pasquier, Etienne-Denis, Baron (1767–1862): Trained as a lawyer, he became a counsellor to the Paris parliament. He was arrested during the Terror, but released after the fall of Robespierre. He resumed his career in 1795 and served the Empire, the Restoration and the July Monarchy in a succession of high government posts before being made chancellor of France in 1837. In their later years he and Adèle were a devoted couple and some believe they were secretly married.

Piozzi, Gabriel Mario (1740–1809): An Italian singer and music teacher, who taught Mrs Thrale's eldest daughter, Queeney. In 1784, to the disgust of Dr Johnson and the disapprobation of Fanny, he married Mrs Thrale, causing a breach for many years in Fanny's friendship with her.

Piozzi, Mrs (see Thrale, Hester Lynch)

Pozzo di Burgo, Charles-André (1764–1842): A Corsican who supported Corsican independence and refused to serve Napoleon. He entered the service of the Tsar of Russia and became his ambassador in Paris during the Restoration. He was a good friend of Adèle's and was close to her during the July 1830 Revolution.

Prince Regent (see George IV)

Récamier, Juliette, Mme de (1777–1849): Reputed to be the most beautiful woman of her time, she married a rich banker, Jacques Récamier, at the age of 15, and until the end of the July Monarchy her salon, at which Chateaubriand often read extracts of his works, attracted the elite of Parisian political and intellectual society. She was said to have many admirers, but no lovers, and was a friend of Adèle's for many years.

Reynolds, Sir Joshua (1723–92): The most famous English portrait painter of his day, he became the first president of the Royal Academy in 1768 and was a close friend of the Burneys' and Dr Johnson's and David Garrick's. Fanny much admired him.

Schwellenberg, Elizabeth Juliana (1728–97): German-born Keeper of the Robes to Queen Charlotte, she was an unsympathetic superior to Fanny when she was Second Keeper of the Robes, but behaved in a more understanding way when Fanny was let down by Mr Digby and was clearly ill towards the end of her service at court.

Sheridan, Richard Brinsley (1751–1816): An Anglo-Irish dramatist and friend of Fanny's and Dr Burney's, whose house he often visited. His most celebrated plays were *The Rivals* and *School for Scandal,* and from 1780 to 1812 he was a Whig MP renowned for his oratory in Parliament.

Staël, Germaine, Mme de (1766–1817): Daughter of the rich Swiss banker and former minister of finance to Louis XVI, Jacques Necker, she married a Swedish diplomat and for many years held the most celebrated salon in Paris, although she was banned from France by Napoleon during the Empire. She published many novels and political and historical works, the most influential being her *Considérations sur la revolution française.* She was a close friend of Adèle's and met Fanny in early 1793 at Juniper Hall when she was a member of the group of French exiles staying there. Fanny much admired her but, under pressure from her father and others, sought to avoid her company.

Talleyrand-Périgord, Charles-Maurice de (1754–1838): Originally a bishop, he became, apart from Napoleon, the most outstanding French statesman of his day, serving successive administrations, including that of Napoleon himself, in a range of high offices, particularly as foreign minister. He was a brilliant negotiator and served France well at the Congress of Vienna in 1814–15. He even negotiated with Pope Gregory XVI a reconciliation with the Catholic Church on his deathbed. Adèle knew him for many years, and Fanny met him as a member of the Juniper Hall set in 1793.

Thrale, Hester Lynch (1741–1821): After marrying Henry Thrale, a rich brewer, in 1763, she established a literary circle at their home in Streatham, which attracted many of London's literary and cultural elite, including Dr Johnson and David Garrick. Her friendship with Dr Burney led to her patronage of Fanny, on whose life this association became a major influence. Following her husband's death in 1781 she married an Italian music teacher, Gabriel Piozzi, which caused a breach in her friendship with both Fanny and Johnson. Her *Anecdotes of Samuel Johnson* provides valuable insight into Johnson's life.

Wellington, Duke of (1769–1852): The dominant military figure in Europe after Napoleon. Born Arthur Wellesley, after successful campaigns in India from 1799 to 1803 and victory over the French in the Peninsular War from 1808 to 1813, he was created the first Duke of Wellington and was the principal architect of Napoleon's defeat at Waterloo in June 1815. After remaining in Paris for a time as generalissimo of the occupying allied forces, where Adèle often came into contact with him, he returned to British politics and became prime minister from 1828 to 1831. He remained a revered national figure until his peaceful death as Warden of the Cinque Ports at Walmer castle in Kent in September 1852.

A TALE IN TWO CITIES

Fanny Burney &
Adèle, Comtesse de Boigne

INTRODUCTION

This book is a story, largely told in their own words, about the lives and experiences of two remarkable women who lived in the second half of the eighteenth, and the first half of the nineteenth centuries, which was by any standards a remarkable period of European history. In *Napoleon's Master*, a biography of the great diplomat and statesman Charles-Maurice de Talleyrand-Périgord, David Lawday called it 'the most pulse-racing age in Europe's history'.[1] The women in question are Frances Burney, later Mme d'Arblay, to be known here simply as Fanny; and Adèle d'Osmond, later la Comtesse de Boigne, but to be called here just Adèle. Their tale is of two countries, England and France, at war for much of the period; of two great cities, London and Paris, in which both of them lived for long periods; and of many of the events, great and small, and people, famous and less-well-known, that helped to shape that dramatic era. During her lifetime, Fanny was better known as a novelist, but it is to her diaries and journals, started when she was only a child, that we have recourse in this book. Adèle had no pretensions to being an author or historian and only started writing seriously in her fifties out of a sense of duty to posterity, but once started, she never stopped, and her memoirs are a brilliant record of the age.

It is sad that, so far as we know, Fanny and Adèle never met each other. But their exceptionally long lives were linked by many events and coincidences. Brought up in a thoroughly English household, Fanny married a Frenchman, whom she met when he was one of a group of exiled French aristocrats – mostly well-known to Adèle – who sought refuge from the Revolution in the leafy tranquillity of Juniper Hall in Surrey in early 1793. Among them were the celebrated Mme de Staël and the great Talleyrand himself, tales of whom fill many pages of both our authors' diaries and memoirs. Adèle in turn married in London – at the same Sardinian embassy chapel at which Fanny and her husband had undergone a Catholic marriage ceremony some years earlier – a rich and much older French general, who had obtained British citizenship. Through these and other circumstances, they came to meet, observe and write about some of the most influential figures of their time, many of whom they each knew, some intimately, both at the same and at different times. They ranged from the great captains, such as Napoleon and Wellington, who had a profound impact on their lives and whom they both saw at close quarters in war and in peace, to the respective English and French monarchies and the leading artists and intellectuals of their day, such as Dr Johnson, Joshua Reynolds, David Garrick, Mmes de Staël and Récamier, Jacques-Louis David, and the writer and would-be statesman François-René Chateaubriand.

What an eventful period it was. The greatest event of the time was, of course, the French Revolution, and the Revolutionary and Napoleonic wars that followed it. They not only shattered the peace of Europe, causing massive loss of life and acute economic strains (it has been estimated that over 2 million people died as a result of Napoleon's adventures), but also spread the disturbing rights-of-man gospel like a bush fire across the rest of Europe, awakening political consciousness everywhere. For Adèle personally, the Revolution meant desperate flight from France, just in time, followed by many years in exile – mostly in London – until Napoleon seized power, initially as first consul, and then as emperor, and it was safe to return to Paris to live in uneasy compromise with his regime. For Fanny, the influx of aristocratic refugees from France created her first links with Adèle's world, and, through her marriage to Alexandre d'Arblay, led to her own subsequent decade of virtual exile as an alien with him in Paris, while their two countries remained at war. This in turn culminated in her flight to Brussels during the Hundred Days and a time of agonizing fear and uncertainty until Napoleon's defeat at Waterloo, when she was finally able to return to England with her sick and wounded husband.

Fanny's life after Waterloo was much less eventful than her pre-marriage days when she had served her five years' hard service at court and, through her father and Mrs Thrale's Streatham circle, associated with the cream of London's intellectual and cultural elite, including Dr Johnson, and gained fame as a tyro novelist. She continued to write and edit, though mainly now her own journals and her father's memoirs, and occasionally renewed her contacts with the royal family. But she was more concerned with domestic affairs, and her later years were saddened by the deaths of those dearest to her, including her husband in 1818 and her only son, Alexander, three years before her own death in 1840. For Adèle, however, the end of Napoleon was the beginning of an active, new political and social life. After three years in London, supporting her ambassador father, she was a regular presence at the restored Bourbon Court; played an important personal part in putting the Bourgeois King, Louis-Philippe, on the throne in 1830; stayed close to him and his queen, her dear friend Marie-Amélie; and remained an influential figure in politics and in her salon, until she withdrew to end her days quietly in the country after the fall of Louis-Philippe in 1848.

It is the vividness and immediacy of the pictures they paint, and the perspective they give us on both the countries in which they lived, that make their journals and memoirs so fascinating. Fanny holds up a mirror to the fashionable London intellectual life of the late eighteenth century, to the Hanoverian court under George III and the Prince Regent, and later to imperial Paris under Napoleon, whom we see reviewing his troops on the Tuileries parade ground. Adèle takes us inside Versailles under the *Ancien Régime*, to London during her exile years, to occupied Paris and London again after Waterloo, and into the streets and over the barricades during the 1830 revolution. Fanny gives us her impressions of Paris as a city – generally unfavourable compared with London – but she is much less interested in political affairs than Adèle who, despite her denials, was a political animal to the core.

Adèle's comments on post-Waterloo England are especially interesting. The cost to both countries of Napoleon's adventures had been enormous. Despite the many administrative, legal and other reforms that he had introduced, and the booty and tribute he had seized from conquered countries, France was drained of manpower and resources. Her economy was increasingly crippled as the blockade of British commerce, the so-called 'Continental System', backfired as a result of the stranglehold on French trade by the dominant Royal Navy, which had destroyed the French and Spanish fleets at Trafalgar. England, whose population was only about a third of the 30 million or so of France at the beginning of the wars, and had started the conflict with a standing army of only some 45,000 men to face the imminent threat of invasion, had also suffered severe financial strain as it subsidized successive allied coalitions and was the first to feel obliged to introduce an income tax. But by virtue of the developing industrial revolution, accelerated investment in transport infrastructure and a rate of growth in agricultural productivity estimated to be more then two and a half times greater than that of France, it survived the wars in better economic shape and achieved a general level of prosperity unrivalled by France or other Continental countries until the end of the nineteenth century. It also, by a gradual process of electoral and other reforms, largely managed to escape the extreme political disturbances that characterized France and swept through many other areas of Europe, culminating in the Year of Revolutions in 1848.

When Adèle returned with her father to London in 1816 after a long absence, she had lost what she had earlier called her anglomania. But, although she was critical of the polluted quality of the air in London, which loomed over the city like a dirty, dark cloud, she was struck by the general prosperity of the country – the well-maintained roads, the excellent state of housing, the well-dressed children outside their neat cottages in the countryside – and wondered aloud why France had lagged so far behind. In spite of her anger with the continued occupation of Paris by allied troops under their generalissimo, the Duke of Wellington, she also praised the English system of constitutional monarchy and the rule of law. Under the latter she believed the most humble country peasant had the same access to his legal rights as the local squire. Although this was a somewhat idealized view, coming from such an acute and intelligent observer it casts a fascinating light on how a war-weary and still socially and economically divided Britain was seen by a representative of her greatest traditional enemy at that time.

ONE

FANNY

Frances Burney was born on 13 June 1752 at King's Lynn in Norfolk, the second daughter of the musician and musicologist Charles Burney, by his first wife, Esther Sleepe. There has been a good deal of academic discussion about the correct form of addressing Frances Burney. None of her novels showed her name on the title page – indeed, her first novel, *Evelina*, did not even use the conventional form, 'By a Lady' – and, for reasons we shall come to later, she took elaborate steps to conceal her authorship from her father, her friends and the public for a long period. Later novels were simply attributed to 'the author of *Evelina*', and her diaries, published posthumously, were issued under her married title, Mme d'Arblay, until the publication in 1889 of the *Early Diary*, which for the first time introduced her baptismal name, 'Frances Burney'. But 'Fanny' is the name by which she has been commonly known by critics, scholars, biographers and the general reader, and that is the name we shall use in the following chapters.

FAMILY BACKGROUND AND CHILDHOOD

Fanny was one of a large well-to-do family, characteristic of its time. It was not, unlike that of the aristocratic Adèle, in the top echelons of society, but progressively well connected and renowned for its intellectual and cultural qualities, particularly in the field of music. Older siblings were Esther (generally known as Hetty) and James. Then, after Fanny, followed Susanna (who became by far the closest to her of all her brothers and sisters), Charles, Henry Edward (who died in infancy) and Charlotte. The household ranks were swelled by two children, Richard and Sarah, born out of their father's second marriage in 1767 to Elizabeth Allen of King's Lynn, who also brought with her Maria, Stephen and Elizabeth from her own first marriage.

Fanny's father, Charles, was born in 1726 in Shrewsbury, the son of a respectable portrait painter, James MacBurney (despite their Scottish origins, the family dropped the 'Mac' and Charles inherited the simple 'Burney'), and after attending the local grammar school in Chester, where his father had moved, and serving for a time as deputy to the cathedral organist, he became the pupil of his half-brother, James, the organist of St Margaret's church at Shrewsbury. At the age of 18 he was taken on as the apprentice of the celebrated Thomas Arne – the composer of, among other things, the great patriotic song 'Rule, Britannia!' – whom he met by chance while on a visit back to Chester. Arne was on his way from Dublin to take up the post of composer at Drury Lane Theatre, and Charles worked for him in London in a somewhat more menial capacity than he had perhaps envisaged, transcribing large quantities of music, teaching junior pupils and sometimes playing in the Drury Lane orchestra or singing in the choir. It was not quite the debut and role in London he might have hoped for, but at least it gave him a foothold in the rich musical world of the capital, where he made new friends and at the house of Arne's sister, the actress Susannah Cibber, met many notables of the day, such as the incomparable Handel, the great actor David Garrick, and leading men and ladies from Drury Lane and Covent Garden theatres. This was the start of what Claire Harman has described as his 'career as an arch-networker among London's bohemians.'[1]

He was, however, rescued from what he found an increasingly frustrating apprenticeship when in 1746 he met the rich Mr Fulke Greville, a descendant of Sir Philip Sidney's friend, the famous Fulke Greville of Queen Elizabeth's day. Greville obviously took a liking to him and for £300 paid off his apprenticeship articles with Arne and took him as his companion and music-maker to his grand country seat at Wilbury House in Wiltshire. It was here that he met, courted and in 1749 married Esther Sleepe, an accomplished young professional musician herself, shortly after the birth of their first child, also named Esther (he may well have been living with Esther as man and wife for some time before the wedding). They initially moved back to live in London, but in 1751, after a brief period earning a miserly salary of £30 a year as organist at St Dionis Backchurch in the City (a church rebuilt by Wren after the Great Fire), they moved to King's Lynn in Norfolk, where Charles took over the post of organist at St Margaret's church at the higher annual salary of £100 and gave music lessons to pupils in many of the great Norfolk country houses.

The family remained in the healthy seaside atmosphere of King's Lynn for about nine years. Fanny arrived on the scene on 13 June 1752, to be followed by Susanna in January 1755 and Charles in December 1757. Fanny was by no means the brightest or seemingly most talented of the growing young family. Her older sister Hetty was rapidly displaying a precocious musical talent and was often called on to perform on private occasions before guests; meanwhile James, who showed great mathematical ability, was sent to the local Lynn Grammar School, where he laid the foundation for a distinguished career in the Royal Navy. Starting as a midshipman he finished his career as an admiral and twice voyaged round the world with Captain James Cook. James sailed with him, and distinguished himself when Cook was killed during his third world voyage in a dispute with Hawaiians in 1779. By contrast, Fanny was short – some five foot two inches in height – plain, short-sighted, very shy and, like Adèle de Boigne, always conscious of her lack of conventional physical attractiveness. Unlike Adèle, however, she had no formal education during her childhood – until much later she was effectively an autodidact – and therefore remained relatively backward. According to her father, 'She was wholly unnoticed in the nursery for any talents or quickness of study.'[2] At eight years of age she had not even learned properly to read and, if we are to believe her father's memoirs, her brother James used to tease her by pretending to teach her how to read by giving her a book upside down, which she failed to realize.

LONDON LIFE

One of the reasons for staying in King's Lynn was the benefit of the sea air to the health of Charles Burney, who had in his youth suffered from a lung ailment, and also to that of the rest of the family. However, after many promptings from his former London friends, who wanted him back in the capital, a now restored and healthy Charles moved the family back to London in early 1760, where they found a house in the then fashionable neighbourhood of Poland Street. This was the beginning of Fanny's exposure to the big, wide world of the capital city. Charles Burney rapidly won a high reputation as a music teacher and, through his pupils, acquired an increasing circle of influential and fashionable friends, many of whom frequently visited the new Burney household.

Among the early visitors were David Garrick and his wife Eva Marie Veigel, the actress Sarah Siddons, the painter Sir Joshua Reynolds, the playwrights Richard Brinsley Sheridan and Oliver Goldsmith, the politician and writer Edmund Burke, Swift's editor and author of *Cook's First Voyages* Dr John Hawkesworth, the engraver Sir Robert Strange and, crucially, Mr Samuel 'Daddy' Crisp, a well-connected gentleman of independent means and art connoisseur and collector, some 20 years older than Charles Burney, who had travelled widely on the Continent and had influential contacts in the art world. Fanny later described him as 'a scholar of the highest order; a critic of the cleverest acumen; possessing with equal delicacy of discrimination, a taste for literature and the arts'.[3] For the next 20 years he was to be the most important influence on Fanny's life, after her father. Fanny spent frequent periods in retreat at his residence at Chessington (then known as Chesington) Hall, situated in a then remote area on a 'trackless' common between Epsom and Kingston in Surrey, and, in a regular correspondence with him until his death, sought his guidance – although she did not always accept it – on almost every aspect of her personal and literary life. To Mr Crisp she was always his little 'Fannikin'. He was clearly a role model for the Revd Mr Villars, the wise and benevolent correspondent of Fanny's heroine in her epistolary novel, *Evelina*.

Like her future acquaintance – the French author and intellectual, Mme Germaine de Staël, who was reputed to sit on a stool at her mother's feet, listening to the conversation of her distinguished father's visitors – Fanny observed and absorbed the learning emanating from her father's guests. Despite being a slow starter, she revealed herself as a meticulous observer and recorder of all that took place around her. She seemed to have a compulsion to write from her earliest days and, like Adèle de Boigne, she had a prodigious memory and was the first among the children to start a diary. Her father once said of her, 'You carry bird lime in your brain – for everything that lights there sticks';[4] and in *Memoirs of Doctor Burney* she records him noting that when she was very young 'she used, after having seen a play in Mrs Garrick's box, to take the actor off, and compose speeches for their characters; for she could not read them'.[5] She later said of her own capacity to memorize, in reference to her extraordinary verbatim account of a speech by the prosecution in the trial of Warren Hastings in Westminster Hall, which she attended in 1788, 'My memory was not more stored with the very words than my voice with the intonations of all that had passed.'[6]

The Burney household did not have long to settle down together in London; it was shattered by the early death of Mrs Burney on 27 September 1762 after a long illness, no doubt induced and exacerbated by years of frequent child bearing (nine pregnancies in 12 years). During the last week of her illness, Fanny, Susan and Charles (then aged ten, seven and four years old respectively) were sent away to Mrs Sheeles's boarding school in Queen Square, and Fanny's grief was so intense that Mrs Sheeles said afterwards that 'of the Hundred children she had had the care of, she never saw such affliction in one before – that [Fanny] would take no comfort and was almost killed with crying'.[7] Charles Burney was equally grief-stricken and sought in the classical way to overcome and suppress his grief by burying himself in hard work – he had for some time been planning to write a major new history of music – and after temporarily bedding the children out with London friends, he placed Hetty and Susanna in a school in Paris, leaving Fanny, who became increasingly dependent on Daddy Crisp, largely to fend for herself in London. Fanny regretted that she had not been able to emulate Hetty and Susanna by living in Paris and learning French with them, and for a long time was extremely self-conscious about speaking French in public, although she gradually taught herself to understand the language and even took lessons from Susanna.

The family situation changed once again when Mr Burney got married for a second time to Elizabeth Allen, the widow of a rich King's Lynn wine merchant who had been a close friend of the first Mrs Burney's when they lived there. Fanny was now 15 and, like her sisters, found it difficult to reconcile herself to

her new stepmother, whom they resented and secretly called 'The Lady'. A bonus
of the marriage, however, was a dower house in the garden of her stepmother's
retained house at Lynn, which, during her frequent visits to Lynn in later years,
Fanny was able to use as a sort of literary asylum within sight and earshot of the
sea, the sailors and the ships in the harbour. Shortly after the marriage Fanny
decided, when her stepmother and father were both away, to make a bonfire
of all her secret writings so far. The bonfire consisted of a great heap of manuscript 'Elegies, Odes, Plays, Songs, Stories, Farces, Tragedies and Epic Poems',
and a novel, *The History of Caroline Evelyn*.[8] The only witness to this somewhat
melodramatic event was Susanna, who wept at such a mass destruction. It is not
absolutely clear why Fanny did this. It could have resulted from remarks made
by the new Mrs Burney. In the introduction to his great 1904 edition of Fanny's
diary and letters, Austin Dobson blames it squarely on Mrs Burney, arguing that
'her good sense, acting upon general principles, led her to inveigh very frequently
and seriously against the evil of a scribbling turn in young ladies – the loss of
time, the waste of thought, in idle cruel inventions – and the (at that time) utter
discredit of being known as a female writer of novels or romances'.[9] If this is true,
then it is no wonder that the second Mrs Burney was not as popular with Fanny
and her sisters as her predecessor.

In 1770, largely prompted by Mrs Burney, who found the house in Poland
Street too small, the family moved yet again, to a bigger house in Queen Square,
Bloomsbury, which at that time looked across open fields as far as Highgate and
Hampstead. At the top of the house, up two flights of stairs, was a small closet or
playroom where Fanny could now retire in private to compose her diary, which
she had discreetly resumed writing in 1768. She now had more time to do this
as her father was often away – he made two long tours abroad to Germany and
the Netherlands, collecting material for his great history of music. To add to his
status and professional reputation in the meantime, he was now entitled to call
himself Dr Burney, having received a Doctor of Music degree from the University
of Oxford in 1769.

When she resumed her private diary in 1768, Fanny gave as her reason in the
opening sentence: 'To have some account of my thoughts, manners, acquaintance and actions, when the hour arrives at which time is more nimble than
memory, is the reason which induces me to keep a Journal: a Journal in which I
must open my whole heart.'[10] Perhaps mindful of the stratagem that Odysseus

used to deceive and escape from the Cyclops Polyphemus in the Odyssey (he called himself 'Nobody', so that when Polyphemus cried out that 'Nobody' had blinded him and was escaping, none of the other Cyclopes rushed to help him), she decided to dedicate the diary to Nobody, since

> to Nobody can I be wholly unreserved – to Nobody can I reveal every thought, every wish of my heart, with the most unlimited confidence, the most unremitting sincerity to the end of my life. For what chance, what accident can end my connections with Nobody? No secret can I conceal from No-body, and to No-body can I be *ever* unreserved. Disagreement cannot stop our affection. Time itself has no power to end our friendship.[11]

Whether Fanny remained quite true to this ideal in later life is somewhat doubtful – in her later years she became an inveterate rewriter and censor, particularly when she came to edit her father's voluminous papers – but at least she set out with virtuous and transparent intentions.

Our knowledge of the rest of Fanny's life is now largely derived from this diary and from her letters that were first published posthumously in a seven-volume selection of *The Diary and Letters of Madame d'Arblay (1842–6)*, edited by her niece Charlotte Barrett and later supplemented by the two-volume *Early Diary of Frances Burney (1889)*, edited by Annie Raine Ellis. There have been a number of modern complete editions and selections since then, the most notable being Austin Dobson's great six-volume edition of 1904, but a convenient and comprehensive reference collection can be found in the Penguin Classics 2001 edition *Frances Burney: Journals and Letters*, selected and introduced by Peter Sabor and Lars E. Troide. This selection was chosen to present representative passages 'which reflect the great range and variety of Burney's journals and letters, giving the reader a sense of Burney – her life and thought – and of the world, events and personalities she presents to us',[12] and the rest of the present book will draw heavily on this selection.

The widening circle of interesting and eminent friends that the growing reputation of Dr Burney as a music teacher and musicologist attracted to their house in Queen Square – and later to yet another house in St Martin's Street, Leicester Square, to which the family moved in October 1774 – provided a wide variety of rich raw material for Fanny's diary and was a fundamental part of her early education. At the top of the new house was a small wooden turret, which was claimed, probably erroneously, to have at one time been Sir Isaac Newton's observatory. Like the dower house at King's Lynn and the playroom at the top of Queen Square, Fanny was able to take refuge in this as her retreat and scriptorium. As Fanny herself said, 'His [Newton's] Observatory is my favourite sitting place, where I can retire to read any of my private fancies or vagaries.'[13]

In addition to Dr Burney's musical, theatrical and artistic friends, a kaleidoscope of other fascinating and sometimes bizarre figures from other walks of life now began to crowd the pages of her diary. Among them are the towering James Bruce, the famous African explorer who in 1768, setting out from Cairo, reached Lake Tana, the source of the Blue Nile; the even taller Count Alexei Grigoryevich Orlov, Prince of the Roman Empire and allegedly the leader of the group of conspirators who assassinated Tsar Peter III, the husband of Catherine the Great; and most curiously, at the invitation of Fanny's brother – the naval officer James – Omai, a South Seas tribal chief from Tahiti, a 'noble savage' who was taken to court to meet King George III and was presented by him with a ceremonial sword. Omai arrived at the Burney house in full court dress after his attendance at St James's Palace, and Fanny was fascinated by and immensely impressed with him.

> He is tall and very well made. Much Darker than I expected to see him, but had a pleasing Countenance. He makes *remarkably* good Bows – not for *him*, but for *any body*, however long under a Dancing Master's care. Indeed he seems to shame Education, for his manners are so extremely graceful, and he is so polite, attentive, and easy, that you would have thought he came from some foreign Court.[14]

Fanny was not the only one to be impressed with Omai. In his great biography, James Boswell records that Dr Johnson also once met Omai at dinner in London in 1776 and 'was struck by the elegance of his behaviour'.[15] So far as Fanny is concerned, no details of these exotic visitors to her father's house escaped her observant eye and diligent pen.

EVELINA

Much of Fanny's time was now taken up by acting as secretary and amanuensis for her father, on whom she doted. Indeed, if she had allowed it, she might well have found herself marooned in this role for much of the rest of her life. But during his absences researching his book both in Britain and on the Continent, she was able secretly to begin work on a novel in addition to continuing her letters and diary. It is not clear exactly when she started it. She initially kept it a strict secret even from her family, but later confided in Susanna and Charles. The story had probably been accumulating in her mind since she destroyed the manuscript novel *Caroline Evelyn* among all the other works in the bonfire at Poland Street nearly a decade earlier. Much of the writing must have taken place during her 'retreat' visits to Daddy Crisp at Chessington, or when she was able to escape upstairs to 'Newton's observatory'.

The story of the publication of *Evelina* is remarkable. Fanny had previously had some contact with publishers as a result of her transcription of her father's *General History of Music*. Using this experience, but disguising her writing in case it was identified, on the advice of her brother Charles, she sent the manuscript – still unfinished and anonymous – to the reputable bookseller Dodsley. Not entirely surprisingly, he turned it down, and after further consultation with Susanna and Charles, she offered the book, still anonymous, to the publisher Thomas Lowndes. She still went to extraordinary lengths to conceal her identity, even requesting his answer to be addressed to a 'Mr King' and left at the Orange Coffee House. Lowndes agreed to read the manuscript, which was delivered by Charles in disguise, and subsequently agreed to publish it, provided the third and final volume of the novel was completed. Fanny was disconcerted by this, as she did not know how she could find the time to finish it quickly, and preferred in any case to test the market by publishing only the first two volumes. Finally, however, she accepted Lowndes's terms, completed the third volume, which was this time delivered by her other brother, Edward, and in November 1777 he offered her 20 guineas (later amended to £20) and an assurance of early publication. In January 1778, playing along with the author's continued wish for anonymity, he sent the unbound proof copies to a 'Mr Grafton' at the Orange Coffee House; only three weeks later, bound copies were available at Bell's Circulating Library on the Strand and for sale with booksellers in London.

Fanny's reluctance to reveal her identity was not surprising, although it did contrast with her initiative and enterprise in getting the novel published. She was naturally shy, diffident and hypersensitive, and dreaded a disapproving reception from family, friends or critics – above all from her beloved father. She confided in her diary: 'I am frightened out of my wits from the terror of being attacked *as an author*, and therefore *shirk*, instead of *seeking*, all occasions of being drawn into notice.'[16] And although at that time there was a growing number of young female writers and intellectuals, it was still exceptional, and regarded in some circles as not really socially respectable, for a well-brought-up middle-class young woman to embark on a career as a novelist. We must be thankful that Jane Austen, a great admirer of Fanny's novels, took no notice of this convention a few years later.

The publication of *Evelina, or The History of a Young Lady's Entrance into the World*, which, in epistolary form, tells of the adventures of a 17-year-old girl from a sheltered country upbringing who is introduced to London society, was a huge success and took the London literary world by storm. It seemed to capture vividly, as seen through the eyes of its young heroine, much of the life and times of eighteenth-century England. The first edition consisted of 800 copies, and was followed by a second of 500 and a third of 1,000, and copies appeared almost at once on the Continent. There was great speculation as to the identity of the author, and when Fanny was finally revealed as such she became the centre of great interest and celebrity. Her greatest relief was when her father – 'the author of my being' as she put it in the dedicatory verses to *Evelina* – lavished his praise on it. Her description of his declaration of approval to her when they met at Chessington – when she was almost overcome with anxiety – is quite touching. 'I have read your Book, Fanny – but you need not blush at it. – It is full of merit – it is really extraordinary.'[17] Fanny was so relieved that she fell on his neck and sobbed on his shoulder. Susanna even reported that he thought it 'the best novel I know excepting Fielding's *Amelia*, and in some respects it is better than his',[18] although it is doubtful whether Dr Burney had ever had the time or inclination to read many novels. It attracted many admirers, and new doors and experiences were now opened to Fanny.

THE THRALES AND DR JOHNSON

The most crucial and influential contact at this time for Fanny's future career was through an acquaintance with Mrs Hester Lynch Thrale, a friend of Dr Burney's. Dr Burney was the music teacher of Mrs Thrale's daughter Esther – known as Queeney – who was later to become the wife of the great Admiral Lord Keith, who, as commander-in-chief at Plymouth, broke the news to Napoleon in July 1815 that he was to be sent as a prisoner to St Helena. The young author of *Evelina* was taken up by Mrs Thrale and invited to visit and stay at the spacious Thrale house in the then countryside of Streatham. Mrs Thrale was the vivacious, well-educated and highly cultured wife of a wealthy brewer and Member of Parliament, Henry Thrale, who also became High Sheriff for Surrey. While her gatherings were perhaps not quite in the same salon league as those in Paris of Adèle's close friends and leading intellectuals, Mme de Staël and Mme Récamier, the former of whom Fanny was to meet in quite different circumstances a few years later, they brought some extremely talented people, male and female, together and were in a sense a London society equivalent.

The star of Mrs Thrale's circle was the great wit, conversationalist, poet, lexicographer and polymath Dr Samuel Johnson, who was sometimes accompanied by his biographer James Boswell. This was not in fact the first contact between the Burney family and Dr Johnson. As a relatively young, unknown musician, Fanny's father had taken the initiative in writing to him from King's Lynn in 1755 to enquire about his project for a great dictionary of the English language. Johnson had much appreciated this, and they had maintained a correspondence and kept in regular touch since then, and Johnson became a regular visitor at the Burney home. This was, however, Fanny's first really close acquaintance with the great man, who had read *Evelina* enthusiastically and praised it highly, claiming that the great novelist Henry Fielding 'never did anything equal to the 2nd volume of *Evelina*', and that 'there were passages in it which might do honour to Richardson'[19] – although it has to be said that Dr Johnson was, according to Mrs Thrale, not renowned for being a great admirer of Richardson. However, on meeting Fanny, Dr Johnson took an instant liking to her – as he was accustomed to do to a number of young female writers – which developed into a lasting friendship until his death.

Apart from Dr Johnson, whose relationship with Mrs Thrale is also the subject of Beryl Bainbridge's perceptive and entertaining novel *According to Queeney*, in which Fanny and her father feature prominently, Fanny was put on show before an ever growing circle of admiring friends. Encouraged by Mrs Thrale, Dr Johnson, Richard Brinsley Sheridan and Sir Joshua Reynolds, she started writing a comedy for the stage, entitled *The Witlings*. They believed that the ear for dialogue and the wit she had displayed in *Evelina* would equip her admirably for writing a stage comedy. She was enthusiastic about this but reluctantly dropped the idea in the face of rather stuffy opposition from her father and Daddy Crisp. Despite their own friendship with David Garrick, Mrs Siddons, Richard Brinsley Sheridan and Oliver Goldsmith as well as other actors and playwrights, they did not fancy their innocent young Fanny becoming too involved with the common theatrical crowd. Fanny nevertheless preserved the manuscript in case there was an opportunity to dust it down and bring it forward again in later years.

In 1780 she accompanied the Thrale family on a visit to the spa city of Bath, where she was introduced in grand style to fashionable society there. While at Bath, reports reached them of serious disturbances in London, which were in fact the so-called Gordon Riots, later immortalized by Charles Dickens in his novel *Barnaby Rudge*. They were led by Lord George Gordon, a fanatical anti-Catholic, as a protestant protest against the Catholic Relief Act of 1778, which had relaxed a number of legal discriminations against Catholics. The riots caused huge damage in London. Over 100 properties were destroyed and it has been estimated that some 850 people in all lost their lives – indeed more damage to property was caused in one week than in Paris during the whole of the French Revolution. The prisons of Newgate, the Fleet, the Marshalsea, the King's Bench, Wood Street Compter, Clerkenwell and Brideswell were burnt down or otherwise destroyed and the prisoners released. Several Catholic chapels were also destroyed, but the rioters failed to seize one of their main objectives, the Bank of England. According to Boswell's account of the disturbances, 'one might see the glare of conflagration fill the sky from many parts. The sight was dreadful.'[20] Although Fanny was not, unlike Adèle in Paris during the 1830 Revolution that put Louis-Philippe on the throne, actually present in London during the disturbances, she and the Thrale party in Bath were terrified by the reports they received from Susanna and others in London. They feared fire-bombing threats to Mr Thrale's business properties in Southwark, because of unfounded rumours that he was a secret Catholic, and, according to Susanna, Dr Burney had to shout out 'No Popery' to prevent a mob attacking his own house in St Martin's Street which was surrounded by Catholic families. They were also alarmed by the arrival in Bath of stagecoaches from London 'chalked over with No Popery' and by the setting on fire of the Roman Catholic Chapel in Bath.[21]

The riots in London were quickly crushed when the king himself ordered in the troops in the absence of any positive action by his ministers or the civil magistrates – rather like the personal intervention of Charles II during the Great Fire of London – and the disturbances did not spread seriously to the rest of the country. The Thrale party, however, decided to remove to the safer surroundings of the seaside resort Brighton, or Brighthelmstone, as it was then called. At that time it was still a relatively small seaside town, but becoming increasingly fashionable. Despite all this movement and excitement, Fanny had still managed to find time to start a new novel, on which she worked hard during the rest of the summer of 1780, particularly during a long-promised visit to the Crisp establishment at Chessington. This time there was less need for secrecy or subterfuge and Dr Burney, now openly proud of his successful author daughter, arranged for it to be published by the printer and bookseller Thomas Payne.

Cecilia, or the Memoirs of an Heiress came out on 12 June 1782 and, like *Evelina*, was an instant success. It told the story of Cecilia Beverley, who had inherited a large fortune on the condition that, if she married, her husband must take her name. She fell in love with Mortimer Delville, who came from an old family, who were strongly opposed to losing the family name. After a variety of sub-plots and tribulations, a way through the dilemma was finally found and the couple were able to marry happily. The first edition of 2,000 copies quickly sold out and booksellers could not satisfy their customers. Queen Charlotte was reported to like it so much that she gave copies to the royal princesses to read, and the historian Edward Gibbon – another friend of the Burneys' – said that he had read all five volumes in one day. It must also have made a great impression in due course on Jane Austen, who frequently referred to Fanny Burney's work in her own novels and probably adopted the words 'pride and prejudice' from the last chapter of *Cecilia* as the title of her own most famous novel.

At the age of 30 this was probably the peak of Fanny's literary fame. She then, however, suffered a series of blows, which caused her great grief and distress. In April 1783 her beloved mentor, Daddy Crisp, died, aged 76. Fanny travelled to Chessington just in time to 'close the Eyes of the kindest – Wisest – most scrupulously sincere and honourable, and most deeply sagacious, and most partially affectionate of Friends'.[22] She had not always taken his advice, which was often very conservative and over-protective, but she missed him and now had only her father to look to. In the summer of 1784 she also suffered what was tantamount to another bereavement. Following the death of her husband three years previously, after two strokes and a severe over-eating disorder, her friend and patron Mrs Thrale fell in love with, and decided to marry, an Italian singer and music teacher, Gabriel Piozzi, who had been a frequent visitor to the Thrale household and also taught their daughter Queeney. Both Fanny and Dr Johnson strongly disapproved of the marriage. Fanny sent her a very emotional letter in late June 1874, begging her to think again: 'O reflect a little before this fatal final answer with which you terrify me is given.'[23] This, and her half-hearted congratulations after the wedding, caused a breach in their friendship for many years which was never properly healed.

The reaction of Dr Johnson to the Piozzi marriage was much more violent. It is not entirely clear why. It could have been sheer jealousy, since Piozzi would now replace him as the first man in Mrs Thrale's life. He may even have had aspirations to marry Mrs Thrale himself. It could also partly have been prejudice against a foreigner – Boswell once, with reference on this occasion to Frenchmen, spoke of Johnson's 'unjust contempt for foreigners';[24] or he may have felt, as a genuine admirer of the late Henry Thrale's, that Piozzi could in no way be worthy of filling that good friend's bed or shoes. He also no doubt feared, at the more practical level, that with Henry Thrale gone he would no longer enjoy the same hospitality and patronage as in the past. He really had done very well out of the Thrales. Once he was established with them, he generally spent from Monday to Friday at Streatham, or at their house near the brewery in Southwark, being fetched and returned in Mr Thrale's carriage; he was extremely well fed and comfortably accommodated (his appetite as he grew older was legendary, not least his passion for peaches); he was given £100 by Mr Thrale to establish a library in the Streatham house, and he even had a summer house built by Mrs Thrale for him to work in the garden and a small laboratory for his experiments. All this might have ceased, and there is certainly evidence that after Thrale's death Johnson's relationship with Mrs Thrale began to cool off. Boswell comments that when 'the manly authority of the husband no longer curbed the lively exuberance of that lady; and as her vanity had been fully gratified by having the Colossus of Literature attached to her for many years, she gradually became less assiduous to please him.'[25]

It was probably a combination of all these factors, but whatever the precise reason, his immediate reaction was to break off all relations with the now to-be Mrs Piozzi. He told Fanny: 'She has disgraced herself, disgraced her friends and connexions, disgraced her sex, and disgraced all the expectations of mankind! If I meet with one of her letters I burn it instantly. I have burnt all that I can find. I never speak of her and I desire never to hear of her more.'[26]

Johnson's extreme reaction, and Fanny's surprisingly uncharitable though more moderate one, did neither of them any credit at the time. In their anger and disappointment – exacerbated in Johnson's case because the first he heard of Mrs Thrale's decision to marry Piozzi was not from her personally, but in a formal legal letter sent to all the trustees of her husband's estate – neither showed much appreciation of the loveless nature of Mrs Thrale's first marriage to a man who, however hospitable, generous and intellectually worthy of their company, appears to have been a demanding and even bullying husband. Although she was kept in luxury and prosperity, allowed to indulge her literary tastes and run her circle, and inherited from him a large fortune, Hester Thrale was permitted little say in the running of the household and throughout her marriage was in effect used as a breeding machine, without ever being able to produce the surviving male heir that her husband so wanted.

The episode is perhaps one of the less attractive in Fanny's long life. To his credit, however, Johnson did reconsider. He agreed to be an executor for Henry Thrale's will, which left Mrs Thrale a very rich widow after she eventually sold the brewery for £135,000 pounds (from which Johnson himself only received an executor's fee of £200), and soon after his angry outburst he wrote again to the now Mrs Piozzi in the following more friendly terms:

> I wish that God may grant you every blessing, that you may be happy in this world for its short continuance, and eternally happy in a better state; and whatever I can contribute to your happiness I am very ready to repay, for that kindness which soothed twenty years of a life radically wretched.[27]

It is satisfying to end the episode on this note, for Johnson was not really at heart a man to bear malice, and he owed so much to the former Mrs Thrale. But sadly, for Fanny, all this was overtaken by Johnson's death, after several years of declining health, on 13 December 1784 at the age of 74. Fanny had become very close to him and, having seen him only four days before his death, she was grief-stricken at not being permitted to visit him at his sickbed on the day before he died.

In 1782 Fanny had also suffered a further double-edged loss. Her favourite and closest sister, Susanna, had left home to marry Captain Molesworth Phillips, a marine comrade of her brother James, who had also accompanied Captain Cook on his last, fatal voyage and displayed great personal heroism by returning, when already wounded himself, to rescue a fellow shipmate in danger of drowning in the incident in which Cook was killed. This deprived Fanny of Susanna's company at home but, after initially moving to live in Boulogne, which caused Fanny and her father concern, the Phillipses settled in a cottage in the small village of Mickleham, at the foot of Box Hill in Surrey, near Dorking, which had a profound effect on Fanny's later life. But before this happened came an extraordinary period in Fanny's life as a result of being introduced in society to the elderly Mrs Mary Delaney, the widow of Dr Patrick Delaney, a friend of Jonathan Swift's. Mrs Delaney was a favourite of King George III's and Queen Charlotte's, who not only gave her a small house near the gates of Windsor Castle when she gave up her home in London, but also a pension of £300 a year.

SECOND KEEPER OF THE ROBES AT WINDSOR

In December 1785 Fanny was invited by Mrs Delaney to stay with her at Windsor. Mrs Delaney had praised Fanny's novels highly to the king and queen, and on 16 December, while Fanny was in the drawing room of Mrs Delaney's cottage after dinner with Mrs Delaney and friends, there was a knock on the door and 'a large man, in deep mourning, appeared in it – entering, and shutting it himself, without speaking'.[28] It was the king, in mourning for the death of his brother-in-law, Prince George of Mecklenburg-Strelitz. Fanny was terrified. 'A Ghost could not more have scared me [...] O mercy! thought I, that I were but out of the Room! which way shall I escape? and how pass unnoticed? – There is but a single Door at which he entered in the Room!'

She could not, however, escape the king, who engaged her in a long conversation about herself, her family, her novels – especially how she had been able to write and publish *Evelina* without her father's knowledge – and whether she intended to write more. Shortly afterwards, Queen Charlotte also entered the room and, after being briefed by the king on his conversation with Fanny, spoke to Fanny too. For Fanny it was all totally unreal. In a letter to Susanna she described the scene in the following terms:

> It seemed to me we were *acting a Play*; there is something so little like common and real life, in every body's standing, while talking, in a Room full of Chairs, and standing, too, so aloof from each other, that I almost thought myself upon a stage, assisting in the representation of a Tragedy, in which the King played his own part, of the King, Mrs Delaney that of a veritable confident, Mr Bernard, his respectful attendant; Miss Port, a suppliant virgin, waiting encouragement to bring forward some petition; Miss Dewes, a young Orphan, intended to move the Royal compassion; and myself, – a very solemn, sober, and decent *Muse*.

This was a wonderfully amusing and satirical description of Fanny's first encounter with the king and queen. Little, however, did she imagine that this, and subsequent contacts while she was staying with Mrs Delaney at Windsor, would lead to the unexpected, and unwelcome, offer in June 1786 of the position of Second Keeper of the Robes to Queen Charlotte at a salary of £200 a year. The queen had obviously taken a great fancy to Fanny. Fanny, however, did not want the position and was 'extremely frightened and full of alarms at a change of situation so great, so unexpected, so unthought-of',[29] but it was an offer she thought she could not turn down. She needed the money to contribute to the family income, and the position at court might enable her to help her father's career – he was disappointed at having been passed over for the position of Master of the King's Band – and also that of her brother James, whose career in the navy had stalled. She therefore, with great misgivings, accepted the offer and reported for duty at the Queen's Lodge, Windsor, in July 1786.

The next five years were among the most unhappy of Fanny's life. Unlike Adèle, who was born into the purple at the court of Louis XVI and Marie-Antoinette at Versailles, Fanny had royalty, as it were, thrust upon her. She had no experience of court manners or etiquette and, apart from her secretarial duties for her father, had lived a free-moving, free-thinking and free-talking life. Although Queen Charlotte was kind and considerate herself, Fanny was under the direct authority of Mrs Juliana Schwellenberg, the queen's senior Keeper of the Robes, whom the queen had brought with her on her marriage journey to London from Germany in August 1761. Mrs Schwellenberg turned out to be a harsh and unsympathetic taskmaster, whom even the generally tolerant king came to find very tiresome. The rigid court routine and lack of personal freedom became more and more oppressive to Fanny, and the strain told on her health. She also suffered greatly from a disappointed relationship with a senior courtier, Colonel the Hon. Stephen Digby, who appeared to be close to making an offer of marriage to her. In the end it was with great difficulty, and only when at last her father realized how damaging her position was becoming to her health, that Fanny persuaded the queen in July 1791 to accept her resignation. At a tearful final interview, the queen expressed her appreciation and, to Fanny's surprise, granted her from her personal account an annual pension of £100. Fanny was now free, though much wounded in health and spirits. But this miserable interlude in her life provided the raw material for some of the most remarkable entries in her letters and diaries, describing in intimate detail life at court and in the royal household, including fascinating accounts of her encounters and relationship with George III during the onset and continuation of his illness.

THE JUNIPER COLONY

As Fanny began to recover her health and spirits, and found more time for writing, she took advantage of visits to Susanna in her cottage at Mickleham, and to their wealthy neighbours and patrons William and Frederica Lock,[30] whom she had first met with Susanna before she took up her post with Queen Charlotte. Indeed, Frederica Lock had written to her on an almost daily basis during her darkest days with the royal family and done a great deal to help sustain her morale. The Locks, as well as having a fashionable town house in Portland Place in London, had in 1774 built Norbury Park, a large country house that looks southward across the Mole Valley – which now houses Denbies, the largest vineyard in England – to the steep chalk slopes, the Whites, of Box Hill, which Jane Austen came to know so well a few years later and used as the site of the famous picnic in *Emma*. William Lock was a well-known and generous art connoisseur, who had brought a copy of the *Discobolus* of the Greek sculptor Myron to Britain; Frederica Lock came from an extremely well-connected family – her godfather was Frederick the Great. Together with Susanna they introduced Fanny to the 'Juniper Colony', as the group of distinguished French exiled aristocrats who had rented as a refuge the nearby Juniper Hall became known.

Originally a large coaching inn, called the Royal Oak, Juniper Hall was built in the seventeenth century and developed in the mid eighteenth century into a substantial country house with a classical portico, tall arched windows and delicate plasterwork inside. The most distinguished feature of the house was a sculptured drawing room, designed in the Adam manner by an amateur artist, Lady Templeton, whose walls were covered with relief panels of classical scenes and figures, centring on a tall carved fireplace in grey-and-white marble. The house stands in a glorious valley, close to Mickleham village, nestling between the nearby hills, and is now a Field Studies Centre owned by the Field Studies Council. It now echoes to the voices of children enjoying nature-study courses and rambles rather than to those of exiled French aristocrats. But it is not difficult for a visitor still to feel or imagine the ghostly presence of those exiled companions, who strolled across its lawns and congregated in the elegant drawing room over 200 years ago…

The house was let to the group of French émigrés by a Mr Jenkinson, described by Constance Hill in her 1904 history, *Juniper Hall*, as 'an affluent lottery-office keeper'[31] (having vacated the house he built another one for himself, Juniper Hill, on a nearby hillside, which still remains as a private residence). Another émigré family, headed by Mme de Broglie, also took a small cottage in nearby Mickleham village. We do not know why they chose Mickleham and Juniper, except that they were reasonably close to and convenient for London, but also tucked away in beautiful countryside where they could hope to rest, escape notice and keep a low profile. As supporters in principle of the Revolution, although opposed to its violence and excesses and in favour of a constitutional monarchy, they were nevertheless politically suspect in government circles in London and apprehensive about their ability to remain as refugees in England. As we shall note later, Fanny was warned by her father and others against being seen to associate with them too closely, and the most celebrated of them, Charles-Maurice de Talleyrand-Périgord, was later expelled by Pitt under the new Aliens Act.

Fanny first heard about them when in September 1792 Susanna wrote to her: 'We shall shortly, I believe, have a little colony of unfortunate French noblesse in our neighbourhood.'[32] 'Unfortunate' was an understatement, as most of the refugees had had their estates in France confiscated and were liable to the death penalty if they returned to France. Indeed, most of them were lucky to have escaped France with their lives, and it is hard to overstate the violence, horrors and arbitrary lawlessness that they had been exposed to in Paris. The kind of hazards they faced are graphically described in the journal of the notorious Grace Dalrymple Elliott, a Scottish courtesan, socialite and sometime mistress of the Prince of Wales, who settled in Paris in 1786 and became the mistress of the Duc d'Orléans. She was arrested in 1793, held for several months in various prisons at Versailles and in Paris awaiting death by the guillotine, saw many of her aristocratic friends summarily removed and executed, but was mercifully released after the death of Robespierre. At one stage she shared a cell with Josephine Beauharnais, the future empress and wife of Napoleon.

In her letter from September 1792, Susanna went on to explain to Fanny that the French party had taken Juniper Hall and that 'our dear Mr Lock'[33] had sent word to the landlord that he would pay the rent. The main members of the party as it eventually formed were Mme de Staël, the leading socialite and liberal intellectual of her day (who had used her diplomatic status as wife of the Swedish ambassador in Paris to help many of the others to escape); the great diplomat and statesman-to-be, Charles-Maurice de Talleyrand-Périgord, the former Bishop of Autun; the former French Minister of War, Louis, Comte de Narbonne, who was at the time Mme de Staël's lover; the former French parliamentary deputy the Marquis de Lally-Tollendal and his mistress, the Princesse d'Hénin; the Marquise de la Châtre and her lover, François de Jaucourt; and, most significantly, Alexandre d'Arblay, a handsome artillery officer who was a close friend of de Narbonne's and had served as chief of staff to the French Revolutionary general and politician, the Marquis de Lafayette.

By November 1792 Susanna was writing to Fanny: 'It gratifies me very much that I have been able to interest you for our amiable and charming neighbours.'[34] Fanny needed little further persuasion. She had already been intrigued by Susanna's accounts of the brilliant wit and conversation of this group and was soon swept into their circle, introduced to them by both Susanna and the Locks. 'Ah what days were those of conversational perfection, of wit, gaiety, repartee, information, badinage and eloquence,'[35] Fanny later wrote. Fanny was dazzled by their high-born background and status, as well as the romantic circumstances of their flight from revolutionary France and the near loss of their lives; to them she was a famous and best-selling authoress. She was nevertheless increasingly cautious about her relationship with the formidable Mme de Staël in view of her 'immoral' relationship with de Narbonne (which also seemed to shock some of the local Mickleham residents) and her radical political views. She began to find, however, that she was increasingly attracted to the soldier, Alexandre d'Arblay, who with his 'very fine figure and face'[36] reciprocated her feelings. Soon they agreed to tutor each other in their respective languages, and in a letter of February 1793 to her father, who was extremely unhappy about this relationship, Fanny wrote

> Mr d'Arblay is one of the most singularly interesting Characters that can ever have been formed. He has a sincerity, a frankness, an ingenious open-ness of nature that I had been unjust enough to think could not belong to a French Man. With all this [...] he is passionately fond of literature, a most delicate critic in his own language, well versed in both Italian and German, and a very elegant poet.[37]

Fanny was clearly aware of where their blossoming relationship might lead and was anxious to win her father's approval. She was reluctant to commit herself, however, as she was also concerned – as with the relationship with Mme de Staël – that the possibility of marrying a Frenchman should not prejudice her standing at court and threaten her pension. Alexandre d'Arblay was, however, an assiduous and romantic wooer. On one occasion he even walked all the way from Juniper Hall to Chelsea – well over 20 miles – to present a rose tree to Fanny, only to find that she was not at home. After much hesitation and soul-searching (which induced some of the Juniper set to label her a prude), Fanny finally consented to marry him, despite her father's continuing opposition and the fact that they would not have much more than £120 a year to live on – the income, nevertheless, she was told, of a moderately well-paid clergyman. This was a very important decision by Fanny and, apart from her determination to continue her writing, a strong assertion of her independence.

MME D'ARBLAY

The marriage of the now 40-year-old Fanny to Mr d'Arblay accordingly took place on 28 July in the beautiful St Michael's church in Mickleham, directly opposite the

Running Horses coaching inn. There is a plaque to commemorate the wedding on the right-hand wall of the porch as you enter the church, on which is inscribed 'And never, never was union more blessed and felicitous'. Sadly, Dr Burney did not attend the wedding, but Susanna and Captain Molesworth Phillips, Fanny's brother James, and Mr and Mrs Lock were present, and Fanny received letters of congratulations from both Mme de Staël and Talleyrand. In order to ensure that Fanny would not be excluded from any family property rights that d'Arblay might recover were there to be a counter-revolution in France, a second ceremony took place in the chapel of the Sardinian ambassador in London on 30 July. It is an extraordinary coincidence that the marriage of Adèle d'Osmond and General de Boigne also took place at the same location some five years later.

Fanny now embarked on her new life as Mme d'Arblay. The couple first lived in Surrey, in rented accommodation in Mickleham village, and then in the village of Great Bookham only a few miles away, but eventually moved to a cottage designed and partly built by d'Arblay on a five-acre plot of land on the Norbury estate at West Humble (a hamlet on the other side of the Mole Valley, opposite Mickleham and Box Hill) given to them as a wedding present by William Lock. It was named Camilla Cottage, after the novel *Camilla, or A Picture of Youth* – Fanny's third – which she published in July 1796 and with whose proceeds the cottage was largely financed. In order to raise money up front, and on the advice of her brother Charles, who acted as her agent, Fanny published the novel by subscription. It was dedicated to Queen Charlotte, and among the subscribers were 'Miss J. Austen of Steventon Rectory' and, surprisingly, Mrs Schwellenberg. She also sold the copyright to Messrs Payne and Cadell of Mews-Gate and the Strand for £1,000. The first edition of 4,000 copies, led by the subscription, sold out in just three months, but later sales were slower and it was not reprinted until 1802. It dealt with the matrimonial concerns of a group of young people and centred on the love affair of Camilla Tyrold with her suitor, Edgar Mandlebert. Its strength lay in the comic situations and absurd characters, which Fanny excelled in depicting, but, in five volumes, it was far too long. Fanny was conscious of this and in presenting specially bound copies to the king and queen and royal princesses – she travelled specially to Windsor to do this – she apologized to the royal family for its excessive length. This occasion was a very important one for Fanny since it was her first visit to Queen Charlotte since her marriage. She was much relieved to be received kindly and graciously.

Giving birth to her third novel was not Fanny's only preoccupation at this time. In December 1794, at the dangerously late age of 42, she gave birth to their first and only child, Alexander, and now had the young baby to care for. In addition to the work on *Camilla* she had also resumed other writings. These included an unsuccessful play, *Edwy and Elgiva*, which lasted only one night at Drury Lane after terrible reviews in March 1795, and, as an act of filial duty, a long pamphlet for a charitable cause supported by her father entitled *Brief Reflexions Relative to the Emigrant French Clergy*. Fanny was upset at the failure of her play, but she should not have taken it too badly, as the great Dr Johnson's first play, *Irene*, had been an equal failure too – it lasted for just three nights – when David Garrick staged it, also at Drury Lane, in 1749. On the whole, however, this was a happy time in Fanny's life. While she looked after little Alex, visited Susanna and the Locks and got on with her writing, her husband worked hard on their garden, of which they were immensely proud. A stained-glass window by Harry Stammers, mounted on a the wall of the main staircase at Juniper Hall, has a delightful image of d'Arblay offering a cabbage to Fanny. There is a wonderful description by Fanny of d'Arblay attempting to cut the hedges with his army sabre:

> I wish you had seen him, yesterday, mowing down our Hedge – with his *Sabre*! – and with an air, and attitudes so military, that if he had been hewing down other legions than those he encountered – i.e. of spiders – he could hardly have had a mien more tremendous, or have demanded an Arm more mighty.[38]

Alas, however, all the hard work was almost entirely negated when one day horses and other animals from a neighbouring farm broke in to the garden. Fanny described the scene of destruction in a letter to her father of 22 March 1800:

> The Horses of our next neighbouring Farmer broke through our Hedges, and have made a kind of bog of our Meadow, by scampering in it during the wet; the sheep followed, who have eaten up All our Greens – Every sprout and Cabbage and Lettuce, destined for the Winter – while the Horses dug up our Turnips and carrots, and the swine, pursuing such examples, have trod down all the young plants, besides devouring whatever the others left of vegetables! Our potatoes, left – from our abrupt departure, in the Ground,

are all rotten or frost-bitten – and utterly spoilt; and not a single thing has our whole Ground produced us since we came home. A few dried Carrots, which remain from the in-doors collection, are all we have to temper our viands.[39]

It was a very sad and discouraging setback to their ambition of self-sufficiency and the joys of country life.

The eventual fate of the cottage was also a sad one. While d'Arblay was back in Paris in 1814, seeking a place in the royal army, Fanny was left to sort out their affairs in England and received a solicitor's letter informing them that Camilla Cottage was to be sold. Apparently William Lock's son and heir, another William (who changed the spelling of his name to 'Locke') had decided that for financial reasons the Norbury Park estate had to be put on the market, and it was discovered that there had in fact been no legal agreement between the two families over the land on which the cottage had been built, and that it therefore had to be sold as part of the whole estate. Despite strong protestations to William by d'Arblay, the sale went ahead and the d'Arblays received only £700 as compensation – much less than they had spent on building and furnishing the cottage. It also, of course, left them with the problem of where to live when they settled back for good, as Fanny hoped they would, in England. It was an unhappy ending to their Surrey idyll. Even more sadly, Camilla Cottage was destroyed in a fire in 1919, although there is a commemorative plaque on a wall facing the present Box Hill and West Humble station.

This was, however, well in the future, and in January 1800 Fanny suffered a most grievous blow in the death of her beloved sister and most frequent correspondent, Susanna, who was returning from an enforced stay in Ireland with her by now estranged husband, who owned family property there. For some time the marriage had been an unhappy one, and Susanna had been reluctant to go there in the first place, but she had in effect been blackmailed by Captain Phillips, who had threatened to take the children away from her if she did not do so. Fanny's intense grief was compounded by the fact that, as a result of a misunderstanding about which port in Wales Susanna would arrive at, she failed to meet her before she died. At the same time, Fanny was becoming increasingly worried that her husband, whose name had been struck off the official list of French émigrés, and who could therefore return with impunity to France where Napoleon was now first consul, would wish to do so in order to try to retrieve at least some part of his own family fortune. She was particularly concerned that he might also, out of a misplaced (in her view) sense of honour and duty, seek to resume service in the French army, having fervently hoped that he had given up soldiering for good.

LIVING IN PARIS

After an abortive attempt in November 1800 to cross to France via Rotterdam, d'Arblay finally got there after enduring a terrible crossing from Deal, near Dover, to Calais in October 1801. His visit, however, was unsuccessful. He only secured a trivial amount of the family fortune, and the only military post offered to him was the command of a brigade in the disastrous expedition to Saint-Domingue (now Haiti) to crush the rebellion led by Toussaint Louverture against French colonial rule. Some two thirds of a French army of 34,000 sent there died, mainly of disease (Adèle's father's brother had also been killed there during this campaign), and if Alexandre d'Arblay had gone there he would probably not have escaped that fate. Thankfully (for Fanny), even if her husband had accepted the offer he would not in the event have been allowed to take it up since, to Napoleon's great displeasure, he stipulated as a somewhat unreal condition of serving in the French army that he would never take up arms against the people of his adopted home, Britain. The first consul clearly could not accept this. Disappointed, d'Arblay returned to England, but went back again to France in February 1802, followed by Fanny and Alex in April. The d'Arblays first established themselves in a rented apartment near the Champs-Elysées, but later, for reasons of both health and economy, moved a mile or two out of Paris to a small house in the village of Passy, overlooking the Seine.

Fanny was not at first much impressed with Paris, which in her view bore no comparison with London. However, when peace between England and France was restored with the Treaty of Amiens in March 1802 and Napoleon was elected first consul for life in August of the same year, something of Paris's former cultural and social life began to return. The d'Arblays could not afford to entertain expensively, but they saw many friends, including some of the old Juniper Hall set. Among them was Mme de Staël, now the most celebrated salon hostess in the capital, but Fanny found herself playing a somewhat embarrassing game of hide-and-seek in attempting to avoid her, reminiscent of the time when, at her father's insistence, she had tried to break off contact with her at Juniper Hall.

As Fanny did not have access in Napoleonic France to her royal pension, d'Arblay took a modest and poorly paid office job at the Ministry of the Interior to supplement his own meagre army pension. It is unlikely that Fanny would have remained voluntarily in France – unlike her husband, who wanted to bring Alex up as a soldier, she was not eager to see her son educated as a young Frenchman, either in the army or in a civil career – but in the event she had no choice. The Amiens peace treaty between England and France soon broke down, and as an English citizen she became a virtual prisoner for a decade until she managed to obtain a passage for herself and Alex to England aboard an American ship, the *Mary Ann*, in August 1812. In fact, in order to deceive the French authorities, the ship was officially scheduled as sailing to the United States, but the captain had agreed to disembark Fanny en route at an English port. Given the state of war now existing between Britain and the United States, however, it was intercepted and seized by an English warship, which took Fanny and Alex safely to Deal. As she had explained in a letter to her father as early as 14 May 1803, although she had managed to escape, it was 'completely impossible for him [d'Arblay] to quit his country during a war'.[40]

Our detailed knowledge of her life in Paris during this long period is more limited since the war made communications difficult and dangerous, especially for aliens, and there are fewer letters from this time. The d'Arblays were also preoccupied with managing everyday life on a small income and organizing the education and future of their son Alex. However, a letter to her father of May 1802[41] (before Britain revoked the Treaty of Amiens and declared war once again) gives a vivid picture of seeing Napoleon review his troops on the Tuileries Palace parade ground, and her journal also describes a much later (undated) visit to the studio of Napoleon's official court painter, Jacques-Louis David, at the invitation of Mme David, to view two new portraits of Napoleon that were on display. It is interesting to speculate whether Fanny might unwittingly have come into contact with Adèle in Paris during this period – it was perfectly possible, as they were both resident in Paris – but there is no evidence of any meeting.

In September 1811, however, Fanny suffered a very serious and dangerous operation, described at length in a letter written between March and June 2012 to her sister Hetty. For some years Fanny had been suffering from inflammation of her right breast and she was eventually advised by her doctors that 'a small operation would be necessary to avert evil consequences'.[42] With unbelievable courage Fanny agreed to the operation, and on 30 September 1811 Baron Larrey, the eminent military surgeon, performed a mastectomy on her. Fanny's long account of the operation in a letter to her sister Hetty some months later[43] makes almost unbearable reading and it is not surprising that it was omitted from the first edition of her journals. We shall return to it in more detail later...

As already stated, in August 1812 Fanny returned to England with Alex, and in March 1814 she published her last and longest novel, *The Wanderer, or Female Difficulties*, on which she had been working in Paris. Although profitable – it was said that she earned £7,000 from it, although this is probably a substantial overstatement – it was not a success, and despite the first edition being sold out three days before publication, more than half of the second edition remained unsold. It was exceptionally long and rambling, as befits the title, and critics and admirers of Fanny's earlier novels were largely disappointed. They had expected her to give them a greater insight into life in Paris and a denunciation of imperial France under Napoleon, whereas what they got was more an exposé of regency Britain. The eminent essayist and critic William Hazlitt gave it a particularly scathing review in the journal *Edinburgh*, for which Fanny and her friends never forgave him. However, Fanny recognized the reasons for the disappointment: she wrote, 'I attribute it to the false expectation that the Book would be a picture of France', but she declared herself 'very harshly mangled'.[44]

BRUSSELS AND THE HUNDRED DAYS

Fanny had, however, been preoccupied by other concerns, including the illness and death of her beloved 88 year old father in April 1814. She was also very worried about her husband, who had remained in France, and in November 1814 she returned once more to France herself to join him. After another unpleasant and stormy crossing, disaster struck at Calais, where d'Arblay, who had come to meet her at the quayside, was seriously injured when he was struck and knocked over by a runaway cart. According to Fanny, 'he was not only renversé, the brancard [shaft] striking him upon his breast, but flung to some distance by the force of the blow'.[45] With great difficulty Fanny managed to get him back to Paris and treated by Baron Larrey, but she was also desperately concerned that his sense of honour and duty would, despite his injury and his generally weak and dispirited condition, lead him to seek service in the royalist army again.

This was indeed the case; d'Arblay accepted a commission as a sub-lieutenant in the Garde du Corps of the restored Louis XVIII. The formal rank was low, and the salary meagre, but he regarded it as a great honour. Their world, like everyone else's, was, however, turned upside down by Napoleon's daring escape from Elba and return to Paris after the astonishing march from Cannes in March 1815. Although Fanny at first did not take the crisis too seriously, she still had a curious confidence in Napoleon, who she thought must know exactly what he was doing. When guns were eventually heard on the outskirts of Paris, d'Arblay rushed home from his office to tell Fanny that Napoleon's troops could be seen encamped just outside the city gates. They knelt together to pray for each other's preservation and then separated. D'Arblay, like a modern Don Quixote, gathered up his military paraphernalia – helmet, pistols, bayonet and ammunition – mounted his horse, and on 13 May – his birthday – rode out of the courtyard crying, 'Vive le roi.' Fanny was desperately worried. D'Arblay was far from well. She wrote of 'his shattered health, and fading Form for-ever before my Eyes'.[46] She was then left to plan her own escape and, after swiftly packing in a bag a few necessaries and rushing to a friend's apartment, she managed to obtain a lift to the Belgian border in the carriage of their old Juniper Hall friend, the Princess d'Hénin.

After travelling for two days and nights without stopping, except to change horses, they eventually reached Brussels via Tournai, Fanny disguising herself as her friend's chambermaid in case they met officials hostile to the English along the way. In the meantime d'Arblay reported for duty at a review of the royalist troops on the Champs de Mars, but was disappointed when, after it had become clear that there had been an almost complete desertion of the royalist army to Napoleon, the king fled to Lille as news of the Napoleon's imminent arrival in Paris reached him. He was then instructed to proceed to Trier to try to muster deserters from Napoleon's army into a force to fight for the French king. His own journey made him ill. He rode for 26 hours in driving rain and was so weak that on arrival he had to rest in bed for two days.

The following weeks were a nightmare of harrying anxiety for Fanny in Brussels and are described vividly in her 'Waterloo Journal' and in other letters of the period. Conflicting rumours about the dispositions of Napoleon's and Wellington's armies ran rife in the city, which, in Fanny's words, became a walking hospital. Maimed and Wounded unhappy men of War are met at every step, either entering, carried in Carts, from the Fields of Battle, or the adjoining Villages, to be placed in Infirmaries, Work houses, Churches, and also at private houses. Every body is ordered to receive all their Dwelling will hold. It is even written on the doors of most houses how many are refuged in them. The Belgians behave with the utmost humanity to the miserable objects of fallen Ambition.[47]

On the evening of 15 June, Fanny was awakened by confused noises and bugle sounds in the street outside. Nobody knew whether the continual ebb and flow of troops through the streets – some bloody and badly wounded – signalled victory or defeat for the allied forces, until in the early hours of 19 June positive news arrived from a British officer that Napoleon had been routed and Brussels saved.

Even then Fanny had no idea what had happened to her husband. He was supposed to be in Trier, rallying royalist troops, but for all she knew he could have returned to Waterloo and even be lying among the piles of mutilated dead and dying still scattered over the battlefield. Early in July, however, she received a message that he had remained in Trier but, somewhat unheroically, had again been severely injured in an accident. On this occasion he had been kicked on the leg by a horse, and septicaemia had set in in the wound. She set off immediately to join him, and after an extremely hazardous journey of six days (again described in detail in her journal),[48] with little money or papers, and harassed at nearly every point by hostile policemen and border officials, she finally arrived in Trier on 24 July to find d'Arblay still seriously ill. With great difficulty, as he was still reluctant to leave France, she finally persuaded him to return with her to England where, after yet another unpleasant Channel crossing, they arrived on 17 October and took lodgings in Bath. Poor d'Arblay never really recovered his health after this unlucky accident.

LAST YEARS IN ENGLAND

Although Fanny lived for another 27 years, she remained in England and her life was generally less eventful, apart from an occasion on 24 September 1817, when she was nearly drowned when marooned with her dog in a cave at Ilfracombe in

Devon, where she had gone on holiday with her husband and Alex. She wrote a brilliant set-piece account of this in 1823 (initially in French, but later translated into English) and it is worth dwelling on what she described as 'my extraordinary adventure'.[49]

She set off for a walk on the beach with her husband's favourite little dog, Diane, searching for interesting rocks and pebbles. In the course of this, she penetrated into a cave with a large open-topped chamber within and started to climb up the rocks on one side in order to get at a shining white piece of rock that she could see at a higher level. Unfortunately, when she began to clamber down she found that the tide had turned and waves were flooding into the entrance of the cave and blocking her exit. With a now frightened and whining little dog, and the water level in the cave rising, she had no option but to try to climb back up the rocky side of the cave and find a ledge where she could rest above the water level. Although she claims that she was terrified ('the prospect of this terrific premature death struck me with dread') and that her clothes were now torn and her feet and hands scratched ('My Hands were wounded, my Knees were bruised, and my feet were cut; for I could only scramble up by clinging to the Rock on all fours'), she managed to cling on and by 'perilous climbing' eventually reached a slab of rock where she could rest. She then, however, had to deal with her frightened and yapping dog which was still below her and unable to scramble up to reach her. She eventually solved this – despite having lost both shoes in the process – by hooking the handle of her parasol in its collar and hauling it up beside her.

Having reached this extremely uncomfortable but relatively safe and dry position, she settled down, with the dog cowering between her feet, to await the next turning of the tide or rescue. By now it was getting dark and Alex, dreadfully alarmed at his mother's absence, had organized a search party after unsuccessfully enquiring after her at every house in the village and even, through a student friend, ordered a boat to sail round the coast. Fanny eventually heard cries (which she at first feared might be 'Banditti' – thought why she thought they were operating in this quiet corner of Devon is never explained) and then recognized Alex's voice. She was enormously relieved, although, as she reports:

> I had great difficulty to dismount, for I was no longer insensible, now, to hurts, bruises, scratches, cuts or torn clothes, or lost shoes; and I was so numbed and stiff that my joints seemed out of play, and I could hardly

move – but, with all that, how happy did I then feel! How gay in spirits, how thankful at heart!

She was soon helped down by Alex and his friends – the sea having largely receded from the cave – and taken back to the house in which they were staying for rest and dinner and welcomed by everyone as if she had risen from the dead. As Kate Chisholm remarks in her excellent biography of Fanny, she was never one to minimize a drama, but, even allowing for exaggeration, the picture of this tough and diminutive 65-year-old, wandering alone along the beach, scrambling up a rocky cave side, losing her shoes and narrowly escaping drowning, but still having the wit to save her dog by using her umbrella to pull it to safety, is a remarkable one. It was nothing, however, compared with the operation she had suffered in Paris a few years earlier.

There were no more adventures quite of this kind. In Bath she met again and achieved a partial reconciliation with her erstwhile friend, the now widowed Mrs Piozzi, and d'Arblay's disappointment at not having been given a higher command in the French royalist forces had been somewhat compensated for by his being promoted by King Louis XVIII to lieutenant general and made a count. Fanny could now formally rival Adèle de Boigne in status and call herself a countess and wife of a general, though, except in her will later, she never used the title. As she said in an unpublished letter of 26 June 1827 to her nephew Dr C.P. Burney,[50] she did not use it

because I have no Fortune to meet it, and because my Son relinquished his hereditary claims of succession – though he might, on certain conditions, resume them – on becoming a Clergyman of the Church of England. But I have never disclaimed my Rights, as I owe them to no Honours of my own, but to a Partnership in those which belonged to the revered Husband who, for twenty-four years, made the grateful Happiness of my Life.

It is nice to recall, however, that when Fanny had the honour of being presented to King Louis XVIII in London in 1814 he complimented her 'in very pretty English' on her writings and, in bidding her farewell, addressed her as 'Madame la Comtesse'.[51] This must have given her enormous pleasure.

After the death of her 'revered Husband' in May 1818, poignantly described in her journal,[52] Fanny moved back to Bolton Street, Piccadilly, with Alex, and devoted herself to helping him in his clerical career and to working on her father's voluminous memoirs, which were eventually published in November 1832. They were, however, so selective and bowdlerized that they were treated with scorn by some critics. 'Surely such a quantity of unmixed nonsense never was written before,'[53] Fanny's former friend, Ann Waddington, now Baroness Bunsen, wrote to her mother. It is not clear why Fanny chose to censor and alter her father's papers so much. It may have been partly filial piety, or, as some hostile critics claimed, her own egoism in wanting to exaggerate her own role in her father's life. But it was certainly not senility as, despite failing hearing and eyesight, she continued working actively on her own papers and entertaining those of her friends who had also survived. The year 1832 was otherwise a sad year for her as it brought the deaths of her sister Hetty and her close friend from Mickleham days, Frederica Lock. The bitterest blow of all, however, was the death in January 1827 of Alex, who, despite the brilliant promise of his youth and at Cambridge, had never achieved a settled career or lived up to Fanny's or his father's expectations. Alex had become engaged to a Mary Ann Smith shortly before he died and she came to live with Fanny as a companion until the latter's death, which occurred at Bolton Street on 6 June 1840, aged 87, after a long period of being confined to bed.

In her will Fanny left her own papers to her niece, Charlotte Barrett, and her father's remaining letters and memoranda to her brother Charles's son, Charles Burney. No doubt in memory of her late husband, she signed the will 'La Comtesse Veuve Piochard d'Arblay', the only occasion that she used this title. In the hope of restoring Fanny's literary reputation, which had been savaged by the publication of her father's memoirs, Charlotte edited and published Fanny's diaries in seven volumes between 1842 and 1846. They were well received and, judging her as a diarist, there is perhaps no better tribute and memorial to her vivid portraiture and extraordinary capacity for recall than that in the following review by the great novelist William Makepeace Thackeray:

> You get portraits sketched from life of many famous personages, who, though they figured but fifty years back, belong to a society as different and remote from ours, as that of Queen Anne or the Restoration – as different as a minuet is from a polka, or the Calais Packet, which was four-and-twenty hours on its journey to Calais from Dover, to the iron steamer that can rush hither and thither and back half a dozen times a day.[54]

TWO

ADÈLE

W hile Fanny Burney was brought up in the stimulating intellectual atmosphere of a bustling musical, theatrical and literary middle-class home and had royalty, as it were, reluctantly thrust upon her in later life, Adèle de Boigne was a true-blue aristocrat by birth and upbringing. Born Charlotte Louise Eléonore Adélaïde d'Osmond on 10 February 1781, she descended on her father's side from the d'Osmonds, who traced their lineage back to the tenth century. Indeed, one of her ancestors, the Comte de Sées, had accompanied William the Conqueror to England in 1066 and had progressively become Duke of Dorset, Chancellor of England and finally Bishop of Salisbury, where he was buried in 1099. Adèle, though politically a liberal and constitutional royalist – she believed in kings, but not in their divine or absolute right to rule – was immensely proud and ever conscious of this illustrious aristocratic pedigree and was always very aware of both her French and English origins.

Her father, the Marquis d'Osmond, was born in the French colony of Saint-Domingue. He was, however, sent to France at the age of three and educated, with his brothers, under the supervision of the Bishop of Comminges at the 'best college'[1] in Paris. He pursued a military career and at the relatively young age of 25, with royal patronage, was appointed lieutenant colonel of his regiment and soon afterwards met his bride-to-be at the watering place of Barèges. Adèle was always fiercely proud of him and described him at this stage of his career as '*un homme extrêmement agréable de formes, remarquablement aimable, fort bon militaire, aimant beaucoup son métier et adoré dans son régiment* [a man extremely agreeable in appearance, remarkably likeable, a very good soldier, who loved his profession and was adored in his regiment].'[2] He subsequently left the army in order to pursue a diplomatic career in the service of King Louis XVI, and at the beginning of the Revolution was about to be posted to the French embassy in St Petersburg. Adèle's mother, Eléonore Dillon, was the daughter of Robert Dillon, a Catholic Irishman of the Dillons of Roscommon and had been born in Worcestershire before the family emigrated to France and acquired property and a grand house in Bordeaux. When Robert Dillon died suddenly at the age of 32, Eléonore's mother was left with 13 children to bring up, but friends and family rallied round to enable her to do so while maintaining her position and household.

The marriage between Adèle's parents was delayed as a result of d'Osmond family objections related to the bride's lack of a fortune. These were, however, overcome when the Marquis d'Osmond's father pledged his financial support, and they were married two years later in 1778. Eléonore d'Osmond was said to be very beautiful and charming – Adèle subsequently wrote that at that period '*elle était extrêmement belle, avait très grand air, même un peu dédaigneux et elle savait se laisser adorer à perfection* [she was extremely beautiful, of a proud and even haughty disposition, and could invite admiration to perfection]'[3] – and, after being introduced at court by another member of the Dillon family, Arthur Dillon, the Archbishop of Narbonne, she was soon appointed 'dame' (lady-in-waiting) to Mme Adélaïde, a daughter of Louis XV's. Despite her husband's '*très grande répugnance au séjour de la Cour* [very strong dislike of court life]'[4] – which he later overcame as he became used to court etiquette – the couple settled at Versailles, where Adèle was born on 19 February 1781.

Our knowledge of Adèle's extraordinary life thereafter derives largely from her own *Mémoires* which cover the period from the 1780s to the 1840s but which were not published until much later. Astonishingly, unlike Fanny, who began her diaries and journals at an early age, she did not begin to write them until 1835, when she was in her early fifties. Reflecting on the tragic death of a young boy whom she had brought up as guardian (she had no children of her own) she decided that, for the sake of her family and descendants, she ought to record the remarkable events of her past life, beginning with her childhood and family life at Versailles. In the frank but modest and disarming fashion that characterizes all her writing, she claimed no particular literary merits for her work and relied on her remarkable memory alone. As she put it, she wrote: '*n'ayant consulté aucun document, il y a probablement beaucoup d'erreurs de dates, de lieux, peut-être même de faits* [I have consulted no document and there are probably many wrong dates, places and perhaps even facts].'[5] But with a detailed recall of even the tiniest events that rivals if not exceeds that of Fanny, the frankness, vividness and self-deprecating nature of her memoirs make them ring fundamentally true throughout.

She dedicated them to her great nephew, the ten-year-old Rainulphe d'Osmond, and typically, in line with her character, described them as merely '*une causerie de vieille femme, un ravaudage de salon* [...] *mon manuscrit arrivera à mes héritiers comme un vieux fauteuil de plus* [the chat of an old woman, a bit of botched-together furniture [...] of which the manuscript will be handed on to my heirs as if it were an extra armchair].'[6] She also formally entitled them *Récits d'une tante*[7] [Tales of an Aunt] and the manuscript was deposited in the library of the Château d'Osmond, the home of her ancestors, where she herself was eventually buried. They were eventually published in four volumes in 1907 by a friend of Rainulphe's, Charles Nicoullaud, who realized that they were of great public interest and ought to be made accessible to historians. Among the first to acknowledge them was Marcel Proust, who wrote an article about them in *Le Figaro* of 20 March 1907, just after they had been published. He admired the picture she painted of a society in constant flux and praised the incisiveness of the characters she portrayed and the way in which she brought them to life for readers of the present day. Indeed, he subsequently based part of the character of Mme de Beausergent in *A la recherche du temps perdu* on Adèle. Like Adèle she wrote her memoirs, loved to tell stories about her father, claimed to have no social prejudices and passed the twilight of her life with her old lover, a retired diplomat. It is surprising that so few other great French writers or historians have taken their cue from Proust and made use of Adèle's memoirs.

LIFE AT VERSAILLES

The *Mémoires* start with life in the court at Versailles, where Adèle was born. She became a favourite of the royal household and was brought up virtually as a member of the royal family: *'J'ai été littéralement élevée sur les genoux de la famille royale* [I was literally brought up on the knees of the royal family]'.[8] She played with the young royal children – she described herself as *'la poupée des princes et de la Cour* [the doll of the princes and the court]'[9] – and was often entertained by the king himself, who was once said to have prevented one of the royal guards from killing her little dog. She became a particular favourite of Mme Adélaïde's, the king's aunt, on whom her mother attended and who often took her for walks in the Versailles gardens. Her fascinating portraits of Louis XVIII and Marie-Antoinette and other members of the court at Versailles, and of the rigid court protocol of the time, relate to this period.

The comfortable d'Osmond family life was shattered, however, when in 1789 the Revolution broke out in earnest and the sans-culottes descended on Versailles. As Adèle put it: *'Les malheurs de la Révolution mirent un terme à mes succès de Cour* [the misfortunes of the Revolution put an end to my success at court].'[10] Her parents did not live in the palace of Versailles itself, where accommodation was restricted, but in a nearby apartment in the town. As rumours of disturbances began to spread, Adèle's father set off to the palace to discover what was happening, but

> *bientôt après son départ, les rues de Versailles furent inondées de gens effroyables à voir, poussant des cris effrénés auxquels se joignaient les bruits de coups de fusil dans l'éloignement.*

> [shortly after his departure, the streets of Versailles were filled with a flood of terrifying-looking people uttering wild cries, while gunshots could be heard in the distance.][11]

Communications with the palace were cut off, and the terrified Mme d'Osmond retreated to a dark room in their apartment with the shutters closed, clutching the infant Adèle on her knees. When Adèle had eventually gone to sleep, Mme d'Osmond bravely but recklessly went out to the gates of the palace in search of her husband, but was sensibly sent back by one of the few members of the National Guard still remaining loyally on duty and once more returned to their apartment in the town.

EXILE

At midnight d'Osmond came back with the news that the king and queen were preparing to leave for Rambouillet. He gathered up his pistols, ordered horses to be saddled and preparations made for instant departure, and initially set out to accompany the king himself, while Mme d'Osmond and Adèle escaped separately. In the event, the king's departure was frustrated – news of it had leaked and the mob prevented his carriage from leaving the stables – and after Mme d'Osmond had made a final visit to say farewell to the royal princesses, Adélaïde and Victoire, who were hiding in terror in a shuttered room in the ground floor of the palace, at whose windows shots had already been fired, d'Osmond swept his family away in great haste and arranged travel to the coast and a passage across the Channel to Brighton.

Adèle's experiences were not unlike those of another refugee aristocrat, Henriette-Lucie Dillon, Marquise de La Tour du Pin, who in her *Journal d'une femme de cinquante ans*, which, like Adèle's memoirs, was not published until early in the nineteenth century, described the terrifying ordeals that she and her husband endured in escaping the guillotine early in 1794 and fleeing to America. Indeed, in her journal there are many fascinating parallels with the experiences of both Adèle and Fanny. The marquise came from Adèle's mother's family, the Dillons; she also spent much of her early life at Versailles, where, like Adèle's mother, she was close to Marie-Antoinette and became a 'dame du palais', and among her close friends were several members of the Juniper Hall set, known to both Adèle and Fanny, such as Mme de Staël, Talleyrand, Lally-Tollendal, and her aunt, Mme d'Hénin. When she returned to France after the Revolution she even took lodgings in Rue de Miroménil, where Fanny and her husband lived for a time during their long stay in Paris from 1802.

Adèle, whose memoirs are usually very good on journeys, for once says that her recollections of their flight across the Channel were scant; we have few details, but after all she was only a child then. However, with one of those coincidences that recur throughout Adèle's memoirs, on disembarking at Brighton they met on the jetty the notorious Mrs Fitzherbert, yet another of Mme d'Osmond's cousins and the current mistress of the Prince Regent – she and he inhabited together a little house in Brighton 'en simples particuliers [like ordinary citizens]'.[12] They received a warm reception and generous hospitality – 'mes parents furent très fêtés [my parents were very warmly welcomed]'[13] – not only from Mrs Fitzherbert, but also from other old friends who were eager to help aristocratic refugees from the dreaded Revolution across the Channel, and stayed there for several days. Thus ended the first dramatic chapter of Adèle's life and thus also began her introduction to the country which for many years she regarded as her second, if not equal, home.

Apart from a brief return to France in January 1790, when Adèle had her last meeting with Marie-Antoinette and her father became dangerously involved in the king's abortive flight to Varennes, the d'Osmond family's exile outside France lasted until September 1804. By then the Terror was long over; Napoleon had consolidated his personal power and in May 1804, with the Pope sitting idly by as a mere spectator, crowned himself Emperor of the French in Notre-Dame cathedral. During that time momentous events – horrifying to the d'Osmonds – had occurred, including the guillotining of Louis XVI and Marie-Antoinette in January and October 1793 respectively, the arbitrary executions of aristocrats during the Terror and the extension of the war by France against a coalition comprising Britain, Russia and Spain. However, during this period also, with only Adèle to look after, the d'Osmonds were able to devote much of their time to ensuring that she received a first-class all-round education, in contrast to Fanny, who to a large extent during her childhood had to fend for herself. She became trilingual, with knowledge of French, English and Italian, and studied literature, history and economics, even reading Adam Smith.

In 1790, after their brief return visit to France, the d'Osmonds had initially sought refuge in Italy. They moved down to Naples, where they were received and entertained by yet another family friend, Queen Marie Caroline, the daughter of Francis I, Emperor of Austria; they seemed to have highly placed friends and connexions wherever they went. During their nine-month stay there, Adèle began her friendship with the Queen's daughter, Princess Amélie, who later married Louis-Philippe, the Duc d'Orléans, and in 1830 herself became Queen Marie-Amélie of France. This close friendship lasted for most of Adèle's life. While in Naples she also came across the celebrated Lady Hamilton, the wife of the British ambassador and mistress of Lord Nelson. Although Adèle expressed some admiration for her ability to dress up and arrange artistic, mainly classical, tableaux (in which Adèle herself was sometimes constrained to join), she thought little of her out of costume, dismissing her with the comment '*rien n'était plus vulgaire et plus commun que lady Hamilton* [nothing was more vulgar and common than Lady Hamilton]'.[14]

From Naples the family returned to England with the help of a rich English friend, Sir John Legard, who financed their journey, which included a hair-raising trek on horseback over the snow-covered St Gotthard Pass – for Adèle the first of many arduous and dangerous land and sea journeys of the kind that both she and Fanny intrepidly took in their stride. After staying for two years in Sir John's house in Yorkshire, where much of Adèle's further education took place, they moved to London in 1796, where the adolescent Adèle was introduced to London society, which by then included many other impoverished French refugee aristocrats. To Adèle's surprise many of those of high birth were working in quite menial low-paid jobs by day and dressing up to maintain appearances for society events at night. Their position was strikingly similar to that of the Tsarist refugees who fled, many of them to Paris, from the Bolshevik revolution in Russia over 100 years later, when former generals, high-ranking court officials and even royal dukes and duchesses found work to eke out a living as commissionaires, cloak-room attendants and cab drivers (a situation vividly depicted in the well-researched novels of the Russian-born French novelist and biographer Henri Troyat).

MARRIAGE

In 1798 Adèle contracted the marriage that set a framework for much of the remainder of her life. She begins Chapter IV of the second volume of her memoirs by jumping with breathtaking frankness into the story of this marriage. She was normally extremely reticent about her personal life, but the circumstances of the marriage were so exceptional that she felt compelled to say more about it. She declares:

Je ne raconterai pas le roman de ma vie, car chacun a le sien et, avec de la vérité et du talent, on peut le rendre intéressant, mais le talent me manque. Je

ne dirai de moi que ce qui est indispensable pour faire comprendre de quelles
fenêtres je me suis trouvée assister aux spectacles que je tenterai de décrire, et
comment j'y suis arrivée. Pour cela, il me faut entrer dans quelques détails sur
mon mariage.

[I do not intend to relate the story of my life, since everyone has their
own, which can be made interesting with truth and talent, but I have no
talent. I shall only say so much of myself as is necessary to explain through
what windows I became a spectator of the scenes I shall try to describe
and how I reached that point. For that reason, I must give a few details
about my marriage.][15]

The 'few details', in brief, are as follows. At a soirée given by her parents in
London, Adèle met General Comte Benoît de Boigne, then aged 49, the French
equivalent of a British nabob who, commanding huge armies, had made a for-
tune in India in the service of the ruler of the Maratha Empire, the Maharaja of
Gwalior. Although he was of relatively low birth (he was the son of a furrier in
Chambéry in Savoie, which was not then a part of France but was located in the
Kingdom of Sardinia), he had risen through the ranks of the Irish Brigade of the
French army and, after service in many parts of the world, distinguished himself
in India. It is perhaps an ironic coincidence that some years later many of the best
Indian troops that de Boigne had organized and trained were crushingly defeated
at the battles of Assaye and Laswari by the future Duke of Wellington, Arthur
Wellesley (the younger brother of the then Governor General of India, Richard
Wellesley), with whom Adèle became so disenchanted when he became allied
generalissimo in Paris after Waterloo.

   During his service in India, General de Boigne took care to maintain good relations with British army officers and high-ranking officials, including the governor
general of Bengal, Warren Hastings. This paid off. After leaving India in 1796, he
moved to England, rented a grand house in Portland Place and in January 1798
was granted English nationality by George III. He wished to establish a position
in society commensurate with his wealth and status, and was looking for a talented and presentable wife to share his bed, head his table and become mistress
of his household. He was immediately much attracted to Adèle, whom he met
at a soirée at her parents' house. Although she was not regarded as exceptionally

good-looking, she had a beautiful singing voice, was precociously well-educated and articulate for her age, and, of course, had an impeccable aristocratic pedigree. On the day after meeting Adèle, he made an offer of marriage to her through an old Irish army friend from India, Colonel Daniel O'Connell.

With incredible coolness, and a business sense well beyond her years, Adèle, fully 17 years old, asked for a day to consider the offer, arranged another meeting with him, laid down her terms and told him that if he was willing to guarantee both her and her parents' future financial independence she would agree to marry him, 'sans répugnance'.[16] But she also made it absolutely clear that this was a business arrangement – a marriage of convenience – and that he could expect no love or affection from her. In her own words:

> Si ce sentiment lui suffisait, je donnais mon consentement; s'il prétendait à un autre, j'étais trop franche pour le lui promettre, ni dans le présent, ni dans l'avenir. Il m'assura ne point se flatter d'en inspirer un plus vif.

> [If this feeling was enough for him, I would give my consent, but if he sought anything more, I was too honest to promise it to him either now or in the future. He assured me that he did not flatter himself that he would be able to inspire any deeper feeling.][17]

General de Boigne accepted the deal, settling on Adèle the immediate sum of £70,000, which would generate for her an annual income of £400, making an immediate grant of £500 to her parents and furthermore undertaking to leave an income of £2,500 to Adèle on his death, or £2,000 if they had no children (in fact, he made the latter sum available to her in 1799 after their first separation).[18]

On this absolutely calculating and mercenary note, though entirely for the future welfare of her beloved parents, the 17-year-old Adèle married a battle-seasoned general, over 20 years her elder, a few days later on 8 June 1798 at the chapel of the Sardinian embassy in London (where coincidentally Fanny Burney and General d'Arblay in 1793 had also undergone their Catholic marriage ceremony). A number of titled French and English notables were present, together with de Boigne's friend O'Connell and another former governor general of India, Lord Teignmouth. Adèle's audacity, decisiveness and sheer bargaining skills were breathtaking – such a contrast with the months of agonizing and hesitation that the more mature Fanny Burney endured before finally agreeing to marry her French general, with whom she was deeply in love. About her decision Adèle commented casually:

> *Très probablement, à vingt ans, je n'aurais pas eu ce courage, mais, à seize ans* [sic], *on ne sait pas encore qu'on met en jeu le reste de sa vie.*

[At the age of twenty I should very probably not have had the courage, but at sixteen [sic] one does not yet know that the rest of one's life is at stake.][19]

It was an extraordinary arrangement. Despite its many upsets – Adèle described it as '*une union très orageuse* [a very stormy union]',[20] and there were several separations; according to Adèle, he left her for good five or six times – it was probably not always quite as unpleasant and disharmonious as Adèle portrays it in its earlier stages, and it certainly secured her future and that of her parents for many years, and indeed enabled her to live a life of considerable comfort and luxury. But despite her claim to provide a 'few details' about the marriage, she gives us relatively little information about de Boigne's background. Indeed, she claims: '*il me trompa sur tous ses antécédents: sur son nom, sur sa famille, sur son existence passée* [he deceived me on his antecedents, on his name, on his family and on his past life].'[21] This is perhaps not surprising, as we know from other sources that he had contracted a marriage in India to an Hélène Bennet and had had two children by her, Anne and Charles-Alexandre. He brought them with him to England and on arrival settled her with a generous income in a house in Enfield (moving her in 1805 to a rather grander property in Lower Beeding in Sussex), and entrusted the education of the two children to her. In return she apparently agreed to keep quiet about their earlier marriage and not pursue her relationship with him, but it is not clear whether the marriage was formally dissolved or not. It is difficult to believe that Adèle had no knowledge of this background, but there is no inkling in her memoirs that she knew about it at the time of her marriage, and if she had been aware of it she may perhaps have felt it more prudent to say nothing about it.

She sometimes, however, wrote frankly and critically about de Boigne's character. According to her, his *disposition à la désobligeance, exploitée avec toute l'aristocratie de l'argent la plus hostile de toutes, rendait son commerce si odieux qu'il n'a jamais pu s'attacher un individu quelconque, dans aucune classe de la société, quoiqu'il ait répandu de nombreux bienfaits.*

[disagreeable disposition, exploited with all the ostentation of wealth, the most repellent of all forms of outward display, made association with him so odious that he was never able to secure the friendship of any single individual, in any class of society, despite all his numerous benefactions.][22]

Adèle was not always quite so disparaging about her husband as this, but what a contrast it was with Fanny Burney's adoring descriptions of her own beloved, but penniless, husband.

The early years of the marriage were indeed stormy. After ten months Adèle, by mutual consent, returned to live with her parents, but the pair were reunited a few months later at Ramsgate and, from their base in England, made an extended tour together of both the British Isles and the Continent until, after a short stay in Bognor (both Adèle and Fanny seemed to have an extraordinary predilection for English seaside resorts and both were among the early pioneers of bathing in the sea), General de Boigne returned to France, where Adèle joined him once more in September 1804. From that date they divided their life between Paris, her husband's residence at nearby Beauregard and his substantial estate at Buisson-Rond, near Chambéry in his native Savoie. Adèle's parents also lived with them for part of this time. In 1812, however, the general, who on any analysis had shown remarkable tolerance and generosity, regularized their divided life by installing himself more permanently at Chambéry, where he was a much-revered local benefactor, and by acquiring a grand late-seventeenth-century mansion for Adèle at Châtenay, near Paris, where she could entertain her parents and friends as she wished and establish her own salon. A close neighbour was now the celebrated diplomat and writer Chateaubriand, which gave rise to a lifelong, if often critical (on her part), friendship.

Adèle is again disarming about her life during this period. She writes:

Ma vie a été si monotone pendant les dix années de l'Empire et j'ai pris si peu part aux grands événements que je n'ai guère de jalons pour fixer les époques.

*Je me bornerai à placer pêle-mêle, et sans égard aux dates, les divers souvenirs
de ce temps qui ont rapport aux personnages de quelque importance, ou qui
peindraient les mœurs du monde où je vivais exclusivement.*

[My life was so monotonous during the ten years of the Empire, and I
was so little involved in great events that I have practically no milestones
by which to guide my chronology. I shall confine myself to recording at
random, without reference to dates, such recollections of this period as
deal with personages of some importance, or depict the manners of that
society in which I exclusively lived.]'[23]

But if Adèle's narrative was a little erratic and out of sequence, it nevertheless
brought to life an absolute galaxy of the star political and intellectual players of
the day.

The years from 1804 to 1814 witnessed the period of the Napoleonic Empire.
Although Adèle and her parents remained resolute constitutional royalists and
fundamentally opposed to Napoleon's growing tyranny, they had enough good
sense to keep their heads down politically and keep their peace with the imperial
court and regime. Adèle begins her account of this period by stating clearly: '*Je ne
voulus pas assister aux fêtes du couronnement; mon héroïsme royaliste en aurait trop
souffert* [I did not wish to be present at the festivities of [Napoleon's] coronation;
my royalist leanings would have been too outraged].'[24] She also went on to say
that her English education had turned her in a direction '*qui a été appelée libérale*
[that has been called liberal]'.[25] She also frequently expressed her admiration of the
British constitutional monarchy. Flitting between the various residences available
to her, and occasionally dutifully joining her husband in Savoie or elsewhere, if
only to preside at his dinner table, she associated closely with most of the great
personalities of French politics and society – mainly from the opposition ranks.
These included Talleyrand and Mme de Staël from Fanny Burney's old Juniper
set and the renowned beauty Mme Juliette Récamier, whose salon was frequented
by her great admirer, Chateaubriand, and a bevy of other adoring female admirers
who, to Adèle's amusement, came to hear him read extracts from his writings
and squabbled over who should pour his tea or coffee for him. Mme Récamier,
whom Adèle regarded as the most beautiful and intelligent woman of her time,
and Mme de Staël became particularly close friends, and Adèle describes in great

detail the ability of the latter, despite her reputedly unattractive physical appearance, to attract male attention by her wit and sheer intellectual brilliance. It is very difficult to reconcile the account of Adèle's varied life in society during this period with her protestation that it was such a monotonous period of her life.

Through family ties with the Dillon family, Adèle was also introduced to the Empress Josephine and her section of the imperial household, and she relates 'une petite circonstance qui confirme ce qui a été souvent dit de la futilité et de la légèreté de l'impératrice Joséphine [a little incident that confirms all that has been often said about the shallowness and fickleness of the Empress Josephine]'.²⁶ In brief, when Mrs Arthur Dillon, a cousin of Josephine's, was once staying with Adèle, she went to visit Josephine at the Château de Saint-Cloud. Josephine, a matchmaker like her husband, led her on to believe she could arrange a grand marriage for her daughter, Fanny, who was coincidentally the younger sister of the Marquise de La Tour du Pin. Anxious to please Josephine, Mme Dillon asked Adèle if she would be willing to give Josephine a beautiful heron plume which her husband had brought back from India. Adèle duly handed one over, but Josephine was so thrilled with it that she asked for another. Adèle once more obliged, but yet another request was made, and in sending the third plume Adèle made it clear that she had no more to give. The sequel to this was that Josephine insisted that in return she would send Adèle a cameo set with valuable precious stones. Adèle was in a tizzy as to how properly to thank the Empress for this, and even called a family council to advise her. In the event, she need not have worried as 'depuis ce jour, je n'ai entendu parler de rien, ni de plumes, ni de pierres, ni de quoi que ce soit [since that day I have heard nothing more at all, neither of plumes nor of precious stones, nor of anything else]'²⁷ – a good example of Josephine's 'futilité' and 'légèreté'.

Josephine's pretensions to matchmaking also had little result. She continued to hold out hopes of a grand marriage for Fanny Dillon, into one of the great European royal, or at least high-ranking aristocratic, houses, and schemed to this effect. But Napoleon, the supreme matchmaker, had other ideas. He wanted her to marry one of his generals, Henri Gratien Bertrand, a distinguished engineer of outstanding loyalty to the emperor. When the feisty and ambitious Fanny heard this she was so disappointed that she exclaimed: 'Bertrand! Bertrand! singe du Pape en son vivant! [Bertrand! Bertrand! Why not the Pope's monkey?]'²⁸ Napoleon was so irritated by this that Adèle says 'ce mot scella son sort [this word sealed her fate]' and she was made to do as she was told and marry General Bertrand. In fact, as Adèle later admitted, Bertrand, who went on to become the grand marshal of Napoleon's court, and accompanied him on most of his crucial campaigns, including Russia in 1812 and Waterloo, and later with Fanny throughout his six years of captivity on St Helena, turned out to be a good and loyal husband, and it seems for the most part to have been a sound and happy marriage. Ironically, Fanny herself, for whom the exile on St Helena was a great trial – she tried to commit suicide by throwing herself into the sea from His Majesty's ship *Bellerophon* at Plymouth in July 1815, when the news was broken to them that the British government had decided to send Napoleon and his entourage to St Helena – had great difficulty on the island in refusing to be drawn into becoming Napoleon's mistress, and this caused a breach in their relationship until shortly before Napoleon's death.

Given the almost incessant succession of wars, Adèle's memoirs of this era are surprisingly thin on the external events of the Empire. She has little to say, for example, about the disastrous invasion of Russia and retreat from Moscow in 1812; she explains this by stating:

Je n'écris pas l'histoire, mais seulement ce que je sais avec quelques détails certains. Lorsque les affaires publiques seront à ma connaissance spéciale, je les dirai avec la même exactitude que les anecdotes de société.

[I am not writing history, but only what I know with certain details. When public affairs come under my special knowledge I will relate them with the same precision as I do my society anecdotes.][29]

This revealing explanation of Adèle's honest approach is not unlike that, at a different level, of the father of history, the Greek historian Herodotus of Halicarnassus. He declared that his purpose was simply to preserve the memory of the past by putting on record the astonishing achievements of our own and other peoples. With the same spirit of modesty and frankness Adèle largely confined herself to recording what she had actually seen and experienced and, like Herodotus, made it clear when she was reporting something related to her by others, the veracity of which her readers must judge for themselves. We must also remember that many important events, especially as French forces began to suffer defeats, were simply not reported as a result of Napoleon's severe suppression and censorship of the press. For example, Adèle records that

> *la bataille de Trafalgar n'a jamais été racontée à la France dans un récit officiel; aucune gazette, par conséquent, n'en a parlé et nous ne l'avons sue que par voies clandestines.*

> [the Battle of Trafalgar was never officially reported in France, so no newspaper mentioned it and we only got to know of it through secret intelligence.][30]

This is also precisely the experience of Fanny when she managed to leave France with her son Alex on an American merchant ship in 1812 and, after interception by a British naval vessel, was put ashore at Deal. At dinner with friends on the night of arrival, she saw a plate decorated with the word 'Trafalgar' written underneath and, on enquiring what this meant, was told about the great victory eight years previously. This is a startling example of news blackout and censorship well before the twentieth century.

THE END OF NAPOLEON

Adèle's reaction to the defeat and abdication of Napoleon in 1814 and the surrender of Paris by one of his most trusted former marshals, Marmont, the Duc de Raguse, whom she came to admire greatly and thought much maligned, was ambivalent. Although she rejoiced to see the tyranny of Napoleon ended, she was distressed as a Frenchwoman to see French armies defeated and Paris occupied by foreign troops, and while she admired him in some respects, she was sceptical about the restoration of the gouty and corpulent Louis XVIII. She said of herself: '*j'étais bien plus antibonapartiste que je n'étais bourbonienne* [I was more anti-Bonapartist than a supporter of the Bourbons].'[31] She was also beginning to identify herself more and more closely with France, where she had lived for the last decade. She commented, '*J'avais perdu en grande partie mon anglomanie; j'étais redevenue française, si ce n'est politiquement du moins socialement* [my anglomania had for the most part disappeared; I had become French again, socially if not politically].'[32] Nevertheless, she continued to admire the English political system, with its constitutional monarchy and, at least in principle, complete equality before the law, describing it as the system 'qu'il y a de plus parfait dans le monde [that is the most perfect in the world]'.[33]

On returning to Paris Adèle and her mother were in fact protected by yet another of the extraordinary connections of the d'Osmond family, another example of the close interrelations between aristocratic families throughout Europe at that time. Looking anxiously out of the first-floor window of their apartment, she and her mother were alarmed when they saw a Russian officer and several mounted Cossacks approaching. After the Russian disaster the Cossacks, who had mercilessly harried the retreating French army, were, of course, among the most feared of foreign troops. When the officer reached the door and asked where Mme de Boigne lived, they recognized him with great relief as an old family acquaintance, Prince Nikita Volkonsky, who had been sent by another old friend, the Russian foreign minister, Count Nesselrode, to find them and assure them of their entire safety and protection. A mounted Cossack was stationed outside their apartment to protect them, and an invitation was extended to both Volkonsky and Nesslerode to dine with them that evening. It was no disadvantage to have friends in high quarters in such troubled times.

With the restoration of Louis XVIII and the Bourbon court, life in Paris changed dramatically yet again. The new Napoleonic aristocracy was out, and Adèle was drawn back into Bourbon court circles. Like Fanny Burney during her years as Second Lady of the Robes to Queen Charlotte, she now found the etiquette of formal court life exceedingly tiresome. At receptions and levees she had to endure long, tedious, cold and uncomfortable waiting periods, often standing for hours on end when she was desperate to get away. On a fascinating side note, she described how the novel custom of shaking hands ('l'usage du shake-hand')[34] had been brought to the French court from England by the Duc de Berry, the son of the Comte d'Artois, the future King Charles X – a reversal of popular belief in Britain about the origins of this 'Continental' custom. Apart from the court, her memoirs also have a good deal to say about great figures such as Talleyrand – now foreign minister – and Tsar Alexander I, Emperor of Russia, who was foolishly snubbed by King Louis on his return to Paris and preferred to associate with members of the previous imperial family, especially Napoleon's stepdaughter and his sister-in-law Hortense Beauharnais, the former Queen of

Holland. The name of Etienne-Denis Pasquier, a rising French statesman who had survived the Terror and gradually risen in the public service under Napoleon, despite his basic commitment to the House of Bourbon, also begins to occur more frequently in Adèle's memoirs. This was the beginning of a deep friendship which lasted into their respective old ages. Adèle also at this time made her first acquaintance with the Duke of Wellington, who was now in Paris, having marched his army there fresh from his victories on the Peninsula.

In September 1814 Adèle's father, to her surprise and disappointment and to the anger of her mother, accepted the post of French ambassador to Piedmont in Turin. He had protested that he would not accept any other diplomatic post than the embassy in Vienna, but he was talked into accepting Turin by Foreign Minister Talleyrand, who told him that the king particularly wanted him to go there, and hinted that if he agreed to this posting the embassy in London might become available for him later on. As Mme d'Osmond was worryingly unwell, Adèle decided to accompany her father to Turin and in effect fulfil the duties of ambassadress – somewhat like Fanny Burney's dedication to acting as her father's amanuensis and secretary. Reporting like a professional diplomat, Adèle found Turin unimpressive and boring – '*le séjour le plus triste et le plus ennuyeux qui existe dans tout l'univers* [the saddest and most boring place to stay in the whole universe]'.[35] Her reaction to the city was remarkably like that of Anthony Trollope, who wrote a few years later that 'of all towns in Italy, Turin has perhaps less of attraction to offer to the solitary visitor than any other. It is very cold in cold weather, very hot in hot weather, and now that it has been robbed of its life as a capital, is as dull and uninteresting as if it were German or English.'[36]

At least when Adèle was there it was still a capital city, but the restored monarchy under King Victor Emmanuel I, who tried to turn the clock back to pre-Napoleonic days, appeared to her ridiculous. Similarly, Turin society seemed to Adèle shallow and stupid, and basic living conditions there were very uncomfortable, except for the house of the British minister, a certain Mr Hill, who had procured a very comfortable residence for himself, but apparently seldom emerged from it. What helped to relieve the tedium, however, was the fact that her father had been instructed to keep a very close watch on the activities of the Bonapartists who were still scattered around Italy, and particularly their communications with Napoleon on Elba. For this purpose d'Osmond made use of an English doctor, Dr Marshall, who had in fact been sent out by the Prince Regent from England to spy on the rather scandalous peregrinations of his estranged legal wife, Caroline, Princess of Wales, whose wanton behaviour even shocked Adèle. In January 1815 Dr Marshall reported to d'Osmond that he had information that Napoleon was planning soon to leave Elba for France, and that there was a movement in France to welcome him back and assist him.

D'Osmond arranged by a variety of channels to convey this information to King Louis in Paris, and, while he and Adèle were on a visit to British-controlled Genoa, news arrived via the French consul in Livorno that Napoleon had indeed left Portoferraio on Elba for France. Again, the ambassador immediately sent dispatches to Talleyrand, who was representing King Louis at the Congress of Vienna, and so began the Hundred Days ending with the defeat of Napoleon by Wellington and Blücher on 18 June. On various occasions during this period, the highly competent Adèle, although she vigorously denied knowing anything about the duties of diplomacy, stood in for her father and held the fort at the embassy in Turin. While Napoleon was assembling his army to meet the British-led and Prussian armies in Belgium, Adèle and her father remained on duty in Piedmont until the news eventually reached them of the battles of Ligny and Waterloo. As a year earlier, on the occasion of Napoleon's first defeat and abdication, Adèle's reaction was again mixed. She wrote in her memoirs:

celles que nous étions contraints à appeler les bonnes nouvelles se succédèrent aussi rapidement que les mauvaises trois mois avant. Il fallait bien s'en réjouir, mais ce n'était pas sans saignement de cœur.

[events that we were obliged to call good news followed as quickly as the bad news three months earlier. We had to rejoice at them, but not without some heartbreak.][37]

It is difficult not to empathize with her reactions.

THE EMBASSY IN LONDON

Adèle was now homesick, and in August 1815 returned alone from Turin to Paris. She found the atmosphere there very different from the previous year, when

Napoleon had abdicated for the first time. The British, Prussian and Russian troops were now there openly as foreign occupiers rather than as welcome liberators. France was truly a defeated – if not disgraced – nation, and Adèle resented their presence. She felt also that the generalissimo, the Duke of Wellington, whom she ironically dubbed 'notre héros',[38] could have made greater use of his prestige and authority to run the troop numbers down more quickly than had formally been agreed; she was also critical of his excessive enthusiasm for stripping the Louvre of its works of art that Napoleon had taken as booty and brought back to Paris. She blamed him too for not using his influence with the king to obtain a reprieve for Marshal Ney, who was found guilty and executed by firing squad for rallying to Napoleon and fighting on his side at Waterloo. Her sadness and frustration at life in Paris under the allied occupation and the shaky rule of the second-time restored Louis XVIII was, however, relieved by her father's appointment in January 1816 as French ambassador in London. Again, particularly because of the poor state of her mother's health, she decided to accompany him to a country and city that she still loved.

Her return to England – 'un vieil ami [an old friend]'[39] – in the spring of 1816 brought her into contact again with many distinguished old friends from former days. Although she had some criticisms of London itself, she was greatly impressed with the general prosperity of the country and even asked herself why France could not have grown as prosperous as her island neighbour. As the daughter of the French ambassador, she was soon launched into London and court society, attending a concert given by the Prince Regent for his mother, Queen Charlotte, who, to Adèle's pleasure, remembered her from a presentation at court on a previous occasion, and a grand ball given by the Marquis of Anglesey, at which she met Byron's mistress, Lady Caroline Lamb. She used her experience of these and other occasions to reflect in her memoirs on social customs in England and in France. Her balanced conclusion was that 'si l'Angleterre avait l'avantage bien marqué dans le matériel de la vie, la sociabilité était mieux comprise en France [although England had a great advantage in material life, social life was better understood in France].'[40]

A particularly poignant episode in her account of high life in England was her description of a later stay for a few days with her father as guests of the Prince Regent's at the Pavilion in Brighton. The prince entertained them at dinner with a touching account of a meeting he had just had with his 'mad' father, King

George III, whom he had not seen for several years. We shall revert to this later. On a different note, demonstrating again her newly asserted French patriotism, Adèle describes with pride how on 18 June 1817, the second anniversary of the Battle of Waterloo, her father declined an invitation to attend a grand ceremony led by the Prince Regent and the Duke of Wellington to open the new Waterloo Bridge over the river Thames. Under the circumstances it was perhaps a rather tactless invitation, and his colleagues in the London diplomatic corps showed solidarity by supporting him and declaring that '*ils ne voulaient pas se séparer de lui dans cette circonstance et que cette cérémonie, étant purement nationale, ne devait point entraîner d'invitation aux étrangers* [they did not wish to stand apart from him on this occasion and that this ceremony, since it was purely national, ought not to involve any invitations to foreigners].'[41]

RETURN TO PARIS AND THE REVOLUTION OF 1830

Early in 1819 Adèle's father decided to retire from the diplomatic service and return to Paris. Adèle and her mother were delighted. Adèle declared that she hated diplomatic life and in any case her mother wanted to be near her son in Paris. She and her mother also felt that her father was no longer able to deal with his heavy load of work as well as he had done in earlier days. He was now well over 60 and showing signs of developing memory loss. Adèle returned to France with him and, after establishing herself in Paris again, spent some time with her husband at his residence in Chambéry before returning once more to Paris to take a house in Rue de Bourbon with her parents. Over the coming years she went from time to time to stay with her husband and, until his death in June 1830, they seem to have reached a more pragmatic basis of mutual understanding that belied the stormy atmosphere of their early married days. In the sensitive appraisal of this marriage in her biography of Adèle, *La Comtesse de Boigne*, Françoise Wagener suggests that, despite the tensions and the terms of the marriage set by Adèle, as time went on the relationship became much less unpleasant and antagonistic: they reached a *modus vivendi* that enabled them both to live their own separate lives but come together as a couple reasonably amicably from time to time.[42]

Adèle's memoirs thereafter chart a rich progression of social and political events, including a dramatic account, given to Adèle by eyewitnesses, of the assassination of the Duc de Berry, the second son of the Comte d'Artois, who was later to succeed to the throne as Charles X, at the Paris opera on 13 February 1820. Adèle was very good at depicting death scenes, which clearly fascinated her, and her tabloid-newspaper-like description of the stricken duke, while not as starkly horrifying as Fanny Burney's account of her mastectomy operation, is positively blood-curdling. Although Adèle in no way sympathized with the Duc de Berry's right-wing views, she did like him personally and was charitable to him on his death, which she says was greatly lamented by the public.

In Paris, at Rue du Bourbon, Adèle gradually established a political salon, attendance at which was much coveted. Despite her protestations at not being a historian, her memoirs describe most of the notable political and social events of the succeeding years, including the death of King Louis XVIII. She had generally expressed a low opinion of his abilities, but she was moved by his death and described how taken aback she was when she went to pay her respects to him shortly before he died – 'Je fus bien frappée de son excessif changement [I was really shocked by the change in his appearance]'.[43] She later paid a moving tribute to him. There was no such lamenting in Paris, however, for the death of Napoleon at the age of 51 on St Helena on 5 May 1821. In sending him to St Helena the British government had hoped that, far away in the South Atlantic, he would gradually fade away from memory and view. Their hopes were partly justified. According to Adèle, 'L'ère de sa popularité posthume n'avait pas commencé pour la France [the era of his posthumous popularity had not begun for France]', and she heard newsboys in the street crying

> La mort de Napoléon Bonaparte, pour deux sols! Son discourse au Général Bertrand, pour deux sols! Les désespoirs de Madame Bertrand, pour deux sols, pour deux sols!

> [The death of Napoleon Bonaparte, two sous! His speech to General Bertrand, two sous! The despair of Mme Bertrand [Adèle's old friend], two sous, two sous!]'[44]

and commented that this produced no more effect in the street than the advertisement for a lost dog.

It was not until the '*retour des cendres* [the return of the ashes]' after the exhumation of Napoleon's body from his grave on St Helena, and their return with pomp and ceremony for burial at Les Invalides in Paris in October 1840, that the Napoleonic eagle soared high once again. Adèle had surprisingly little to say otherwise about Napoleon's captivity on St Helena, but his death did give her an excuse to reveal her sense of humour and relate a wonderful anecdote about the way in which the news was received by King George IV when the foreign secretary, Lord Castlereagh, conveyed it to him. Lord Castlereagh entered his study and said, 'Sir, I come to tell Your Majesty that your mortal enemy is dead', to which the king replied, 'What! Is it possible? Can she be dead?'[45] The king thought he was talking of his estranged wife, Queen Caroline. It is interesting that this story went the rounds and crossed the Channel in such an age of pre-modern communications.

By far the most dramatic episode in which Adèle was personally involved, however, was the July Revolution of 1830, which ended the rule of Charles X and brought the Duc d'Orléans to the throne as King Louis-Philippe, Roi des Français – the so-called Bourgeois King. Adèle was a unique and independent observer and participant, and her account of the events from 26 to 30 July is as vividly descriptive as that of any modern journalist or war correspondent. She is, nevertheless, remarkably modest about both her account and the role she played. She actually wrote this account in 1832, before she began the main part of her memoirs in earnest three years later, and said of it:

> Je ne m'aveugle pas sur leurs défauts. Si je n'ai pas suffisamment de talent pour les éviter, j'ai assez d'intelligence pour les sentir. Le style est lâche; il y a des longueurs infinies.

> [I am well aware of their defects, and if I am not clever enough to remove them, I have enough intelligence to recognize them. The style is lax and there are long boring passages.][46]

However, she justified her failure to correct the alleged defects by claiming that her account had one great merit:

> c'est de m'avoir reportée aux événements et si vivement rappelé mes impressions du moment que j'ai pour ainsi dire revécu les jours de juillet avec toutes

leurs craintes, toutes leurs anxiétés, mais aussi toutes leurs espérances, toutes leurs illusions.

[it lies in the fact that I have gone back to the events and have so vividly recalled my impressions of the moment as almost to have relived those July days, with all their fears, all their anxieties, but also all their hopes and all their illusions.][47]

Nobody reading her authentic and gripping account would contradict this claim. She also went on to play down with unnecessary modesty her own involvement and insisted that she did no more than relate what she had seen for herself.

Political discontent with the regime of Charles X and the excessive influence of right-wing extremists had been building up for some time and came to a head with a by-election defeat for the royalists and the proclamation by the king of four royal ordinances that were designed to reimpose press censorship, dissolve the Chamber of Deputies, modify the electoral law and call new elections. Adèle was first approached by her old friend, Marshal Marmont, Duc de Raguse, the military commander of the city and an old opponent of Wellington's in the Peninsular War, who warned her that serious trouble was brewing and that in his view the Bourbons were finished. On 27 July she learned from workmen at her house that ferment was beginning to spread, but, cool as ever, she went out shopping on the Rue Saint-Denis in the afternoon and called on various friends. By the evening there was news of disorder spreading through the city and Adèle became worried when none of her workmen returned either in the evening or on the following morning. Still undeterred, and despite reports of barricades being erected in the streets, artillery being shifted into position and some people being killed, she intrepidly ventured out to visit her bankers in order to transact some business before a planned visit to the country. She found growing chaos in the streets and – although not until after she had concluded her banking business – returned home and was entreated by her close friend M. Pasquier, now a respected senior political counsellor and later to become chancellor of France, to warn Marshal Marmont not to use the full force of the military against the demonstrators. She entirely agreed with this and sent an appropriate message, commenting: *'Si le Maréchal fait tirer un seul coup de canon, qu'il se fasse tuer, car sa vie ne sera plus qu'une série de malheurs!* [If the Marshal should fire even a single cannon, he had better kill himself since his life will be nothing more than a series of misfortunes!]'[48] It was an extraordinarily confident and imperious message from a woman of no official standing to one of Napoleon's most experienced and respected former marshals, but it was very sound advice.

Events then moved quickly, with Adèle seemingly involved or a witness at virtually every crucial stage. She was in regular contact with a number of influential friends, such as Pasquier, Chateaubriand, Mme Récamier and Talleyrand in addition to Marshal Marmont, and she spent the evening of 28 July either going out into her courtyard or peering through her windows to see what was happening in the street below. The next morning she sent her butler out to visit the barricades and report back on the situation and wrote a further note to Marmont seeking a pass to enable her to leave Paris. Although she received the pass promptly, she was dissuaded from leaving by Pasquier, a strong supporter of the Duc d'Orléans, who could sense a successful outcome to the uprising. She spent more time looking through her windows at the barricades being erected below, but on hearing the news of the capture by the demonstrators of the Louvre and the abandonment of the Tuileries by the royal family, she decided to go out again to see for herself.

She first had to get through the barricades, but 'celles-là étaient fort incommodes à franchir; il fallait escalader les unes, ramper sous les autres [they were very difficult to cross; you had to climb over some, and crawl under others]'.[49] She then had to make her peace with the men and women who manned them. The latter were extraordinary. They had in fact partly dismantled some of the furniture that had been piled up on the barricades, and

> s'étaient emparées de quelques chaises et là, bien mises, bien parées, avec des chapeaux élégants à plumes ou à fleurs, elles étaient tranquillement assises, à l'ombre de leurs ombrelles et de la barricade, comme elles l'auraient été sous les arbres des Tuileries.

> [had seized some of the chairs, and in their best dresses, and wearing hats decorated with feathers or flowers, were calmly sitting under the shade of their parasols and the barricade, just as if they had been sitting under the trees in the Tuileries gardens.][50]

Leaving this bizarre sight – almost reminiscent of the '*tricoteuses*', the knitters who had sat around the guillotine – she made her way to the Russian embassy to see yet another old friend, Pozzo di Burgo, now in post as the Russian ambassador in Paris. Corsican-born, and a lifelong rival and opponent of Napoleon, he was yet another of the extraordinarily wide aristocratic mafia of influential friends the d'Osmonds had made across Europe over the years. Having left Corsica when it failed to win its independence from France – Napoleon, having initially supported the Corsican nationalist movement, had then decided to throw in his lot with France – he entered the service of the Tsar, became – astonishingly – Russian ambassador in Paris and played an important part in coordinating action between Tsar Alexander I and the Duke of Wellington when allied forces entered Paris after Waterloo.

After she had consulted Pozzo, who indicated that he also was on Orléans's side, Adèle then made her hazardous way back home and, having sent a servant out to buy essential provisions such as ham and sacks of rice and flour, she sat back again to await developments. They were not long in coming. The Duc d'Orléans had arrived at the Palais Royal and Charles X was said to be preparing to leave Paris on the road to Versailles. Adèle then performed what she described with her usual modesty as a '*petit rôle politique que j'ai pu jouer dans ces grands événements* [small political role I was able to play in these great events]'.[51] She sent a note by hand of a friend, Mme de Montjoie, to inform the Duc d'Orléans that the Russian ambassador openly supported him.

Since it was most important to know that Russia would back him, this played a crucial part in persuading the Duc d'Orléans to accept the initial post of lieutenant general of the Realm, offered to him by 60 deputies who met at the Palais Bourbon and issued a public proclamation of support for him. General public support for the duc mounted, and Adèle again played her part by visiting her very dear friend, the Duchesse d'Orléans, and urging her to have confidence in and openly support her husband. She urged her:

> *Montez en voiture, madame, avec tous vos enfants, vos voitures de gala, vos grandes livrées. Les barricades s'abaisseront devant elles. Le peuple flatté de cette confiance vous accueillera avec transport; vous arriverez au Palais-Royal au milieu des acclamations; il n'y a pas à hésiter.*

[Ride out in your carriage, madame, with all your children, your state carriage and full livery. The barricades will fall down before you. The people will be flattered by your confidence and will welcome you with enthusiasm, and you will reach the Palais Royal amid acclamation; you must not hesitate.][52]

Amélie was not quite brave enough to do this without her husband's specific endorsement, but she eventually joined her husband at the Palais Royal, where he was acclaimed with enthusiasm by the gathering crowds and in due course crowned Louis-Philippe, Roi des Français.

Adèle's friendship with the Orléans family, and her close contacts with so many other major political, diplomatic and military players, undoubtedly enabled her to hold significant influence over the outcome of the revolution, much though she modestly downplayed it. With her remarkable personal courage, she acted as an invaluable intermediary between the reigning royals and the Orléanses, thoroughly enjoying the role. She admired Louis-Philippe, was extremely fond of the new royal family, and greatly valued her relationship with them in the years to come. As Olivier Barnier put it in his afterword to Muhlstein's abridged English edition of Adèle's memoirs, 'the pleasure with which she writes about her closeness to the new royal family is palpable.'[53]

FINAL DAYS

The 1820s and the 1830 Revolution were perhaps the highlight of Adèle's social and political life. After the Revolution she reopened her salon, which became again a leading centre of Parisian intellectual and cultural activity. For many years it was frequented by most of the leading intellectual figures of the day, including poets and writers such as Sainte-Beuve, Jasmin and de Girardin, as well as her close friend Mme Récamier and many prominent political personalities, including Talleyrand. She also maintained an exceptionally close relationship with the queen and the Orléans household. In one sense it could not have been as close as that of Fanny Burney's daily contact with Queen Charlotte at Windsor, but Fanny's position was, of course, one of dependency, whereas Adèle was a friend and near equal. In June 1830 her husband, General de Boigne, died and despite their past differences and divided married life Adèle spoke kindly of him in her memoirs. Indeed, she had a great deal in the material sense for which to be grateful to him.

From this time on her relationship with Pasquier began to develop into the lifelong friendship that lasted until he died in July 1862 at the great age of 96. This relationship is considered with great authority and understanding in Françoise Wagener's biography of Adèle. Wagener says that from 1830 Adèle

> *concentra sa vie personnelle sur une seconde grande présence masculine, celle du futur chancelier Pasquier, homme d'état prépondérant, admiré pour sa sagacité, sa modération et sa longévité.*

> [concentrated her personal life on a second great masculine presence, that of the future chancellor Pasquier, an outstanding statesman, admired for his wisdom, moderation and longevity.][54]

They became one of France's most celebrated couples – almost a national institution – and some believe that they were secretly married. There are many accounts and even portraits of them together in their declining years, but although they enjoyed a relationship that was a '*miracle permanent de compréhension, d'échange, d'écoute mutuelle, de douceur, de proximité intelligente* [an enduring miracle of understanding, of sharing, of listening to each other, of gentleness, of intelligent closeness]',[55] they never lived together and there is no evidence that they married.

When Adèle was in Paris they met almost every evening in her salon, which was now one of the most influential and sought-after in the city. In her memoirs Adèle is always discreet about their relationship, but after his death in 1862 she paid the following moving tribute to him:

> *Il est impossible de trouver un commerce plus facile et plus charmant que celui de monsieur Pasquier. A un esprit toujours inventif, à une conversation des plus variés, il joignait un incomparable bon sens et une bienveillance naturelle qui, sans être jamais banale, lui faisait constamment tirer le meilleur parti possible des hommes et des choses.*

> [It is impossible to find an easier or more charming relationship than that with M. Pasquier. He combined with an ever inventive spirit and the most

varied conversation an incomparable good sense and a natural benevolence which, without ever being banal, constantly made him see the very best possible in both people and situations.][56]

The language is typically restrained, but makes quite clear her huge affection and respect for the long-standing Derby of later years to her Joan.

In May 1831 she suffered the death of her mother, Eléonore, who had been ailing for many years, but her revered father, to whom, like Fanny, she was always closer, lived on until February 1838. She was never so actively involved again in political affairs during the 1830s, but for the next decade her tireless pen continued to turn out brilliant accounts of contemporary events (she did not stop her writing until 1843). One such, in a specially written memorandum, was that of the farcical landing of the Duchesse de Berry in Provence in April 1832 in an attempt to lead an old royalist insurrection, revive the war in the Vendée, overthrow the July monarchy and put her son, the Duc de Bordeaux, on the throne. The attempted coup was a complete fiasco and Adèle's account of the duchess's capture, which she described as the 'premier acte de cette comédie [first act of this comedy]',[57] is a tragicomic tour de force.

After the failure of the uprising, the Duchess and some of her co-conspirators were tracked down to a large country mansion and took refuge in a secret recess behind a chimney breast, but were literally smoked out when a fire was lit and they could no longer stand the heat and the fumes that began to suffocate them. Adèle recounts that

> ce qui acheva de rendre leur situation intolérable, c'est la fumée épaisse et puante des papiers imprimés. La cachette n'était pas séparée du tuyau de la cheminée jusqu'en haut; elle s'en remplit incontinent et ses malheureux habitants en furent comme asphyxiés.

> [what made them give up their intolerable situation was the thick and smelly smoke coming from the printed papers they had with them. The hiding place was not separated from the chimney flue above, which filled it with unrestrained smoke and virtually asphyxiated its unhappy occupants.][58]

With the good political sense and humanity that she had displayed in warning Marshal Marmont against the excessive use of military force against the July demonstrators in Paris in 1830, Adèle also strongly advised that it would be politically counter-productive to force the Duchess to face the full force of the law and stand trial for treason. Indeed, she thought the best course would be to deport her from France as soon as she was apprehended. In the event, and particularly since it was found to everyone's surprise that the Duchess was pregnant by an undeclared lover, she was allowed to leave the country on a French frigate for Livorno in Italy after a short imprisonment in a fortress at Blaye. Sadly, the baby died in infancy. For vivid and exciting reporting, this racy account from firsthand sources compares with that of the July Revolution and with Fanny's account of her courageous wanderings across Belgium and Germany to find her injured husband after the Battle of Waterloo.

Another tour de force is Adèle's account of the severe cholera epidemic that struck Paris during Lent in 1832 and caused 13,000 deaths in the first month and 18,400 in total by the time it ended in September. It almost ranks with Thucydides' famous account in Book Two of his *History of the Peloponnesian War* of the plague in Athens in 430 BC or Samuel Pepys's description of the plague in London in 1665. The epidemic broke out violently in Paris and took the government completely unawares. Rumours about the cause of the disease ran rife: four innocent people suspected of being poisoners were murdered, other atrocities were committed and accusations were flung right and left, at republicans, legitimists and the government. On the whole, however, the Parisian public reacted well. Ambulances were mobilized to pick up people who had fallen sick in the streets; groups of high-born young men went from dwelling to dwelling, at great risk, to remove corpses; priests went round to administer confessions and last rites to the dying; in the suburbs improvised hospitals were established and food, clothing and beds provided for the sick.

Chacun donnait, même au delà de ses moyens, avec entraînement, et, ce qui est pour le moins autant à remarquer, si le riche était généreux, le pauvre était reconnaissant. Jamais je n'ai vu toutes les classes de la société réunies par un lien plus touchant.

[Everyone gave enthusiastically, even beyond their means, and, what is not the least remarkable aspect, if the rich were generous, the poor were appreciative. I have never seen all classes of society united by a more touching bond.][59]

Adèle was truly proud of the caring behaviour of her fellow countrymen, which she summed up as '*l'honorable conduite tenue par la grande masse de la population. Riches et pauvres, chacun fit son devoir et plus que son devoir* [the honourable conduct displayed by the great mass of the population. Rich and poor, everyone did their duty – indeed, more than their duty].'[60]

As Adèle grew older many of her old friends inevitably passed away, including Chateaubriand in July 1848 and Mme Récamier in the following year. Like many others, she had a love–hate attitude towards the immensely gifted but enigmatic and often frustrated Chateaubriand, and her memoirs contain a lengthy, fascinating and critically perceptive appreciation of what has been called a brilliant literary but disappointing political career. Her old friend Talleyrand, the survivor of so many regimes, also died in 1848, and her long description of his attempt at deathbed reconciliation with the Pope and the Catholic Church makes absorbing reading. The great diplomat, whom Napoleon was once said to have described as 'a lump of shit in a silk stocking'[61] and on St Helena regretted he had not had shot when he could have done, characteristically kept his options for the future life open until the end.

In 1848 Adèle witnessed yet another revolution: the fall of the July monarchy and the assumption of power in a coup d'état, first as president and later as emperor by another Napoleon, Louis, the son of Napoleon Bonaparte's younger brother, also Louis, who for a short time had been the King of Holland. This was in a sense the end of the old world for Adèle. In contrast to July 1830, she was not personally involved in the events of this revolution, but she gives a full and vivid second-hand account of it. Following discontent in the army and growing civil disturbances, including the customary invasion by demonstrators of the Tuileries, Louis-Philippe signed an abdication order, and he and the queen managed to make their way to Harfleur and get an onward passage aboard an English ship to England, where they settled at Claremont, a great house near Esher in Surrey. Adèle, who at this time was partially immobilized by a foot operation, was greatly distressed by these events and at one stage contemplated going into exile with Pasquier. This was really the end of her direct association with great political events, and in 1851 she sold the house her husband had acquired for her at Châtenay and bought a new one at Trouville, close to the sea in Normandy, where she could be nearer to Pasquier. One convenience of modern times was that the first proper passenger railway built in France ended there, so they could travel to or get news from Paris more promptly than elsewhere. She also formed a new friendship there with the young poet Prosper Mérimée, who had been a supporter of Louis-Philippe's and visited, corresponded with and became devoted to her. Without children of her own, it is yet another testimony to her tough but sympathetic and adaptable character that in old age she was able to develop friendships with young people, including her great-nephew, who later became her heir and inherited her papers.

To her great grief her oldest and dearest friend, Queen Marie-Amélie, widow of Louis-Philippe (who had himself died in 1850), died on 24 March 1866 at Claremont House, but the now ailing Adèle soon followed her. For some time she had been severely disabled and unable to walk, and had to be carried to her carriage and to the different rooms in her house or into the garden. With the death of Marie-Amélie, and the earlier death of Pasquier in 1862, she had lost all her old friends and she passed away on 10 May 1866 at the age of 85 – not quite as old as Fanny Burney, but a considerable age for that period. She seemed to be ready to go and expired peacefully: in the words of Marie, her young companion and reader,

avec ses dents de jeune fille et ses beaux cheveux. Avec tout son esprit aussi – forte et noble femme, consciente et responsable jusqu'au terme, ayant accompli son parcours.

[with the teeth of a young girl and beautiful hair. With her spirit intact as well – a strong and noble woman, conscious and responsible to the end, having completed her life's course.][62]

As previously stated, her memoirs were kept in the family and not published until 1907 – an utterly brilliant record of an exceptional person.

THREE

NAPOLEON

The dominant European figure during the lifetimes of Fanny and Adèle was Napoleon Bonaparte. Although he did not start the French Revolution, he took it over, tamed it and turned the republican wars into more than a decade of imperial aggression and expansion, which overwhelmed the rest of Europe. Large tracts of western Russia were laid to waste, with huge loss of life; Britain was under continual threat of invasion; and the map of Europe was drawn and redrawn at Napoleon's whim as he nominated his brothers, sisters and favourite marshals as sovereigns of newly conquered or assimilated territories. To the English, 'Boney' was a nightmarish figure with a huge army waiting at Boulogne to cross the Channel, seize them in their beds and take control of their country. In her delightful memoirs of Napoleon's initial stay for a few weeks at her father's house, the Briars, on St Helena in October and November 1815,[1] the 15-year-old Betsy Balcombe told how she had been taught as a child to believe that he was a 'huge ogre or giant, with one large flaming red eye in the middle of his forehead, and long teeth protruding from his mouth, with which he tore to pieces and devoured naughty little girls, especially those who did not know their lessons'. After living, going for walks and playing children's games with him, she soon learned that he was not so terrible after all, but this image of the tyrant that had been built up in the British press was no doubt why crowds in little boats flocked to catch a real-life glimpse of him when he arrived as a captive at Plymouth and Torbay in July 1815 on His Majesty's ship of the line *Bellerophon*.

Economic life was transformed under Napoleon's impact: in France by the drain of continual warfare on its financial and other resources as well as the effects of the British maritime blockade on its ports and commerce; and in Britain by the sheer cost of re-equipping and maintaining the navy and financing coalition after coalition against the French Empire. And millions of lives had been lost on battlefields all over Europe. Napoleon, unlike the Duke of Wellington, was never sparing of his own troops or those of the enemy. At the end of the wars an economically weakened France was virtually back to its pre-Napoleonic boundaries, while Britain, as was to happen again after the world wars of the twentieth century, had to regroup and cope with the economic penalties of military success.

The lives of both Fanny and Adèle were profoundly affected by these events. After her marriage to Alexandre d'Arblay in 1793, and the subsequent move with him to live in France, Fanny was in effect imprisoned in Paris for a decade (from 1802 to 1812) after the short-lived Peace of Amiens had broken down. English residents in France were treated with suspicion as aliens and prevented from communicating freely with Britain or leaving the country. She also suffered the agonies of having to flee from Paris on Napoleon's return from Elba and survive alone in the fevered war atmosphere of Brussels during the Waterloo campaign, after her ailing and would-be soldier–hero husband had set off on a mission to raise loyalist forces for the restored King Louis XVIII at Trier. With no reliable news of him after the Battle of Waterloo, she finally undertook on her own a hazardous six-day journey through Belgium and Germany to try to find him, not knowing whether he was still alive or dead. In the event, she found him once again severely injured and had great difficulty in getting him back safely to Paris.

By contrast, Adèle and her family were never quite as close as Fanny to serious front-line fighting, except for the early days of the Revolution when the mob invaded Versailles and they narrowly escaped being seized and killed, and also during Adèle's direct forays to the barricades in Paris during the 1830 July

1 *Henry Thrale, by Edward Scriven, after Reynolds*

2 *Sir Joshua Reynolds, by George Clint, after Reynolds*

3 *David Garrick as Richard III, by John Dixon*

4 *A Literary Party at Sir Joshua Reynolds's, by D. George Thompson*

5 *Nine Muses, by Richard Samuel*

6 *Louis XVI, King of France, seized by a revolutionary mob, by John Smith III*

7 *Louis XVIII, King of France, by Charles Turner*

8 *La Famille Royale (Louis XVIII) et les alliées…, published by Décrouant*

9 *Alexander I, Tsar of Russia, published by Colnaghi & Co.*

10 *George IV, by Samuel William Reynolds*

11 *Adèle de Boigne at 83 years. Photograph by Trinquart*

12 *Marquis d'Osmond,*
Adèle's father

13 *Alexandre d'Arblay, by*
Carle and Horace Vernet

14 *Mme de Staël, after*
a portrait by Gérard

15 *Mme Récamier, by Gérard*

16 *Charles-Maurice de Talleyrand, by Thomas Hodgetts*

17 *View of the Trial of Warren Hastings, published by Robert Pollard*

18 *Calais Pier, by J.M.W. Turner*

19 *Camilla Cottage. Sketch by Alexandre d'Arblay*

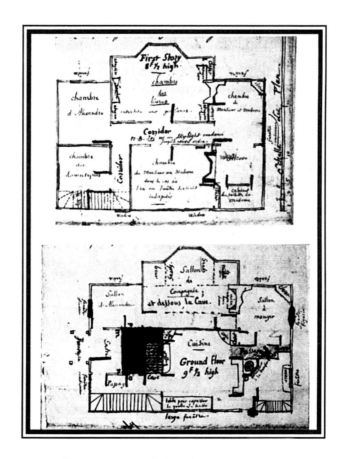

20 *Camilla Cottage ground plan. Sketch by Alexandre d'Arblay*

JUNIPER HALL

This house gave shelter in 1792 to a group of progressive French aristocrats who had fled to England to escape the worst excesses of the French Revolution.
The group included the Princesse de Hénin, the Comtesse de la Châtre, Madame de Staël, Jaucourt, Louis de Narbonne, Lally Tollendal, Alexandre d'Arblay and Talleyrand.
It was here that Fanny Burney the novelist, as a visitor to her sister, Susanna Phillips of Mickleham, met Alexandre d'Arblay to whom she was subsequently married at Mickleham Church.

Given by European School – Brussels I. 1994

IN THIS CHURCH WAS MARRIED
FANNY BURNEY,
NOVELIST AND DIARIST,
TO THE FRENCH EMIGRÉ GENERAL
ALEXANDRE D'ARBLAY,
28th. JULY 1793.
"And never, never was union more blessed and felicitous"

21 *Plaque on wall outside Juniper Hall*

22 *Plaque in Mickleham Church commemorating the marriage of Fanny Burney and Alexandre d'Arblay*

Revolution. But, as 'constitutional' royalists, after having fled from France once during the Revolution, they had to find ways of tempering their opposition and of living with Napoleon's administration during the years of the Empire. As Adèle's father had nailed his royalist colours to the mast by accepting ambassadorial office in Piedmont under the first Bourbon restoration in 1814, they would have been at grave risk if Napoleon's return from Elba had succeeded and he had consolidated his power in Paris. They would no doubt once again have been forced into exile and to seek refuge in England or elsewhere. These and other events gave both Fanny and Adèle many opportunities to view and comment on Napoleon at firsthand, and this chapter will draw on their different accounts of those experiences.

It is often said of great men and women that they were lucky, and Napoleon is no exception. The truth, however, as so often, is that, although he was said to choose lucky generals, he made the most of his own luck, certainly on the battlefield, by a combination of tactical genius, tirelessness, ruthlessness, understanding of human nature and an eye for the critical moment to take a risk and strike. Adèle's memoirs, however, contain accounts of two little-known but fascinating incidents in which luck seems to have been on his side.

The first relates to a journey Adèle's father made in January 1790 when, having left the army two years previously and entered into Louis XVI's diplomatic service, he chartered a felucca in the harbour at Toulon in order to take him over on business to Ajaccio, Napoleon's birthplace in Corsica. He was approached before departure by '*un gentilhomme Corse* [a Corsican gentleman]',[2] who was accompanied by his young son and begged d'Osmond to take them both over with him as passengers to Ajaccio. D'Osmond agreed, and at dinner on the voyage, to which he invited them together with some of his former army colleagues on board, d'Osmond noticed that the boy, who was wearing a military school uniform, was still sitting and reading on his own at the end of the boat. He asked one of the ship's officers, a M. de Belloc, to call the boy over to the dinner table to join them. The boy, however, declined and de Belloc was so irritated that he exclaimed: '*J'ai envie de le jeter dans la mer, ce petit sournois; il a une mauvaise figure. Permettez-vous, mon colonel?* [I should like to throw this sly little chap into the sea; he has an unpleasant face. Will you allow me to do this, colonel?].'[3] D'Osmond laughed and replied:

Non, je ne permets pas, je ne suis pas de votre avis, il a une figure de caractère;
je suis persuadé qu'il fera son chemin.

[No, I won't allow it and I don't share your view; his face shows character
and I am sure he will make his way in the world one day.][4]

Adèle's next sentence then contains the punch line: '*Ce petit sournois, c'était*
l'empereur Napoléon [This sly little chap was the Emperor Napoleon].'[5] There is
some suggestion that the boy was in fact Napoleon's older brother, Joseph, who
was also sent away to a military school in France, but de Belloc stuck to his belief
that it was Napoleon and in later years commented ruefully that if Adèle's father
had only allowed him to throw the young Bonaparte into the sea, he would not
then be turning the world upside down. D'Osmond's view of the boy's potential
showed remarkable prescience, but perhaps on reflection he too might have
regretted that he did not allow de Belloc to do what he wanted.

Adèle interestingly records that following this incident her father, in addition
to meeting for the first time Pozzo di Burgo, who was to feature prominently in
her future life, went to the Bonaparte home in Ajaccio to meet the mother of the
young boy whom he had saved from being thrown into the sea on their crossing
there. This was the formidable and celebrated Letitia, who became known as
Mme Mère under the Empire. Adèle says:

Lors de la visite de mon père, elle était encore une très belle femme; il la trouva
dans sa cuisine, sans bas, avec un simple jupon attaché sur une chemise, occu-
pée à faire des confitures. Malgré sa beauté, elle lui parut digne de son emploi.

[At the time of my father's visit she was still a very beautiful woman.
He found her in the kitchen, without stockings and with a simple apron
over her dress, busy making jam. Despite her beauty, what she was doing
seemed to him appropriate.][6]

This picture of the mother of the emperor-to-be, the matriarch of the large
Bonaparte clan, bare-legged and making jam in the kitchen in spite of her Corsican
aristocratic lineage, is a vivid and touching one and perhaps shows why in later
life she was so revered by Napoleon and the rest of her family.

The second incident is even more startling and relates to the end of February 1815, when d'Osmond was serving as the restored Louis XVIII's ambassador to Piedmont. He and Adèle, who found Turin an extremely boring city, and its inhabitants even more so, travelled to Genoa – then occupied by British forces – where they were invited to attend a demonstration to the king, the restored Victor Emmanuel I, of an awesome new British weapon of war, the Congreve rocket, which had been devised by Sir William Congreve, controller of the army laboratory at Woolwich, who had seen reports of a similar weapon being used by native troops against British forces in India. Although it did feature among the weapons deployed at Waterloo, the Duke of Wellington never really trusted it, as he believed it just as likely to hit his own troops as those of the enemy, but on this occasion it was decided to show it off.

The diplomatic corps and other VIPs were duly conducted to a rocky plateau overlooking the sea just outside the city. They had a wonderful view of the ocean. Moored out at sea, just within their vision, was an old ship anchored there to act as a target for the rockets. Just as the fuses were to be lit and the demonstration begun, they sighted two small ships out in the bay, tacking to get across it and out into the open sea. Instructions were given for the firing to be suspended until the two vessels had succeeded and were safely out of range. Adèle then reports, again delaying the punch line to the end:

> *D'après toutes les circonstances qui sont venues depuis à notre connaisance, il est indisputable que ces deux bricks transportaient Bonaparte et sa fortune aux rivages de Cannes. Combien le hazard d'une de ces fusées, en désemparant ces bâtiments, aurait pu changer le destin du monde!*

[In view of the facts that afterwards came to our knowledge, there can be no doubt at all that these two brigs were carrying Bonaparte and his fortunes to the shores of Cannes. If one of those rockets had happened to strike these boats, how great a change might have been made to the destiny of the world!]'[7]

How great indeed! This story, which there is no reason to doubt, but which has been strangely overlooked by historians, must rank as one of the greatest might-have-beens in history. Napoleon was on his way back from Elba with his little army and in a short time, gathering more troops to him as he marched, was back in power in Paris.

Fanny's first-hand experience of Napoleon did not come until she and her husband were living in Paris, and there is curiously little mention of him in her accounts of the earlier periods of her life, given the shadow he cast over her native country. In May 1802 they were given tickets to watch Napoleon, as first consul, review his troops on the parade ground of the Tuileries Palace. Fanny was lucky enough to be stationed at a window of the audience chamber and she describes how a senior functionary started the proceedings by flinging open a door with a commanding crash and calling out in a loud and authoritative voice: 'Le Premier Consul'.[8] She says that if she had not been allowed to stand at the front (since she was only five foot two inches tall) she would hardly have seen Napoleon. As it was, she had a close-up view and it is worth quoting her description at length:

> I had a view so near, though so brief, of his face, as to be very much struck by it: it is of a deeply impressive cast, pale even to sallowness, while not only in the Eye, but in every feature, Care, Thought, Melancholy, and Meditation are strongly marked, with so much of character, nay, Genius, and so penetrating a seriousness – or rather sadness, as powerfully to sink into an observer's mind: yet, though the Busts and Medallions I have seen are, in general, such good resemblances, that I think I should have known him untold, he has by no means the look to be expected from Bonaparte, – but rather that of a profoundly studious and contemplative Man, who, "o'er Books consumes" – not only the "midnight oil", but his own daily strength, and "wastes the puny body to decay" by abstruse speculations, and theoretic plans, or, rather, visions, ingenious, but not practicable. But the look of the Commander who heads his own army, who fights his own Battles, who conquers every difficulty by personal exertion, who executes all he plans, who performs even all he suggests – whose ambition is of the most enterprising, and whose bravery of the most daring cast – This, which is the look to be expected from his situation, and the exploits which have led to it, the spectator watches for in vain. The plainness, also, of his dress, so conspicuously contrasted by the finery of all around him, conspires forcibly with his countenance, so "Sicklied o'er with the pale hue of Thought", to give him far more the air of a Student than of a Warrier.[9]

Fanny was evidently very impressed and excited by the experience. Although she did not find in Napoleon, on the strength of this one brief close-up, the look of the all-conquering military commander she had expected, she was struck by the studious and contemplative, even melancholy, nature of his appearance on this occasion. It tends to confirm the remarkable ability of Napoleon to fascinate, and almost mesmerize, people with his personal magnetism and charisma. Even veteran sea captains, who had spent most of their lives in the Royal Navy fighting against Napoleon, came away after calling on him on St Helena, in the damp and cramped conditions of Longwood House, captivated by his personality and full of sympathy, if not outrage, for his treatment by the British government and the governor, Sir Hudson Lowe. Similarly, the midshipmen on the *Northumberland*, which took him to St Helena, ended the voyage won over by his personality – they even named one of the ship's great guns after him. On the occasion of this review, Fanny was so excited that she forgot the offer from the friendly wife of a grenadier, whom she called 'Ma Mie', and who was standing near to her, to engage the first consul in conversation as he passed by her to or on his way back from the parade. As for the parade itself, she found it

> far more superb than anything I had ever beheld; but while – with all the pomp and circumstance of war – it animated all others, it only saddened me, and all of past reflection and all of future dread, and all the delusive seduction of the martial music, filled my eyes frequently with tears.[10]

When Napoleon went down to the Tuileries gardens to inspect the troops at close quarters, Fanny was also intrigued that he seemed, by the casual and almost careless manner in which he held the bridle of his rearing, prancing horse, not to be a very good horseman. On reflection, however, she summed up her view of him on parade by saying:

> I am the last to be a *Judge* on this subject but, as a Remarker, he appeared to me as a Man who knew so well he could manage his Animal when he pleased, that he did not deem it worth his while to keep constantly in order what he knew – if urged or provoked, – he could subdue in a moment.[11]

Fanny's remarks were ostensibly addressed to Napoleon's horsemanship, but were clearly intended to be interpreted as a reference to his capacity for command and control generally. Her thoughts were echoed by her neighbour, Ma Mie, who, suspecting that Fanny might not be quite as impressed as she should have been, exclaimed to her:

> *Est-ce que vous ne savez pas cela, Madame? Dès que le premier Consul vient à la parade, le soleil vient aussi! Il a beau pleuvoir tout le matin; c'est égal; le premier Consul n'a qu'à paraître et tout de suite il fait beau.*

> [Don't you know, madam? As soon as the first consul comes on parade, the sun also shines. Although it has rained all morning, that doesn't matter; the first consul has only to appear and suddenly it is fine again.][12]

This was another example of Napoleon's extraordinary charisma and ability to win people over to him, but Fanny wisely 'apologised humbly for [her] ignorance'.

Fanny did not see Napoleon at close quarters again but – as already briefly noted, in a journal entry sometime before, and probably close to, July 1812 – she described how she was invited by Mme David, the wife of Napoleon's official court painter, Jacques-Louis David, to visit his studio and see two new paintings of Napoleon, which had been commissioned for a national exhibition. Fanny should have been a connoisseur of portrait painting, since one of the greatest friends of her father, whose work she had frequently seen and admired, was Sir Joshua Reynolds, the greatest English portrait painter of his day. On this occasion Napoleon had been consulted on the choice of subject and had elected for an equestrian pose and even dictated how he should be presented: 'Faits moi calme, posé, tranquil – sur un cheval fougueux [Show me as calm, posed, tranquil – on a fiery horse].'[13] Fanny was much impressed with the result, and in her journal says:

> And the imperturbable composure of Bonaparte, who seems absorbed in ruminations so abstruse that they lift him up above all personal care, and give him a contempt of all personal danger, contrasted with the fiery spirit and uncontrollable vigour of the wildly unruly animal, produces an effect

so striking between The Horse and Rider, that France seems depicted as retaining all its martial ardour, while governed by a Chief who owes his power and command to his own fearless self-possession.[14]

The old master's magic, as portrayed on canvas through David's art, obviously made the impression on Fanny that Napoleon intended. Here was the great military commander, astride his fiery steed, brought to life.

Fanny was also shown by Mme David another rather different portrait of Napoleon that had in fact been commissioned by an English peer, the Marquis of Douglas and Clydesdale, which was later entitled *L'Empereur debout dans son cabinet* (*The Emperor in His Office*). Again Napoleon, the supreme propagandist himself, had dictated the form of the portrait, which showed him standing 'in his Morning and most undressed military uniform',[15] in front of a table covered in maps, which were also scattered across the floor. He was 'very carelessly arranged, his cravat off or falling, and one stocking down at heel'.[16] His face, however, had

an expression as simple, as unaffected and as unassuming as his attire, and with the fall of his hands, which are very finely finished, he seems to be making an appeal to the British nation, through the British nobleman for whom this representation of their renowned antagonist is designed, that shall cry out: Look at me, Britons! Survey me well! What have you to fear, or doubt? What is there to excite such deadly hatred, in a man as soberly and modestly arrayed as the plainest John Bull amongst yourselves, and as philosophically employed, without state or attendance?[17]

Although Fanny had shown that she was not impervious to Napoleon's personal charm, she had by then lived in Paris for a decade under his absolute rule and was perceptive enough to recognize the propaganda purpose behind this portrait. She was, however, very careful not to reveal to the 'shrewd, penetrating, sagacious and sarcastic'[18] Mme David that she understood that the object of the painting was 'to conquer John Bull's opinion for the attainment of British popularity'. She was also sorry not to have been able to meet the artist David himself, who was out of Paris at the time, but in the course of the viewing she was joined by Mme Larrey, a pupil of David's and the wife of Baron Larrey, the 'Prince of surgeons', who in the previous September had carried out the successful mastectomy operation on her and also attended to her husband in Paris after the injuries he suffered in the accident on the quay at Calais.

Fanny's view of Napoleon began to change – and some of the scales were removed from her eyes – after her return to France to rejoin her husband in November 1814, when their lives were violently disrupted by Napoleon's escape from Elba and seizure of power early the following year. But even then she found it difficult at first fully to appreciate what his return could entail. Habituated to Napoleon's ability to conquer and achieve the seemingly impossible, she wrote:

> the idea of Napoleon was blended with all our thoughts, our projects, our actions. The greatness of his power, the intrepidity of his ambition, the vastness of his conceptions, and the restlessness of his spirit, kept suspense always breathless, and conjecture always at work. [...] how could I for a moment suppose he would re-visit France without a consciousness of success, founded upon some secret conviction that it was infallible. Unmoved, therefore, I reposed in the general apparent repose, which, if it were as real in those with whom I mixed as in myself, I now deem for all a species of infatuation.[19]

This 'infatuation' was, however, soon dispelled when Napoleon and his growing army were reported to be approaching Paris and she received an urgent message from her husband, who had set off to join the royalist forces, to leave Paris as soon as possible. During the subsequent nightmarish days in Brussels, when there was still no news of d'Arblay, she sent a hopeful letter to him saying:

> If he [Napoleon] succeeds, in two years he will again lead us the same dance of death he has so frightfully taught us at this moment. The numbers of dead, whether of Conquerors or Conquered, have not yet been counted! – nor even all the wounded – some are still on the field of Battle, where they are dressed, – their wounds, I mean! – while waiting for carriages, which are constantly on the road![20]

A few weeks later, in a letter to her friend Queeney, the daughter of Mrs Thrale, she was praising Queeney's husband, Admiral Lord Keith, because 'he gives, and in so lordly a manner, the word of command to the late tyrant of Nations and Sovereign of Kings'.[21] This was a reference to the fact that when Napoleon and his small group of loyal companions were brought over to England on the *Bellerophon*, Lord Keith, the naval commander-in-chief at Plymouth, was deputed by the government to inform him that his request for asylum in England had been refused and that he and his party were to be sent to St Helena. The use of the word 'tyrant' in reference to Napoleon at last is significant.

Fanny's views on Napoleon could never be as sophisticated or politically informed as those of Adèle, who had to find ways of coming to terms with the imperial court and had many more opportunities to view and judge Napoleon at close quarters in Paris. Just as Fanny had described in thoughtful detail Napoleon's review of his troops on parade, one of Adèle's first descriptions is of a ball given by the emperor to celebrate the marriage of the Princess of Baden, to which she had been invited (a good example of how she and her family succeeded in remaining *personae gratae* with the court). It was a very grand affair – Napoleon was always anxious to create a court that could be compared favourably with those of the established European royal houses – and the Empress Josephine, the princesses, their ladies-in-waiting and assorted functionaries and chamberlains were all in attendance in full court dress. After the performance of a short ballet, Napoleon did the rounds of the room, talking exclusively to the ladies. He also was in full imperial dress – waistcoat and white-satin knee breeches, white shoes with gold rosettes, a gold-embroidered coat of red velvet cut straight in the style of his future father-in-law, Francis I of Austria, a sword sparkling with diamonds and a cap with feathers held together by a diamond buckle. Adèle, however, was decidedly unimpressed. She writes:

> *Ce costume pouvait être bien dessiné, mais pour lui qui était petit, gros et emprunté dans ses mouvements, il était disgracieux. Peut-être y avait-il prévention; l'Empereur me parut affreux, il avait l'air du roi de carreau.*

> [The costume may have been well designed, but was quite unsuited for him on account of his small size, his corpulence and his clumsiness of movement. I may have been prejudiced, but the emperor seemed to me frightful, and looked like the king of diamonds.][22]

A brilliantly dismissive portrait of the five foot six and a half inches tall and increasingly corpulent Napoleon.

As Napoleon passed along the assembled ranks of ladies, chatting to some of them, he paused and spoke to Adèle, requesting her name, registering his appreciation of her husband's service to his country, asking her age and enquiring:

> *Vous n'avez pas d'enfants? Je sais bien que ce n'est pas votre faute, mais arrangez-vous pour en avoir. Croyez-moi, pensez-y, je vous donne un bon conseil.*

> [You have no children? I know that it is not your fault, but you should arrange to remedy that. Believe me, and think about it, I am giving you good advice.][23]

Although Adèle may have felt flattered by the emperor's attention (despite his questions, he clearly remembered who she was and the circumstances of her marriage), it may also have been a little chilling to know that, with his extensive intelligence network under the powerful police minister Fouché, he knew so much about her personal affairs. It is amusing too that the great matchmaker and marriage fixer also thought it within his compass to determine whether people should have children or not.

Adèle's scathing comments about Napoleon's dress and somewhat ludicrous appearance at the ball were perhaps compensated for by her account of a later occasion when he gave another ball to mark the baptism of his son, whom he had given the title the King of Rome – an occasion which she describes as '*la dernière fête impériale* [the last imperial festivity]'.[24] On this occasion military uniforms were banned and Napoleon was no longer dressed up in his grand imperial costume. He wore

> *un simple uniforme, que lui seul portait au milieu des habits habillés, le rendait encore plus remarquable et parlait plus à l'imagination que ne l'auraient pu faire toutes les broderies du monde. Il voulut être gracieux et obligeant, et me parut infiniment mieux qu'à l'autre bal.*

> [a simple uniform, which he alone wore in the middle of all this formal dress, made him a yet more remarkable figure and spoke more loudly to

the imagination than all the gold lace in the world. He wished to appear gracious and kind and made a far better impression on me than at the other ball.][25]

On the other hand:

L'impératrice Marie-Louise était un beau brin de femme, assez fraîche, mais un peu trop rouge. Malgré sa parure et ses pierreries, elle avait l'air très commun et était dénuée de toute physionomie.

[The empress Marie-Louise was a fine woman, fresh in appearance but a little too red. But despite her dress and her jewels she seemed very common and entirely without distinction.][26]

These remarks reflect the complicated nature of Adèle's reactions to the new aristocracy created by Napoleon. As a genuine old aristocrat, faithful to her family's long and distinguished history dating back to the Norman conquest, she perhaps rather snobbishly mocked the new court, particularly when it dressed and behaved pretentiously. Nor did she believe that the young empress – Marie-Louise, the daughter of Francis I, Emperor of Austria, whom Napoleon had married in place of the divorced Josephine in 1809 in order to produce a male heir and found a Napoleonic dynasty – could add the 'class' necessary to make the parvenu court respectable. Her comments on Marie-Louise may also have reflected some lingering loyalty to the former Empress Josephine, with whom her mother's side of the family, the Dillons, were connected. But her basic patriotic loyalty now was still to France – she had thrown off her former 'anglomania' – and when she saw Napoleon in more modest garb she could not but moderate her comments on her country's head of state. Napoleon cast aside this modesty later, however, when he was detained on St Helena in his final years. In an increasingly desperate attempt to preserve his imperial dignity and status, he insisted on rigid protocol, including full dress uniform every night at dinner in the tiny, claustrophobic dining room in Longwood House, right until the last months of his life when his terminal illness confined him to his bath and bed for much of the time.

A most curious story told by Adèle relating to Napoleon occurs in the context of the elections of 1827 and the fall of the Louis XVIII's principal minister,

Jean-Baptiste de Villèle. She says that in 1827 or 1828 a little girl of two years of age was brought to her with bright-blue eyes, which seemed in no way remarkable at first sight. However, on closer examination the iris appeared to be composed of little filaments forming white letters on a blue background placed around the pupil and making the words 'Napoléon Empereur'. The word 'Napoléon' was apparently equally distinct in either eye, although the first letters of the word 'Empereur' were indistinct in one eye and the last letters in the other. The mother of the little girl, a Lorraine peasant, told Adèle a complicated story to explain the phenomenon, involving a special silver coin given to her as a keepsake by a soldier brother with the above words inscribed on it. Returning from a visit to her brother after an exhausting journey, and having no other money or source of credit, she was forced to use the coin at an inn to obtain refreshment and was distressed at having to part with it. Her husband returned to the inn and managed to get it back, and when he returned home she was so overjoyed that 'l'enfant, qu'elle portait dans son sein, tressaillait et elle se sentait pâmer. Je me sers de son expression [the child that she carried in her womb leaped and, to use her own expression, she felt faint with delight]'.[27] It is an odd story, and Adèle is not normally a credulous witness. But she prefaces it by assuring the reader that it was true, that she had seen it with her own eyes, and that no fraud was possible. It is difficult to know what to make of this story except that at some time everyone seems to have been mesmerized in one way or another by Napoleon.

Adèle's more considered political comments on Napoleon, and on the consequences of his dictatorship for France and Europe, were deeper and more perceptive. As a Frenchwoman, she could not in the end deny his stature and genius, which for some meant that he had to be judged by different standards from other people. Even her friend Chateaubriand, who was often in two minds but came down decisively against Napoleon in the end, said that 'il ne doit pas être jugé d'après les règles que l'on applique aux grands génies [you must not judge him by the rules you apply to other great geniuses]'.[28] But she saw the damage his rule was causing and sensed the growing disenchantment and sheer fatigue of her countrymen, despite the welcome that Napoleon had received – though perhaps largely from the army and dismissed veterans – at the beginning of the Hundred Days on his return from Elba. For example, commenting sceptically on the official reports of military victories she writes:

je crois que les masses étaient devenues profondément indifférentes aux succès militaires. Lorsque le canon nous annonçait le gain de quelque brillante bataille, un petit nombre de personnes s'en affligeait, un nombre un peu plus grand s'en réjouissait, mais la population y restait presque insensible. Elle était rassasiée de gloire et elle savait que de nouveaux succès entraînaient de nouveaux efforts. Une bataille gagnée était l'annonce d'une conscription.

[I believe the masses had become profoundly indifferent to military successes. When the cannon announced to us the victory of some brilliant battle, a small number of people were distressed, a slightly greater number rejoiced, but the general population remained virtually unmoved. They were sated with glory and knew that new successes brought demand for new efforts. A battle won meant the announcement of a new conscription.][29]

As we have seen in the case of the disastrous defeat of the French and Spanish fleets at Trafalgar in 1805, which was not reported in the official bulletin, news was severely censored and doctored. As Adèle records:

Les bulletins ne parlaient jamais que de nos triomphes, l'armée française était toujours victorieuse, l'armée ennemie toujours battue, et pourtant, d'échec en échec, elle était arrivée des rives de la Moscova à celles de la Seine.

[The bulletins only ever talked about our triumphs. The French army was always victorious, the enemy army beaten, and yet successive defeats brought it from the banks of the Moskva to the banks of the Seine.][30]

In more severe vein she says:

A mesure que le théâtre de la guerre se rapprochait, il était plus difficile de cacher la vérité sur l'inutilité des efforts gigantesques faits par Napoléon et son admirable armée; le résultat était inévitable. J'en demande bien pardon à la génération qui s'est élevée depuis dans l'adoration du libéralisme de l'Empereur, mais, à ce moment, amis et ennemis, tout suffoquait sous sa main de fer et sentait un besoin presque égal de la soulever. Franchement, il était détesté: chacun voyait en lui l'obstacle à son repos, et le repos était devenu le premier besoin de tous.

[As the theatre of war came nearer to home, it became more difficult to hide the truth concerning the futility of the gigantic efforts made by Napoleon and his impressive army; the result was inevitable. I must seek the pardon of the generation that has since grown up in adoration of the emperor's *liberal principles*, but, at that moment, friends and enemies were all suffocating beneath his iron hand and felt just as strong a desire to get rid of it. To speak frankly, he was detested: everyone saw him as the obstacle to peace, and peace was the first necessity for everyone.][31]

These were very strong charges – although, as always, Adèle exonerated the army itself and the ordinary soldiers from her strictures – but they must have accurately reflected the majority of popular feeling at the time. It was precisely the same general feeling that Napoleon, despite his initial reception by the army, failed to appreciate when he returned to Paris after Waterloo and, notwithstanding emotional appeals to the Assembly by both himself and his brother Louis, he was told in no short order by the provisional government under Fouché to leave Paris and France.

Adèle also appreciated the corrupting effect of supreme power on Napoleon, particularly in his relationship with subordinates. As the end of the Empire seemed to be in sight, in face of the overwhelming allied coalition, she wrote:

Le joug de Bonaparte devenait intolérable; son alliance avec la maison d'Autriche avait achevé de lui tourner la tête. Il n'écoutait que des flatteurs; toute contradiction lui était insupportable. Il en était arrivé à ce point qu'il ne supportait plus la vérité, même dans les chiffres.

[The yoke of Bonaparte was becoming intolerable; his alliance with the Austrian royal house had succeeded in turning his head. He listened only to flatterers; he could not stand any contradiction. He had reached the point where he could no longer bear the truth, even the truth of the facts and figures.][32]

Sic semper tyrannis!

Nevertheless, in spite of all her rational criticisms, Adèle's deep loyalty to her native country led her in the end to a more balanced judgement on Napoleon, reflecting partly her patriotism and perhaps despite herself succumbing a little, like many others, to his fabled charm. From the overall point of view she thought that history might be kinder to him.

A son tour la postérité oubliera les aberrations de ce sublime génie et ses petitesses [...] Quand une figure comme celle de Napoléon surgit dans les siècles, il ne faut pas conserver les petites obscurités qui pourraient ternir quelques-uns de ses rayons; mais il faut bien expliquer comment les contemporains, tout en étant éblouis, avaient cessé de trouver ces rayons vivifiants et n'en éprouvaient plus qu'un sentiment de souffrance.

[In its turn, posterity will forget the aberrations and little weaknesses of his sublime genius [...] When a figure like that of Napoleon arises amid the centuries we ought not to remember the little shadows that might tarnish some of its splendour, but explain how it was that his contemporaries, who had all been dazzled by him, found his splendour no longer a source of life but rather of pain and grief.][33]

These were charitable words indeed, but the final judgement in her memoirs, as she grew older and the immediate memories of Napoleon perhaps began to fade, was even more forgiving.

Recalling the sheer audacity of his escape from Elba (which she might have seen thwarted, had Congreve let off his rockets at Genoa sooner) and the many other bold strokes during his political and military career, Adèle wrote:

Il était impossible de n'être pas frappé de la grandeur, de la décision, de l'audace dans la marche et de l'habileté prodigieuse déployée par l'Empereur, de Cannes jusqu'à Paris. Il est peu étonnant que ses partisans en aient été électrisés et aient retrempé leur zèle à ce foyer du génie. C'est peut-être le plus grand fait personnel accompli par le plus grand homme des temps modernes.

[It was impossible not to be struck by the grandeur, the decision, the audacity and the prodigious skill that the emperor showed during the march from Cannes to Paris. It is not surprising that his supporters were electrified and that their zeal was reconfirmed by the contact with his genius. It was, perhaps, the greatest personal achievement by the greatest man of modern times.][34]

It was surely this admiration of Napoleon despite herself – her heart overcoming her head – that restrained Adèle from public criticism of him that might have had damaging consequences both for her and for her family. She was once asked, '*Comment n'êtes-vous pas exilée?* [How is it you were never exiled?]' She replied:

> *Ma maison était de celles où l'on parlait le plus librement; je voyais beaucoup de monde de toutes les couleurs, j'étais polie pour tous. Mes opinions étaient connues, mais pas aigrement professées.*

> [My house was one of those where you could talk more freely; I saw many people of every persuasion, and I was polite to everyone. My opinions were well known, but they were not expressed acrimoniously.][35]

With her extraordinary good sense and political acumen – and a sound instinct for self-preservation – Adèle knew how to keep the balance between free speech and discretion.

I wonder whether Adèle, on maturer reflection in old age, would have stood by all her later comments on Napoleon, especially the more favourable ones? She certainly appreciated that after his return from Elba his moral and physical powers were beginning to decline. She comments:

> *Dès que sa position lui fut complètement dévoilée, il désespéra de son succès, et le dégoût qu'il en conçut exerça peut-être quelque influence sur le découragement montré par lui lors de la catastrophe de Waterloo. J'ai lieu de croire que, bien peu de jours après son arrivée aux Tuileries, il cessa de déployer l'énergie qui l'avait accompagné depuis l'île d'Elbe.*

> [When he fully understood the nature of his position, he despaired of success, and the resulting despondency probably had an influence on the discouragement he showed at the time of the Waterloo catastrophe. I have reason to believe that a very few days after his arrival at the Tuileries

he ceased to display the energy that he had shown from the time of his departure from Elba.][36]

This kind of observation about his state of mind and physical health has also often been made by those who sought excuses for his defeat at Waterloo.

Adèle's sentiments were not, however, atypical of other love–hate attitudes towards Napoleon. Her great friend, the diplomat and writer Chateaubriand, to whose views on Napoleon we have already referred, and who was disappointed at not achieving the high positions in government that he had hoped for and thought himself worthy of, found himself in a similar dilemma. In his *Vie de Napoléon*, which constituted books XIX to XXIV of his great work *Mémoires d'outre-tombe*, he set out to investigate both sides of Napoleon's character and life. Putting the two facets together he sought to '*examiner cet homme à deux existences, de peindre le faux et le vrai Napoléon* [examine this man from two dimensions, to paint the false and the true Napoleon]'.[37] His first conclusion was that Napoleon '*était un poète en action, un génie immense dans la guerre, un esprit infatigable, habile et sensé dans l'administration, un législateur laborieux et raisonable* [was a poet in action, a genius in war, a tireless spirit, clever and sensible in government, a hard working and reasonable legislator]'. Nevertheless, as self-delusion and corruption by power set in, '*un orgueil monstrueux et une affectation incessante gâtent le caractère de Napoléon* [a monstrous arrogance and a perpetual affectation spoiled Napoleon's character]' and, paradoxically, for all his pretensions to liberty and equality, he ended up by being '*l'ennemi mortel de l'égalité et le plus grand organisateur de l'aristocratie dans la démocratie* [the mortal enemy of equality and the greatest organizer of aristocracy in a democracy]'. Chateaubriand's final charge sheet of what he labelled '*l'esclavage napoléonien* [Napoleonic slavery]' was

> *le tort que la vraie philosophie ne pardonnera pas à Bonaparte, c'est d'avoir façonné la société á l'obéissance passive, repoussé l'humanité vers les temps de dégradation morale, et peut-être abâtardi les caractères de manières qu'il serait impossible de dire quand les cœurs commenceront à palpiter de sentiments généreux.*

[the sin for which true philosophy will not pardon Bonaparte is to have moulded society into passive obedience, thrust humanity back into an era of moral degradation, and perhaps caused people to degenerate in such a way that it becomes impossible to say when hearts will again beat with generous feelings.]

These views, though more fully and vividly expressed, were not far in substance from those expressed by Adèle. Chateaubriand also found expression for his disenchantment with Napoleon by stating that in 1821 it would have been better to leave Napoleon to rest in his lonely and unmarked grave, deep in the ground on St Helena, than to exhume his remains and bring them back in triumph to Paris and set the eagle soaring aloft again. This was not unlike the reaction of the Duke of Wellington who, when consulted on the French government's request in 1840 to exhume Napoleon and take him back for burial in France, said that 'he does not care one twopenny damn what becomes of the ashes of Napoleon Bonaparte'.[38]

I suspect that Adèle, who wrote equally critically of the dual nature of Chateaubriand's own character, would not in general have dissented from these remarks, which could be suitably applied to most dictators in history. Given the ambivalence of these two intellectual heavyweights, we can easily forgive Fanny Burney for being fascinated by Napoleon's complex personality, at least on first acquaintance.

FOUR

WELLINGTON

The other dominating European military figure of the age during which Fanny and Adèle lived was the Duke of Wellington. In a sense he cannot be compared in overall stature with Napoleon, though many historians, like Andrew Roberts in his excellent book, *Napoleon and Wellington*, have sought to do so. Apart from his short-lasting and generally unremarkable premiership from 1828 to 1830, and an even shorter spell as de facto head of government, though not technically prime minister, in 1834, he never exercised political power equivalent to that of Napoleon at the highest level, although he remained almost to his death in 1852 a revered figure whom governments felt it necessary to consult on matters of national importance both great and small (ranging from whether in 1821 France should be allowed to exhume Napoleon on St Helena and take his remains back for burial in Paris to how to deal with the problem of sparrows inside the great Crystal Palace Exhibition in 1851 – he is said to have urged Queen Victoria to try sparrow hawks!). He remained essentially a loyal servant of the Crown, describing himself as a 'Nimmukwallah', or, as he put it, 'I have eaten of the King's salt, and, therefore, I conceive it my duty to serve and with unhesitating zeal and cheerfulness, when and wherever the King or his Government may think it proper to employ me.'[1] It is inconceivable to imagine Napoleon subscribing to this, even when he was a junior officer.

As a military commander, however, he proved himself Napoleon's equal, although Napoleon would never accept this and generally spoke of him in disparaging terms. Before the Battle of Waterloo, when his marshals were warning him of Wellington's formidable ability with British infantry to hold a defensive position, he dismissed him as just a sepoy general – one who had earned his reputation by beating inferior native troops in India – and said that the battle would be no more than the affair of a '*déjeuner* [breakfast]'. He defeated the best of Napoleon's marshals in the long Peninsular campaign from 1808 to 1813 and with a somewhat improvised allied army, stiffened by a core of British infantry veterans, and with the critical intervention of Blücher and the Prussians, he was victorious over Napoleon at Waterloo. They were the same age, 46, at Waterloo, but Wellington long outlived Napoleon. While Napoleon suffered a squalid and painful death from stomach cancer on St Helena only six years later, Wellington died peacefully in his sleep in 1852, as Warden of the Cinque Ports, in his favourite armchair at Walmer Castle in Kent at the age of 82. Debate will continue as to whether Wellington was a superior general compared to Napoleon. Until the Waterloo campaign he had never commanded such large armies as Napoleon and had fought fewer battles. But he won them all and he was certainly one of the greatest generals that Britain has ever had. He was necessarily more cautious and sparing of his troops than Napoleon was – he had to be because he only had one army and, unlike Napoleon, he could not summon up tens of thousands of replacements by simply ordering yet another conscription.

Whereas Napoleon cast his shadow over long periods of the lives of Fanny and Adèle, Wellington did not really make a direct impact on their lives until the Waterloo campaign, when he was commander-in-chief of the allied armies in Belgium and, especially for Adèle, when he was appointed British ambassador in Paris during the first Bourbon restoration in August 1814 and, more significantly, during the period immediately following Waterloo. He was then appointed commander-in-chief, or generalissimo of the army of occupation in Paris, and, with Tsar Alexander I of Russia, was the most powerful and prestigious figure in Europe. One of his significant acts when ambassador in 1814 had been to purchase from Napoleon's sister, Pauline Borghese, the magnificent Hôtel de Charost in the Rue du Faubourg Saint-Honoré, which, to the envy of the rest of the diplomatic corps, remains the British ambassador's residence in Paris to this day.

Fanny's acquaintance with Wellington was much more limited than that of Adèle and largely confined to her *Waterloo Journal*, which covered the events of April to July 1815, as seen from Brussels. This is perhaps not surprising since Fanny's earlier life in London, except for her five years at court, had mainly been spent in literary, musical, theatrical and intellectual circles, while Wellington – as Arthur Wesley, later Wellesley – had been a relatively unknown young army officer earning a growing reputation for his successful campaigns thousands of miles away in India. In 1801 he defeated Tipu Sahib, Sultan of Mysore, in the Fourth Mysore War and in 1803 won outstanding victories – some of the hardest he ever fought – over enemy armies that had a vast numerical superiority at the battles of Assaye and Argaum in the Second Mahratta War. He returned to England with the rank of major-general in September 1805, and for a time entered politics, becoming chief secretary to the Lord Lieutenant of Ireland. After active service as a brigade commander in an expedition under Lord Cathcart to Copenhagen in 1807, he was sent with a force of 9,000 men to Portugal in 1808 and thus began the start of his protracted but eventually victorious campaigns against Napoleon's marshals from 1808 to 1813 in the Peninsula. During most of this time, however, Fanny, with her husband and Alex, was virtually a prisoner in Paris and news, especially of French defeats, was strictly censored.

There is one intriguing episode related by Fanny, however, that shows that at least some news of Wellington's exploits in the Peninsula filtered through. In August 1812 Fanny was detained with her son Alex in Dunkirk for nearly six weeks, trying to arrange a passage back to England. As an alien, she was under close scrutiny by the French authorities, and she had a particularly unnerving experience when she was threatened with confiscation of the precious manuscript, in three volumes, of her new novel *The Wanderer*, which she was carrying in a large portmanteau specially made for the purpose by her husband, who had remained in Paris. As Fanny describes it, on opening the portmanteau and seeing these suspicious papers, the French police officer at the custom house began a rant of indignation and amazement, at a sight so unexpected and prohibited, that made him incapable to enquire or hear the meaning of such a freight. He sputtered at the Mouth, and stamped with his feet, so forcibly and vociferously, that no endeavours I could use could palliate the supposed offence sufficiently to induce him to stop his accusations of traitorous designs, till tired of the attempt, I ceased both explanation and entreaty, and stood before him with calm taciturnity.[2]

Fortunately, Fanny, fearing the destruction of what she called the 'Fourth Child of my Brain',[3] managed to secure the intervention of a certain Mr Gregory, who happened to be at hand and was apparently a respected English merchant long settled in Dunkirk. He vouched for her and persuaded the French authorities to let her keep and embark with the manuscript.

After this early incident Fanny imprudently sailed much closer to the wind in Dunkirk by showing a dangerous interest in a large group of Spanish prisoners who were under close guard and were marched out every day to do hard manual labour. She felt great sympathy for them, 'knowing that they were Men with and for whom our own English and the Immortal Wellington were then fighting' and, moreover, 'They were mostly strongly built and vigorous, of solemn, almost stately Deportment, and with fine dark Eyes, full of meaning, rolling around them as if in watchfull Expectation of insult'.[4] Fanny was so far carried away by the good looks of the prisoners, and her rather romantic perception of England's Peninsular allies, that she cast caution aside and engaged in conversation with them, in a mixture of French and English, and 'enquired whence they came and whether they knew General Wellington'. She was delighted when they 'smiled and nodded at his Name, and expressed infinite delight that I was English', and she subsequently emptied her purse of all her small change 'to distribute to my new and completely dilapidated friends'.[5]

In doing so she took a great risk, as she found herself being observed by

an Officer of the Police, in full gold trappings, and wearing his Badge of authority, and his head covered, and half a yard beyond it, with an enormous Gold Laced cocked Hat, furiously darting forward from a small house at the entrance upon the Quay, which I afterwards learned was his official dwelling.[6]

Luckily for Fanny, following a terrifying interrogation – which revealed that she was English, had a French husband working in a Ministry in Paris, and was in Dunkirk to embark on an American vessel – and after being ordered by the French official to accompany him to a small hotel for further questioning, she was saved once again by the intervention of Mr Gregory. All this arose because she had excited suspicion by 'merely speaking, from curiosity, to the Spanish prisoners'. But Fanny later wrote that 'this adventure, in the terrors to which it gave rise, was one of the most severe to my apprehensions, during several minutes, that I have ever experienced in my life'.[7] It is, however, a touching picture of how this tiny but brave 60-year-old English lady, stranded and, except for the good Mr Gregory, friendless in Dunkirk, was prepared to run a high risk by extending sympathy and practical help to some of her country's less fortunate allies imprisoned in France. It is interesting also, given the censorship of news by Napoleon, that she seemed well informed of Wellington's exploits in the Peninsula.

After this hazardous brush with the French police and customs in Dunkirk, and yet another rough Channel crossing aboard an American ship, which lasted two days and nights and left Fanny so exhausted that 'I was literally and utterly unable to rise from my hammock',[8] she eventually, by courtesy of an intercepting Royal Navy vessel, reached safety and friends at the port of Deal. Her stay in England was, however, a relatively short one. After arranging the publication of *The Wanderer* and coping with the death in April of her beloved father, she returned once more to France to rejoin her husband in November 1814, leaving Alex behind at Cambridge. Her stay in Paris, however, was even shorter as she was compelled to take flight to Brussels in March 1815, in order to escape from the returning Napoleon. In Brussels the great figure of the Duke of Wellington now loomed much larger and more prominently in her life, as recorded in the pages of her *Waterloo Journal*.

Her first, almost reverential, description of the great man was occasioned by a grand concert on 27 April at which the famous Italian opera singer Angelica Catalani was due to perform. Among the prominent guests were Queen Wilhelmina of the Netherlands and 'the King of Warriors, Marshall Lord Wellington surrounded by his Etat major [general staff] and all the officers and first persons here, whether Belgians, Prussians, Hanoverians or English'. Just as she had been impressed by Napoleon in 1802 when she saw him review his troops on horseback on the parade ground of the Tuileries Palace, so she was even more struck by her first close sight of the duke. 'I looked at him watchfully all night', she records,

> and was charmed with every turn of his countenance, with his noble and singular physiognomy, and his Eagle eye, and Aquiline, forcible Nose. He was gay even to sportiveness all the Evening, conversing with the officers around him on terms of intimacy and pleasantry. He never was seated, not even for a moment, though I saw seats vacated to offer him frequently.

With his penchant for attractive Italian opera singers, 'he seemed enthusiastically charmed with Catalani, ardently applauding whenever she sang'. However, when she began to sing 'Rule, Britannia!', the duke 'with sagacious reserve listened in utter silence'. According to Fanny 'he felt it was injudicious, in every country but our own, to give out a Chorus of Rule, Britannia! Britannia, Rule the Waves!' and, when some officers started shouting for an encore, 'he instantly crushed it, by a commanding air of disapprobation; and thus offered me an opportunity of seeing how magnificently he could quit his convivial familiarity for imperious dominion, when occasion might call for the transformation'.[9]

This was hero worship of a high order and perhaps an indication of why the duke's very presence in Brussels created such confidence, despite the many rumours about the successful advance of Napoleon's army over the frontier into Belgium. It is a pity that Fanny was not also present at the Duchess of Richmond's famous ball on the eve of Waterloo, as she would no doubt have left us an equally lively and detailed account of that occasion. Fanny must have been especially pleased when her husband, having received his order from the king to go to raise royalist forces at Trier, succeeded in obtaining a lengthy audience in Brussels with the duke, with whom he thought it necessary to concert his plans. As for the 'Rule, Britannia!' incident, Fanny may have taken a special interest in this, recalling that it had been written by Thomas Arne, who was her father's first music teacher and patron at Drury Lane when he moved from Chester to London at the age of 18.

After her husband left her and Brussels was awash with anxious rumours about how the war was going, Fanny needed all the more to maintain her faith in the duke's ability to emerge victorious. Her admiration for him was now boundless.

On Saturday, 17 June 1815, when it was rumoured that victory was imminent but nobody knew with any certainty on which side, and while many of her friends were already fleeing Brussels, Fanny retained her faith in Wellington and decided to stay put. Finally, however, on hearing a report that Napoleon had in fact won a victory (this was presumably a reference to his partial defeat of Marshal Blücher and the Prussians at Ligny on the previous day), she packed a few belongings and joined the family of a British banker, William Boyd, who had promised to take her with them by canal barge to Antwerp. When they got to the mooring place, they found to their dismay that all the canal and other means of transport had already been commandeered by the duke for his army and they had to return to the city centre. By now the sound of nearby cannons could be heard clearly in the city and, still frightened, bewildered and not knowing what was happening, Fanny went out again courageously into the streets – rather like Adèle on the barricades during the July Revolution in Paris in 1830 – in order to try to get some concrete first-hand news. She fortunately met an Englishman who reassured her in the following terms that her hero was in command:

> He [the Duke of Wellington] was everywhere, he said; the Eye could turn
> in no direction that it did not perceive him, either at hand, or at a distance;
> galloping to charge the enemy, or darting across the Field to issue, or to
> change some orders [...] He seemed as impervious for safety as he was
> dauntless for courage, while Danger all the time relentlessly environed him,
> and Wounds, fractures, dislocations, loss of limbs, or Death continually
> robbed him of the services of some of the bravest and dearest of those who
> were nearest to him. But he suffered nothing to check, or appal, or engage
> him, that belonged to personal interest or feeling: his entire concentrated
> attention, exclusive aim, and intense thought were devoted [...] to the
> WHOLE, the ALL.[10]

This picture of the duke on the Waterloo battlefield, though perhaps somewhat romanticized, accords with many other eyewitness accounts of his conduct on that day. In contrast to Napoleon, who remained strangely inactive for most of the day in the rear of the battlefield near his headquarters at the inn, La Belle Alliance, the duke was, or appeared to be, everywhere, even at one stage riding down to the crucial stronghold of the besieged chateau farm of Hougoumont on his right flank to encourage its guards garrison at the height of its crisis and to give orders for its reinforcement. This gave enormous confidence to his troops – the sort of confidence that Fanny herself had felt through his presence in Brussels. As the duke is reputed to have said himself after the battle, 'By God, it's a good job I was there'[11] – a sentiment that Fanny and the whole of the expatriate population of Brussels and the allied army would have strongly endorsed. Captain John Kinkaid of the 95th Rifles even said, 'We would rather see his long nose in a fight than a reinforcement of ten thousand men any day'.[12]

By the next morning it was confirmed in Brussels that Wellington and Blücher were victorious and that Napoleon and his army were in full retreat. Fanny was overjoyed. In a letter of 26 June to her husband (although she did not know whether he was in Trier, or had left it, or even whether he was still alive) she wrote: 'Why have I not a Balloon to be the first to tell you this enchanting news! Or, rather, Wings to fly to you with it myself! Buonaparte has yielded to Lord Wellington.'[13] She had also learned by this stage that her hero had dismissed Napoleon's request, on arrival in Paris, to be allowed to abdicate in favour of his young son the King of Rome and a regency, or in favour of his stepson Prince Eugène or the Duc d'Orléans. She wrote proudly: 'The Duke sent him word that he must yield at Discretion, or Fight. He had nothing to do with Abdicating, for he was Nothing. He had already abdicated, when he was Emperor'. Praising further Wellington's firmness, she also noted that 'The [French] army then sent a deputation, demanding a Truce to prepare a Peace, for sparing the further effusion of human blood. The Duke answered, Their King might spare it, when reseated on his Throne; but that for Them, and from Them, the application was too late'.[14] All this was a far cry from her one-time faith in the omnipotent and all-conquering Napoleon, but she now felt secure in the knowledge that her new hero had defeated the tyrant. Nevertheless, she also now had to undertake her lone journey from the 'Walking Hospital' of Brussels in search of her husband at Trier, some 160 miles away, or wherever else he might have got to.

Adèle's perspective of the duke was, of course, quite different from that of Fanny. After the scales had fallen from Fanny's eyes as regards Napoleon, Wellington became her hero and saviour. Adèle's views were necessarily more complex. She could not but welcome him in 1814 as the victor over the tyrant, but as a French patriot, recovered from her earlier anglomania, his position as generalissimo of the occupying forces in Paris after Waterloo was a perpetual reminder to her of France's defeat and humiliation. The comments on his conduct in her diaries thus tended to become increasingly critical.

The first appearance of Wellington in Paris to be noted by Adèle was not in fact until the middle of 1814, during the period of the first Bourbon restoration and before Napoleon escaped from Elba and was defeated at Waterloo. She was present at a grand ball given by the English commissioner to the allied armies, Sir Charles Stewart, the brother of the foreign secretary, Lord Castlereagh. Although a glittering galaxy of royalty was present, including the French royal family, the King of Prussia and the very tall Tsar Alexander I of Russia, Adèle's eyes seemed to be fixed only on the duke. She described his appearance in the following terms:

> C'est au milieu de ce bal que parut pour la première fois à Paris le duc de Wellington. Je le vois encore y entrer, ses deux nièces, lady Burgersh et miss Pole, pendues à ses bras. Il n'y eut plus d'yeux que pour lui, et dans ce bal, pavé de grandeurs, toutes s'éclipsèrent pour faire place à la gloire militaire. Celle du duc de Wellington était brillante, pure et accrue de tout l'intérêt qu'on portait depuis longtemps à la cause de la nation espagnole.

> [It was in the middle of this ball that the Duke of Wellington made his first appearance in Paris. I can still see him now entering the room with his two nieces, Lady Burgersh and Miss Pole, hanging on his arms. There were no eyes for any one else, and at this ball, where grandeur abounded, everything gave way to military glory. That of the Duke of Wellington was brilliant and unalloyed, and a lustre was added to it by the interest that had long been felt in the cause of the Spanish nation.][15]

So far, so good; it is a sign of the pre-eminence of the duke's reputation, even at this stage, that for Adèle he should be such a focus of attention, without a hint of resentment or criticism. Her views, however, began steadily to change after Waterloo, when the allied armies, of which Wellington had been appointed commander-in-chief, were no longer seen as liberators but as an alien occupying force. She began to resent and find increasingly humiliating their presence in the streets of Paris, and found more reason to criticize Wellington, both for his personal conduct and for not using his great prestige and influence to ease France's lot. Two episodes attracted her particular censure.

The first was the extraordinary personal and practical role that the duke took in carrying out the 'spoliations', or retrieval of booty and works of art looted by Napoleon from various quarters of his empire, that were demanded by the allies. Adèle could hardly believe her eyes and described how

> *Notre héros, le duc de Wellington, se fit l'exécuteur des spoliations matérielles imposées par les Alliés. Sous prétexte que les Anglais n'avaient rien à réclamer en ce genre, il trouva généreux d'aller de ses mains triomphantes décrocher les tableaux de nos musées. Ceci ne doit pas être pris comme une forme de rhétorique, c'est le récit d'un fait. On l'a vu sur une échelle, donnant lui-même l'exemple. Le jour où l'on descendit les chevaux de Venise de dessus l'arc du Carrousel, il passa la matinée perché sur le monument, vis-à-vis les fenêtres du Roi, à surveiller ce travail.*

> [Our hero, the Duke of Wellington, took it upon himself to carry out the spoliations demanded by the Allies. Under the pretext that the English had no claims of this kind to make, he was so generous as to come and take down the pictures from our museums with his own victorious hands. What I write should not be mistaken as rhetoric, for it is a true account. He was seen on a ladder setting an example. On the day when the *Horses of Venice* were taken down from the arch of the Carousel, he spent the morning perched on this monument opposite the king's windows, super-vising the work.][16]

She was not alone in resenting the duke's personal role in this. In a sarcastic reference to his behaviour in Paris during this period, Chateaubriand described him as '*Wellington devenu dictateur au Louvre* [Wellington who had become the dictator of the Louvre]'.[17]

Adèle's indignation, not least her ironic use again of the expression '*Notre héros*', is evident in every line. This picture of the duke up a stepladder, taking the works of art from the wall with his own hands, is so different from that normally presented in most portraits or biographies of the great man. She was also not only angry with the duke's own behaviour, but with the encouragement it gave to others to follow his example. She wrote: '*La conduite du duc donnait le signal aux impertinences des sous-ordres* [The duke's conduct was the signal for his subordinates to display their impertinence]'; and went on to castigate an army paymaster, '*un certain vulgaire animal du nom de Mackenzie* [a certain vulgar animal by the name of Mackenzie]', for making light of the serious indemnities imposed on France. She concluded: '*Je l'aurais tué d'un regard* [I could have killed him with a look].'[18] So far had she come from her admiration of the duke only a few months previously.

The other, and more serious, grievance that Adèle held against the duke concerned the trial and execution of Marshal Michel Ney, known as 'le Rougeaud' for his red hair and ruddy complexion. The trial took place before the Chamber of Peers from 21 November to 6 December 1815, when he was declared guilty of high treason by 139 votes to 17, with five abstentions. He was shot shortly after the trial on 8 December. Although in dictating his memoirs to Emmanuel, Comte de Las Cases, on St Helena, Napoleon described Ney as '*toujours une pauvre tête* [always muddle-headed]'[19] and laid much of the blame for the defeat at Waterloo on him for leading his finest cavalry, the flower of the Grande Armée, to destruction by launching them at Wellington's centre without infantry in support, Napoleon had previously ennobled him as Prince of Moscow for his outstanding courage during the disastrous Russian campaign and given him the title of the bravest of the brave. During the retreat from Moscow Napoleon is said to have exclaimed, 'I have three hundred million in francs at the Tuileries. I'd give them all up to save Ney. What a soldier! The army of France is full of brave men, but Michel Ney is truly the bravest of the brave.'[20] However, after Napoleon's first defeat and abdication in 1814, Ney, who had been prominent among those urging Napoleon to abdicate, had switched allegiance to the side of the restored King Louis and was made a peer by him. On Napoleon's escape from Elba and landing in Provence at the end of February 1815, the marshal famously promised the king to stop his march and bring him back to Paris in an iron cage. In the event he changed sides again and fought on the losing side at Waterloo. He was subsequently arrested at his country estate and brought to trial.

General sentiment in Paris was hostile to Ney. Adèle describes how in high political circles there were many who demanded that an example be made of him in order to deter future traitors. Her own sympathies, however, were clearly with Ney, and she was angry to see members of her own class in high society volunteering to help guard the marshal in prison and even sleep there in order to ensure that he could not escape. It is arguable that if he had had sufficient courage the king could have pardoned him, but Louis XVIII had not been a party to the

St Cloud Convention, which granted an amnesty to those who had fought for Napoleon, and, as Adèle pointed out, the penalty of death for treason was regarded in France as natural. She wrote: '*On a fort reproché au Roi de ne lui avoir pas fait grâce. Je doute qu'il le pût; je doute aussi qu'il le voulût* [The king has been greatly reproached for not pardoning him. I doubt whether he had either the power or the wish to do so].'[21] She further commented that if the king had intervened, '*il risquait une émeute populaire; sa vie pouvait y succomber, mais non pas son pouvoir* [he risked a popular uprising, in which his life, but not his power, could be lost]'. Instead, Adèle laid the principal blame for not pardoning him on the Duke of Wellington. She claimed that, with his immense prestige, '*La grâce du maréchal était dans ses mains, bien plus que dans celles de Louis XVIII* [The marshal's pardon was much more in his hands than in those of King Louis]'.[22] In any case she did not think it was reasonable to expect the king to give too much weight to the life of one man when balancing the country's wider interests.

Whether Adèle's charge against Wellington is fair or not is difficult to say. It was not unreasonable for him not to interfere in a matter that was essentially an affair of French domestic politics. In his *Napoleon and Wellington*,[23] Andrew Roberts points out that the duke had been pointedly snubbed by the king shortly before the date of Ney's execution and that Wellington was reputed to have said, 'I could only have asked it as a special favour to myself, and when I had been insulted in this manner, and was not on terms with the King, I could not think of asking favours of him.' There were, however, those of Wellington's political opponents in London who shared Adèle's view of the duke's behaviour. Lord Holland, who was, with his wife, a notorious sympathiser of Napoleon's, and who campaigned against his imprisonment and treatment on St Helena, pleading his cause in the House of Lords, strongly criticized Wellington and implied that he was jealous of Ney's superior reputation for generalship. On the other hand, when the news of Ney's death reached Napoleon on St Helena, he appeared to be quite indifferent to it. For Adèle, it was one more charge to be chalked up against the man who was unwilling to use his position and prestige to act with clemency in what she believed to be her country's interest. Wellington's own case is also weakened by the fact that some years later in 1838 at Stratfield Saye, the country house in Hampshire given to the duke by a grateful Parliament, Lady Salisbury recorded that 'Speaking of Ney, he said it was absolutely necessary to make an example.'[24]

As the occupation of Paris by allied troops – some 30,000 of them – continued,

Adèle's views on the duke became increasingly critical. She was very angry that the duke would not use his influence to accelerate their departure. She wrote:

Le duc de Wellington s'opposait à voir diminuer l'armée d'occupation, en reconnaissant pourtant que la dépense qu'elle occasionait écrasait le pays et rendait plus difficile le remboursement des contributions, réclamées par les puissances, avant de consentir à l'évacuation complète de la France.

[The Duke of Wellington was opposed to seeing the army of occupation reduced, while recognizing that the expense it entailed was crushing the country and making it more difficult to secure the reparation contributions claimed by the allied powers before they would agree to the complete evacuation of France].[25]

She was all the more incensed because she believed that British ministers in London were more sympathetic to a rundown of the forces and that Wellington was concerned that any reduction in the English garrison relative to the other occupying forces might diminish his personal standing. She also believed that Tsar Alexander I would have been more accommodating. Like Napoleon's stepdaughter and later sister-in-law, Hortense de Beauharnais, Adèle was very impressed by the tsar. When he entered Paris in 1814, she said of him: '*On ne peut s'empêcher de reconnaître que la conduite sage, modérée, généreuse de ce souverain justifiait l'enthousiasme que nous lui montrions* [You cannot prevent yourself from acknowledging that the wise, moderate and generous conduct of this sovereign justified the enthusiasm we all showed to him].'[26] It no doubt helped, as she noted also, that he was young, tall, handsome, gentle and imposing.

At the beginning of 1816 her father was appointed to the post he had always wanted, that of ambassador in London, but Adèle decided to remain in Paris until later in the spring. Although most of the foreign troops had by now moved to the garrisons outside Paris assigned to them under the Treaty of Paris, the Duke of Wellington, obviously anxious to remain in command on the spot, stayed in the city. Adèle records that

Le duc de Wellington seul, en sa qualité de généralissime de toutes les armées d'occupation, résidait à Paris et nous en faisait les honneurs à nos frais. Il donnait

assez souvent des fêtes où il était indispensable d'assister. Il tenait à avoir du monde et, notre sort dépendant en grande partie de sa bonne humeur, il fallait supporter ses caprices souvent bizarres.

[The Duke of Wellington alone, as generalissimo of all the armies of occupation, resided in Paris and did the honours of the town at our expense. He frequently gave parties at which attendance was obligatory. He was anxious to attract much of society and, as our future fate depended to a large extent on his good humour, it was necessary to put up with his caprices, which were often bizarre.][27]

Adèle was particularly incensed at the way in which he flaunted in public his relationship with the famous Italian opera singer Giuseppina Grassini, whom she had known in London when she was living there in exile with her parents during the Revolution. Unlike Fanny, who was intensely shy and as a young girl dreaded being asked to perform before other people, Adèle possessed a very good and powerful singing voice and was often asked to sing at private functions. Indeed, this was one of the things that attracted her husband General de Boigne when he first met her in London. As an example of her virtuosity, in her account of that time she recalls that her mother had invited to their house Sappio, the former music master of Marie-Antoinette, who was so enthusiastic about her voice that he persuaded her to sing with his wife, who was also a noted musician. '*Nos voix s'unissaient si heureusement que, lorsque nous chantions ensemble à la tierce, les vitres et les glaces en vibraient* [Our voices blended so harmoniously that when we sang together in thirds the windows and mirrors vibrated].'[28]

She was also invited to sing with the great diva herself, Grassini.

J'ai fait dans ce même temps bien souvent de la musique avec madame Grassini. C'est la première chanteuse qui ait été reçue à Londres précisément comme une personne de la société. Elle ajoutait à un grand talent une extrême beauté.

[I often made music at this same time with Mme Grassini. She was the first singer who was received in London as a society figure. She combined with her great talent extreme beauty.][29]

Giuseppina Grassini was an Italian contralto, who made her debut in Milan in 1794, sang before Napoleon after the Battle of Marengo, then triumphed at the opera in Paris and in due course became Napoleon's mistress. She was known as 'la chanteuse de l'empereur [the emperor's singer]' and is said to have made the contralto voice reach equality in public esteem with the hitherto preferred soprano. Adèle thus had cause to remember her well on many counts and was outraged to see her being paraded brazenly by the Duke of Wellington, whose mistress she also became. Of the occasion which particularly shocked her she wrote:

> Je me rappelle qu'une fois il inventa de faire de la Grassini, alors en possession de ses bonnes grâces, la reine de la soirée. Il la plaça sur un canapé élevé dans la salle de bal, ne quitta pas ses côtés, la fit servir la première, fit ranger tout le monde pour qu'elle vît danser, lui donna la main et la fit passer la première au souper, l'assit près de lui, enfin lui rendit les hommages qui d'ordinaire ne s'accordent guère qu'aux princesses. Heureusement, il y avait quelques grandes dames anglaises à partager ces impertinences, mais elles n'étaient pas obligées de les subir comme nous et leur ressentiment ne pouvait être comparable.

[I recall that on one occasion he conceived the idea of making Grassini, who was then at the height of her attractiveness, the queen of the evening. He placed her on a raised sofa in the ballroom and never left her side, had her served first before anyone else, made people stand back so that she could see the dancing, gave her his hand to take her into supper first, sat her next to him and finally showed her the kind of attentions normally only granted to princesses. Fortunately, some high-born English ladies were there to share these insults, but they were not obliged to submit to them as we were, and their resentment could hardly be compared with ours.][30]

Adèle's outrage spits out from every line of this account of the duke's conduct. There may have been an element of her aristocratic snobbishness in it too. Great divas were all right in their place, which was in the drawing room or singing on the stage of the opera house, but for the all-powerful Duke of Wellington to give her pride of place over both French and English grandes dames at a great social occasion was simply not acceptable – perhaps particularly since it was known that the duke's unhappy and rather unglamorous wife, the former Kitty Pakenham, was not then in Paris to attend these great occasions with him. Adèle's attitude also recalls to some degree the hostile reaction of Fanny to the decision of her patroness, Mrs Thrale, to marry the Italian music teacher, Gabriel Piozzi – another professional singing foreigner. Adèle displayed a similar disapproval of the duke's philandering propensities when on a later occasion she somewhat prudishly criticized his association with Mrs Arbuthnot, the wife of one of his closest friends. Mrs Arbuthnot was probably one of the ladies who, though intimate with the duke, did not become his mistress.

Adèle felt strongly that the Duke of Wellington could have done more to accelerate the run-down and departure of the allied troops occupying Paris. On the day of her return to Paris in September 1815, she wrote:

> *Je reviens à mon arrivée à Paris. Quelque disposée que je fusse à partager la joie que causait le retour du Roi, elle était empoisonnée par la présence des étrangers. Leur attitude y était bien plus hostile que l'année précédente: vainqueurs de Napoléon en 1814, ils s'étaient montrés généreux; alliés de Louis XVIII en 1815, ils poussèrent les exigences jusqu'à l'insulte.*

> [I return to the day of my arrival in Paris. Although I was ready to share in the general joy occasioned by the king's return, my pleasure was poisoned by the foreigners' presence. Their attitude was much more hostile than during the previous year. As the conquerors of Napoleon in 1814 they had shown themselves generous; as allies of Louis XVIII in 1815 they pushed their demands to the point of insult.][31]

Going even further in her criticism she commented that the allies were jealous of and surprised by the relative prosperity with which the defeated France had emerged from the war (though this is not entirely consistent with her observations elsewhere on the superior prosperity of England) and that

> *leur haine fut aveugle, car, s'ils voulaient abaisser la France, ils voulaient en même temps consolider la Restauration. Or, les humiliations de cette époque infligèrent au nouveau gouvernement une flétrissure dont il ne s'est point relevé et qui a été un des motifs de sa chute. La nation n'a jamais complètement pardonné à la famille royale les souffrances imposées par ceux qu'elle appelait ses alliés.*

[their hatred was blind, since, if they wished to humiliate France, they also wanted at the same time to consolidate the Restoration. The humiliations of this period, however, inflicted on the new government a wound from which it never recovered and which was one of the reasons for its downfall. The nation never completely forgave the royal family for the sufferings imposed on it by those it called its *allies*.][32]

This was strong and politically shrewd criticism indeed, which later found a parallel in the plight of Germany after World War I, and there is no doubt that Adèle regarded the Duke of Wellington as one of the principal culprits responsible for it.

It is possible also that Adèle felt a little guilty that she had not at the time been able to intervene with her old family friend, Pozzo di Burgo, in a manoeuvre he had carried out with Wellington, which had ensured that British troops were the first to enter Paris after Waterloo. Pozzo was the Russian ambassador to France and was asked by Tsar Alexander I, who had little sympathy for the Bourbons, to request that the duke hold back the advance of his own forces until the Austro–Russian and Prussian armies were also already in line. Pozzo, who according to Adèle

n'était « brin Russe », et avait grande envie de s'arranger en France une patrie à son goût, en y conservant un souverain qui lui avait des obligations personelles,

[was by no means a 'lover of Russia' and strongly wished to create a nation to his own taste in France by preserving a sovereign who was under personal obligation to himself,][33]

duly spoke to the duke, but only to invite him to endorse a response to the tsar that he himself had already drafted. This stated that it was too late, since the duke had insisted on an immediate march into Paris, taking the king with him and installing him in the Tuileries Palace. The duke went along with his ruse, replying: 'Comptez sur moi; la conférence a eu lieu précisément comme vous la rapportez [Count on me; the conference has taken place exactly as you have reported it].'[34] Fortunately for Pozzo, the tsar appeared to believe his story, exclaiming: 'Ce qui est fait est fait, il n'y a plus à s'en préoccuper; peut-être est-ce pour le mieux [What is done is done, and there is no use in attempting to undo it. Perhaps it is all for the best]',[35] and Wellington with his troops, and accompanied by the king, duly proceeded to be the first to enter the gates of Paris.

Despite her criticisms of the duke's conduct in the early days of the occupation, Adèle, as always, was a little kinder to him in her more mature assessment later on. Early in 1818, when the end of the occupation was in sight, the duke narrowly escaped an assassination attempt. On Tuesday, 10 February, when he was returning from an evening party, as his carriage turned into the entrance of his mansion in the Avenue des Champs-Elysées at about 12.30 a.m., there was a flash and a bang and a glimpse of a blond man running away down the street. The duke was unharmed – he at first thought a sentry had discharged his musket by mistake – and the police eventually identified and arrested the would-be assassin, a veteran soldier named André Nicholas Cantillon, who was fanatically devoted to Napoleon. Adèle's comments on this event were as follows:

> Cet événement pouvait avoir les plus fâcheuses conséquences. Le duc de Wellington était le personnage le plus important de l'époque; tout le monde en était persuadé, mais personne autant que lui. Son mécontentement aurait été une calamité. Tout ce qui tenait au gouvernement fit donc une très grosse affaire de cet attentat et le lendemain le duc était d'assez bonne humeur.

> [This event could have had the most disastrous consequences. The Duke of Wellington was the most important personage of the time; everybody was convinced of it, and no one more so than himself. His displeasure would have been a calamity. Everybody connected with the government made a great outcry concerning this outrage, and the next day the duke was in a fairly good humour again.][36]

While confirming the pre-eminent position that the duke occupied in Paris at the time, Adèle could still not avoid her little dig at the duke's sense of his own importance. But she went on strongly to deny rumours spread by the liberal opposition that, in conjunction with the ultra-right-wing party, he had arranged for a blank shot to be fired at his carriage as a pretext for prolonging the occupation of the country. She wrote:

Il faut rendre justice au duc de Wellington; il était incapable d'entrer dans une pareille machination; mais il conçut beaucoup d'humeur de ces propos, et, il le faut répéter, notre sort dépendait en grande partie de ses bonnes dispositions, car lui seul pouvait prendre l'initiative et affirmer aux souverains que la présence en France de l'armée d'occupation, dont il était généralissime, avait cessé d'être nécessaire au repos de l'Europe.

[We must do justice to the Duke of Wellington; he was incapable of lending himself to such a machination. But he was very angry at this talk, and, it must be repeated, our fate largely depended on the goodness of his temper, as he alone could take the initiative and tell the sovereigns that the presence in France of the occupying army, of which he was the generalissimo, had ceased to be necessary for the peace of Europe.][37]

Although it is by no means certain that the duke would have resisted such a 'machination' if it had suited his purposes, Adèle's final judgement of him in her memoirs shows her usual good, fair sense in political matters, despite her frequent denials that she was interested in politics. It would have been interesting to have had her comments on Napoleon's behaviour on St Helena in April 1821, when, in dictating his will to General de Montholon as he lay dying, he left among many bequests 20,000 francs to the would-be assassin, Lieutenant Cantillon, who, in his view, had as much right to eliminate Wellington as Wellington had to send him to die on St Helena. Wellington's reaction to this was, typically, that it was further proof of Napoleon's 'littleness of mind'.[38] I suspect that at this stage Adèle might just have gone along with the duke. Fanny would certainly have done so.

FIVE

KINGS & QUEENS

As we have seen, both Fanny and Adèle spent significant periods of their lives in the company of royalty. For Fanny this was largely confined to the 'Five Years within Ten Days'[1] from 17 July 1786 to 7 July 1791, when she served Queen Charlotte as a virtually conscripted and very reluctant Second Keeper of the Robes. It was not a job offer she could refuse since, apart from the annual salary of £200 and the personal security this offered, she was under great pressure from her father to take a post that might help him or her brothers Charles and James to gain preferment in their chosen professions. After she had, with great difficulty, obtained her release from this post, Fanny never again lived close to the royal family, although she maintained contact whenever possible with Queen Charlotte, to whom she owed her pension and indeed dedicated her third novel, *Camilla*. Fanny also had little direct contact with royalty during her years in France, which were largely spent under the regime of Napoleon and the empire. She must have been rather envious to hear from her friend Queeney, the eldest daughter of Mrs Thrale, that on a visit to Versailles as a small child with her parents and Dr Johnson she had been noticed and remarked on as a very pretty child by none less than Marie-Antoinette herself.

Adèle, on the other hand, lived in close contact with royalty nearly all her life, including even the English royal family when she accompanied her father to London in 1816 on his appointment as French ambassador. She was brought up at the court of Louis XVI and Marie-Antoinette at Versailles, was a regular presence at the court of the restored Louis XVIII and his successor Charles X from the time of the Bourbon restorations in 1814 and 1815 until the July Revolution of 1830, and remained in intimate contact with the Bourgeois King, Louis-Philippe, and his wife Queen Marie-Amélie until they were forced out and replaced by Louis-Napoléon first as president in 1848 and then emperor in 1852. She retained a lifelong friendship with Marie-Amélie until the latter's death in exile at Claremont House in Surrey in 1866. Moreover, she learned to live in relative harmony with the imperial court during the years of Napoleon's ascendancy. Her direct association with royalty, therefore, stretched over a longer period and involved greater variety than that of Fanny's five intensive years at court, and it was different in nature. Fanny, though on close and friendly terms with the king and queen and their children, was nevertheless an employee – a high-grade servant. Adèle was a friend and, in her childhood, virtually one of the family. As we shall see, however, both suffered from the rigid protocol of court etiquette. Their respective diaries – in Fanny's case the separate section entitled *Court Journals*, which she later edited and bound together – provide an extraordinarily intimate picture of many aspects of life at the French and English courts during the late eighteenth and early nineteenth centuries.

Prior to her service at court, Fanny's life had been almost entirely spent in a musical, literary, theatrical and intellectual environment, first at her father's house in London and later at the house and literary circle of Mrs Thrale. The dramatic new phase in her life was inaugurated by her friendship with the elderly Mrs Mary Delaney, a favourite of the royal family's, who lived in a grace-and-favour dwelling in the grounds of Windsor Castle. It was there that she was first introduced to King George III and Queen Charlotte, and the king, in loud and jovial fashion, with frequent and characteristic cries of 'What, what', quizzed her on *Evelina*, enquiring particularly how she had managed to write and publish it without her father's knowledge, introduced her to the queen and the royal princesses, and pressed her on her future authorship plans.

FANNY AT COURT

The subsequent offer of a permanent post as Second Keeper of the Robes to the queen came as a shock to Fanny. Not only did she not want to join the royal household, she did not want to be committed to anything at all for an indefinite number of years. Among other considerations, she must have feared for the future of her writing. She wrote:

> My greatest terror is lest the Queen […] should make me promise myself to her for a length of years – What can I do to avoid that? – anything that has a period is endurable – but what can I object that will not sound ungrateful to the honour she is doing me and meaning me?[2]

Although Fanny found the queen generally gracious, considerate and charming, she was alarmed at the prospect offered to her. 'I must confess myself extremely frightened and full of alarm at a change of situation so great, so unexpected, so unthought of. Whether I shall suit it or not Heaven only knows, but I have a thousand doubts.'[3]

Fanny's attitude was quite different from that of Adèle towards royalty. For Fanny, behind the formality, the glamour, the ceremony and the glory, it was, especially in her early days at court, a frightening and constricting new world. For Adèle, contact with royalty was the norm for someone brought up by aristocratic parents under the *Ancien Régime* at Versailles. She was even able to treat the 'nouveau' imperial court established by Napoleon with a certain condescension and disdain, bordering on snobbishness, although she retained some regard for the Empress Josephine, with whom her mother's side of the family – the Dillons – had been connected and enjoyed a friendly relationship for many years. It is interesting, in view of Fanny's later romantic love affair with Mr d'Arblay and her earlier youthful yearning to find true love, that she compared her position at court to a marriage. In a letter from Windsor to her sister Susanna in July 1786, she wrote of her new post:

I am married, my dearest Susan – I look upon it in that light – I was averse
to forming the union, and I endeavoured to escape it; but my friends
interfered – they prevailed – and the knot is tied. What then now remains
but to make the best Wife in my power? I am bound to it in Duty, and I
will strain every nerve to succeed.'[4]

These are uncharacteristically bitter and despairing words from Fanny and
cannot but evoke our sympathy and understanding. Adèle would no doubt have
understood the comments on marriage in view of her own loveless marriage for
financial convenience to General de Boigne, but she might have found Fanny's
fear of the royal court more difficult to share.

The two main problems for Fanny at court were firstly the hard and dic-
tatorial oversight exercised by her immediate superior, Mrs Elizabeth Juliana
Schwellenberg, the Keeper of the Robes. Fanny later nicknamed her Cerbera,
the female form of the three-headed dog Cerberus, which guarded the entrance
to Hades. Secondly came the relentless daily court routine and etiquette that
governed almost every moment of her day. Mrs Schwellenberg had come with
the queen from Germany and had spent most of her working life at court. She
was a harsh taskmaster and Fanny was obliged to spend long periods of the day
with her, often to play cards, whether she wanted to or not. She was, at any rate
in Fanny's earlier days, totally unsympathetic to Fanny's problems, even when
her health was manifestly beginning to suffer. For example, in November 1787
when Fanny was travelling with her in a carriage from Windsor to London,
she refused to allow Fanny to draw up the window on her side of the carriage,
despite Fanny's protests that the draught was causing severe pain to her eyes: 'I
had a terrible journey indeed to town, Mrs Schwellenberg finding it expedient
to have the Glass down on my side, where there blew a sharp wind, which so
painfully attacked my eyes, that they were inflamed even before we arrived in
town.'[5] But the particular problem of the relationship with Mrs Schwellenberg
was only one facet of the overall constriction of daily court routine on Fanny's
life. The order of her day was rigidly programmed, almost like a school timetable
or the regime in a convent, and although she was comfortably accommodated at
Windsor, with her own maid and servant, she had few quiet moments to enjoy
her apartment in privacy.

She described the routine in detail in a long entry in her *Court Journals* of

24 July 1786. The nature of her 'general method of passing the day' is illustrated by the following extracts, which are worth quoting at length:[6]

I rise at six o'clock, Dress in a morning Gown and Cap, and wait my first summons, which is at all times from 7 to near 8; but commonly in the exact half hour between them. What time I gain before I am called, I devote to settling Drawers, Dress and my Room, and giving directions to my man and maid, whom I am obliged to watch and instruct as if they were my Children, as I feel answerable for their good behaviour.

The Queen never sends for me till her Hair is Dressed. This, in a morning is always done by her Wardrobe Woman, Mrs Thielky, A German, but who speaks English perfectly well.

[...]

By 8 o'clock, or a little after, for she is extremely expeditious, she is dressed. She then goes out, to join the King, and be joined by the Princesses, and they all proceed to the King's Chapel in the Castle, to Prayers, attended by the Governesses of the Princesses, and the King's Equery. Various others at times, attend; but only these indispensably.

I then return to my own Room, to Breakfast.

I make this meal the most pleasant part of the Day; I have a Book for my companion, and I allow myself an Hour for it.

[...]

At 9 o'clock I send off my Breakfast things, and relinquish my Book, to make a serious and steady examination of every thing I have upon my Hands in the way of *business*; in which *preparations for Dress* are always included, – not for the present Day alone, but for the Court Days, which require a particular Dress, for the next arriving Birth Day of any of the Royal family, every one of which requires new apparel [...] That over, I have my time at my own disposal till a quarter before 12, except on Wednesday and Saturday, when I have it only to a quarter before Eleven.

[...]

A quarter before one is the usual time for the Queen to begin Dressing for the day. Mrs Schwallenberg then constantly attends; so do I. Mrs Thielky of course at all times. We help her off with her Gown, and on with her powdering things, and then the Hair Dresser is admitted. She generally reads the news-papers during that operation.

[…]

It is commonly 3 o'clock when I am thus set at large. And I have then two Hours quite at my own disposal: – but, in the *natural course of things*, not a moment after!

[…]

At 5 we have Dinner. Mrs Schwellenberg and I meet in the Eating Room. We are commonly Tête à Tête: when there is anybody added, it is from her invitation only. Whatever right my place might afford me, of also inviting my friends to the Table, I have now totally lost, by way of courage and spirits to claim it originally.

From this time, *naturally*, I belong to Mrs Schwellenberg wholly. […]

When we have Dined, we go upstairs to her Apartment, which is directly over mine […] Here we sit, *when I behave as I ought to do*, till half past 6, when the Major goes to attend the King to the Terrace. And *here we sit*, also, when, also, I behave as I ought to do, till the Terracing is over; this is at about 8 o'clock. Our Tête à Tête then finishes and we come down again to the Eating room.

[…]

From that time, if Mrs Schwallenberg is alone, I never quit her for a minute, till I come to my little supper, at near Eleven. If she has any body to play at Cards, I steal away for 5 minutes at a time, into my own Room, – which is close by, though not leading to, the Eating Room.

Between Eleven and 12 my last summons usually takes place. Earlier and later occasionally.

Twenty minutes is the customary time then spent with the Queen: Half an Hour I believe is seldom exceeded.

I then come back, and after doing whatever I can to forward my Dress for the next morning, I go to Bed – And to *sleep*, too, believe me, – the early rising, and a long Day's attention to new affairs and occupation, cause a fatigue so bodily, that nothing mental stands against it, and to sleep I fall the moment I have put out my Candle and laid down my Head.

Such was the regular daily routine – which she sometimes described as 'slavery' – to which Fanny was subjected at Windsor. Perhaps the most telling words in her whole description are 'I belong to Mrs Schwellenberg wholly'.[7] Her weariness and sense of oppression and frustration emerge clearly from every line. It is not surprising that her health began to suffer, nor that there is little humour in the narrative of her *Court Journals*. She certainly could not now summon up the satirical spirit that had enabled her, before she took up her post, in a letter of 17 December 1785 to her sister Hetty, to mock the absurdities of court etiquette, which she had presumably learned about in advance while staying with Mrs Delaney. The absurdities were now only too real. She wrote then:[8]

In the first place, you must not Cough. If you find a cough tickling in your throat, you must arrest it from making any sound: if you find yourself choaking with the forbearance, you must choak: but not Cough.

In the 2d place, you must not sneeze. If you have a vehement Cold, you must take no notice of it; if your Nose membranes feel a great irritation, you must hold your breath; if a sneeze still insists upon making its way, you must oppose it by keeping your teeth grinding together; if the violence of the repulse breaks some blood-vessel, you must break the blood-vessel; But not sneeze.

In the 3d place, you must not, upon any account, stir hand or foot. If, by chance, a black pin runs into your Head, you must not take it out. If the pain is very great, you must be sure to bear it without wincing; If it brings the Tears into your Eyes, you must not wipe them off; If they give you a tingling by running down your Cheeks, you must look as if nothing was the matter. If the blood should gush from your Head by means of the black pin, you must let it gush; If you are uneasy to think of making such a blurred appearance, you must be uneasy. If, however, the agony is very great, you may, privately, bite the inside of your Cheek, or of your lips, for a little relief; taking care, meanwhile, to do it so cautiously as to make no apparent dent outwardly. And, with that precaution, if you even gnaw a piece out, it will not be minded, only be sure either to swallow it, or commit it to a corner of the inside of your mouth till they are gone, – for, You must not spit.

ADÈLE AND COURT ETIQUETTE

This was the old Fanny talking, with a sense of fun and ridicule, before what she had sent up as a spoof became an oppressive daily reality. Although accustomed to court life from infancy, Adèle would certainly have had some fellow feeling with her. She too in later life found some of the rigidities of court protocol tedious in the extreme, particularly under the first restoration of Louis XVIII in 1814. In a passage of her memoirs describing the new Bourbon regime, she expressed her dislike of the newly imposed strict rules concerning court dress and etiquette. Mme la Dauphine, the daughter of Louis XVI, who 'en fit une affaire de ces choses [made a very serious business of this]', wanted to go back to the customs of the old court at Versailles and

> on ajouta au costume impérial tout le paraphernalia de l'ancien, ce qui faisait une singulière disparate. Ainsi on attacha à nos coiffures grecques ces ridicules barbes, et on remplaça l'élégant chérusque qui complétait un vêtement copié de Van Dyck par une lourde mantille et une espèce de plastron plissé.

> [to the imperial costume was added all the paraphernalia of the old style, and this was singularly incongruous. To our Grecian style of hairdressing, for example, these ridiculous lappets were added, and the elegant cherusque, which completed a mode of dress copied from Van Dyck, was replaced by a heavy mantilla and a kind of pleated front.][9]

'Madame' was very concerned that everyone should observe these rules to the letter and displeased with anyone who sought to modify them.

Adèle was also critical of the dress code at the English court, to which she found herself subject in London in 1816 when she was there to accompany her ambassador father. She described at great length in her memoirs the incredibly elaborate costume she felt obliged to wear – a plumed headdress, a circlet of pearls, a garland of roses, diamond buckles and comb, tassels of white silk, an enormous hooped skirt laced to her waist, two further skirts of satin and tulle over it and a further large bouquet of flowers that she carried in front of her so that 'j'avais l'air de sortir d'une corbeille de fleurs [I looked as if I was emerging from a basket of flowers]'. She summed it up, with her customary sense of wry amusement, by saying that, when she had seen the immense preparations necessary for this toilet, '*j'étais restée partagée entre l'envie de rire de leur énormité, qui me paraissait boufonne, et le chagrin de m'affubler si ridiculement* [I was uncertain whether to laugh at their enormity, which seemed entirely comical, or to be upset by the necessity of dressing in such a ridiculous style]'. Endearingly, however, as a little personal vanity took over, she had to admit in the end that '*lorsqu'elle fut achevée, je me trouvai assez à mon gré et que ce costume me sembla seyant* [when the costume was complete I was well pleased, and thought that it suited me]'.[10]

Worse for Adèle than the dress code in either Paris or London, however, was the etiquette laid down for precedent and procedure at court levees in Paris, which was determined by the king himself. A strict order of entry was prescribed for appearance before His Majesty. Duchesses led the way, with lesser mortals of the aristocracy following in their train. According to Adèle:

Il faut convenir que les précautions avaient été toutes prises pour rendre la distinction aussi choquante que possible pour celles qui y attachaient quelque importance.

[It must be admitted that precautions had been taken to make the distinction as offensive as possible to those who attached any importance to it.][11]

When the king arrived, he normally spoke only to the duchesses or a favoured few ladies of the highest rank. The rest, like Adèle, were involved in an extraordinary procession, filing past the corpulent king, passing through the Gallery of Diana, into Madame's reception room, where '*elle disait à chacun ce qui convenait* [she said the right thing to everyone]', and into the Pavillon de Flore, which was in effect out into the street. The Pavillon had a cobbled floor and neither doors nor windows, and so was entirely exposed to the weather. Adèle and the other lesser aristocracy were then not allowed to go back under cover through the palace but were obliged to find their way into the windy basement, past the kitchens and then outside to try to find their carriages. But this was not easy.

Dans le premier cas, il fallait faire le trajet sans châle ni pelisse; l'étiquette n'en admettait pas dans le château. Dans le second, il nous fallait aller chercher nos gens jusque dans la place; on ne les laissait pas arriver plus près.

[In the first place we had to go on our way with neither shawl nor cloak, as etiquette did not allow either within the palace. Secondly, we had to go as far as the square for our servants, as they were not allowed to approach any nearer.][12]

So they shivered and frequently got wet.

Despite her background at Versailles and familiarity with old-fashioned court etiquette, these petty restrictions at the newly restored Bourbon court must have seemed particularly irksome and tedious. The whole set-up *était mal arrangée car on n'en sortait jamais qu'ennuyée, fatiguée, mécontente* [...] *C'était une véritable corvée* [was badly organized, for we never left it without feeling bored, tired and discontented [...] It was true drudgery].'[13] She adds: '*J'étais des bien traitées et pourtant je n'y allais qu'en rechignant, le plus rarement qu'il m'était possible* [I was among those who were well treated, and yet I never went willingly, and only as rarely as possible].' Adèle would clearly have found common cause with some of Fanny's frustration at the routine of the Windsor court.

Returning to life at Windsor, the increasing strain to which Fanny was subjected did not, happily, prevent her from recording some memorable and dramatic episodes in court life. A notable one was an attempted assassination on the king in August 1786, the first and perhaps least serious of several attempts on the king's life. It was described by Fanny in a letter to Susanna of 2 August 1786. As Fanny went to her room she found there, with Princess Elizabeth, Mme La Fite, the princess's governess and also reader to the queen in French and German, who told her in great alarm that an attempt had been made on the king's life. When the king, who had been attending a levee in London, arrived back at Windsor in the afternoon, 'he hastened to her [the queen], with a countenance of striking vivacity, and said "here I am! Safe and well – as you see! – but I have very narrowly escaped being stabbed".'[14] He then described the incident.

In brief, as he alighted from his carriage at the garden door of St James's Palace, a 'decently Dressed woman' approached him with a rolled up petition. As she presented it to him with her right hand and the king bent forward to take it, she drew out a knife from it with her left hand and thrust it at his heart. The king started back, as she attempted a second thrust, which just touched his waistcoat, until one of his nearby attendants wrenched the knife from the woman's hand. In the pandemonium that followed, the would-be assassin was seized but was in danger of being lynched by the crowd 'who were now tearing her away, no doubt to fall the instant sacrifice of her murderous purpose'. The king then intervened, calling out: 'The poor creature is mad! Do not hurt her! She has not hurt me!' The king then 'came forward, and shewed himself to all the people, declaring he was perfectly safe and unhurt; and then gave positive orders that the woman should be taken care of, and went into the Palace, and had his levée'.

Fanny was enormously impressed by the king's cool and clement behaviour and wrote:

> There is something in the whole of his behaviour on this occasion, that strikes me as proof indisputable of a true and noble courage; for in a moment so extraordinary, an attack, in this Country, unheard of before, to settle so instantly that it was the effect of insanity, to feel no apprehension of private plot or latent conspiracy, to stay out, fearlessly, among his people, and so benevolently to see himself to the safety of one, who had raised her arm against his life, – these little traits [...] have given me an impression of respect and reverence to the intrinsic worth of their operation that I can never forget, and never think of but with fresh admiration.[15]

Queen Charlotte, however, could not take the incident as calmly as her husband. When Fanny went to her later that day, 'she scarce once opened her lips. Indeed I could not look at her without feeling the tears ready to start into my Eyes. But I was very glad to hear again the voice of the King, though only from the next Apartment, and calling to one of his Dogs.'[16] I suspect that Adèle would not have been quite so shocked or excited as Fanny at this attempt. She was all too familiar with assassination attempts in Paris. Both Napoleon and Wellington had narrow escapes, and there were at least half a dozen attempts on the life of Louis-Philippe during his long reign.

GEORGE III'S MADNESS

Perhaps the most significant passages historically in Fanny's journal of this period are the accounts of the tragic illness of the king, brought to dramatic life in recent years in the play *The Madness of King George* by Alan Bennett and subsequently made into a popular film. Fanny was an eyewitness of the onset of his illness, and she describes it with great affection, sympathy and compassion. It was regarded by the king's doctors simply as insanity or madness, but in more recent years it has generally been diagnosed as a form of porphyria, an inherited metabolic disorder of certain enzymes that can cause complications ranging from skin problems and pains in the limbs to mental disturbance and confusion, leading to delusory fits. One recent theory, however, is that the king was suffering from manic depression, a psychiatric disorder. At that time there was no understanding of the condition and therefore no appropriate cure.

The first serious indications occurred in November 1788, which Fanny described in a letter to Susanna and Mrs Frederica Lock in the following terms:

> O dreadful Day! – my very Heart has so sickened in looking over my memorandum that I was forced to go to other employment. O my dear Friend; what an history! The King at Dinner has broken forth into positive Delirium, which long has been menacing all who saw him most closely; and the Queen was so overpowered as to fall into violent Hysterics.[17]

Fanny went on to describe how on the following day she rose early and was very alarmed to hear men's voices in the king's dressing room. They had been up all night as the king had come into the queen's room to satisfy himself that she had not been taken away from him and he was still there and refusing to be moved away. 'He kept talking unceasingly – his voice was so lost, in hoarseness and weakness, it was rendered almost inarticulate; but its tone was all benevolent – all touching graciousness.'[18]

From this time onwards, 'as the poor King grew worse, general hope seemed universally to abate; and the Prince of Wales now took the government of the house into his own Hands. Nothing was done but by his orders, and he was applied to in every difficulty.'[19] In contrast to his turbulent and generally confrontational relationship with the king and his deliberate support for his political opponents, the Prince Regent's general conduct towards his father during his illness was considerate and widely praised. Fanny was much touched by the great demonstration of public concern for the king. One of the king's doctors, Sir Lucas Pepys, who had coincidentally rented Juniper Hall in September 1793 after the French émigrés had left it, told her that 'none of their own lives would be safe, if the King did not recover, so prodigiously ran the tyde of affection and loyalty'.[20] This affection for the genial sovereign was equally manifested when he recovered in the course of the summer of 1789. Prayers were said for him in the churches, and he was cheered in Weymouth where he went for a period of convalescence and took part in the novel recreation of sea bathing, which Fanny also enjoyed. Fanny describes a wonderful scene where 'the first time of his bathing, he had no sooner popt his Royal head under the water, than a Band of Music, concealed in a neighbouring machine, struck up God Save Great George, our King!'[21] Sea bathing was still a relatively new and wondrous habit in both England and France, and Adèle describes how she too attracted a large crowd when she pioneered it from a bathing machine on the beach at Boulogne, although there was no hidden band to play the Marseillaise to celebrate her own immersion.

Back in 1788 at Windsor, however, the king's condition had so worsened that it was decided to transfer him to Kew Gardens, where, although the accommodation was uncomfortable and inadequate, it was possible to confine him more discreetly. Fanny was in the accompanying party, and the celebrated Dr Francis Willis, a specialist 'of peculiar skill and practice in intellectual maladies',[22] whom Fanny much admired, was also sent for. It was here that one of the most celebrated incidents recorded in Fanny's journals occurred. Fanny had been told that it was safe to walk in the Kew gardens as the king would on that day be away at Richmond. As she duly strolled round the gardens she suddenly saw through the trees a group of two or three figures whom she assumed to be workers or gardeners. She was alarmed, however, when she found herself pursued by them, and heard the voice of the king himself 'loudly and hoarsely calling after her "Miss Burney! Miss Burney!"'[23] She ran on in panic, looking for some escape path from the gardens, while the 'poor hoarse and altered voice' continued to pursue her and 'more and more footsteps resounded frightfully behind me'. Eventually she recognized the voice of Dr Willis, begging her to stop and calling out, 'You *must*, ma'am, it hurts the King to run.'

'Then, indeed I stopt! – in a state of fear really amounting to agony,' wrote Fanny. Eventually the king caught up with her and called out, 'Why did you run away?' In what Fanny describes as 'the greatest effort of personal courage I have ever made', she turned and confronted the king, who put both his hands round her shoulders and embarked on a long and moving personal conversation. He told her how glad he was to see her, asked a great deal about her father 'of whom he spoke with great kindness', reminisced with various anecdotes about Handel, his favourite composer, running over several airs and choruses from his works in a voice that was 'so dreadfully hoarse, that the sound was terrible', and talked sympathetically about Mrs Schwellenberg, whom he called the 'coadjutrix'. He was clearly fully aware of the problems Fanny had with her and said, 'Never mind her. Depend upon me – I will be your Friend – as long as I live – I here pledge myself to be your friend.'

This is an extremely touching picture of George III at the height of his so-called madness and illustrates both his compassionate nature and the genuine sympathy that seemed to exist between him and Fanny right from their very first meeting at Mrs Delaney's house in December 1785. As Fanny put it, 'He opened his whole Heart to me', and his understanding remarks about Mrs Schwellenberg must have resonated particularly with her.

The king's passion for the music of Handel was well known, and his eagerness to talk about him, and to run over some of his music, also brings to mind the moving scene at Brighton in early 1817 described by Adèle. Adèle and her father were staying as guests of the Prince Regent at the Royal Pavilion at Brighton, his famous folly built to accommodate his gluttonous excesses, described by Adèle as 'un chef-d'œuvre de mauvais goût [a masterpiece of bad taste]'.[24] After dinner one night, the prince told his guests the story of his last visit to his father the king, who was in close confinement and whom he had not seen for several years. Only the queen and the Duke of York were normally admitted to the inner chambers to see him. He was now entirely blind and, for most of the time, kept in a padded room in complete silence, as voices were liable to send him into an agitation that could last for several days.

On this occasion, since the queen was not well, the Prince Regent was taken to visit him first. He was shown into a large drawing room where he found his father 'très proprement vêtu, la tête entièrement chauve et portant une longue barbe blanche qui lui tombait sur la poitrine [very neatly dressed, his head entirely bald, with a long white beard that fell down upon his breast]'.[25] He was, astonishingly, purporting to hold a Council of State and talking to a senior minister, and, after this was adjourned, leaning on the arm of a page, he went to talk to his children, and to the queen, who too had now been brought into the same room. Following a short conversation with them he went alone

au piano où il se mit à improviser et à jouer de souvenir de la musique de
Hændel en la chantant d'une voix aussi touchante que sonore.

[to the piano where he sat down and began to improvise and play from
memory some pieces of music from Handel, singing in a voice that was
both sonorous and touching.]

As he was told that his father might well remain at the piano for three hours or
more, the Prince Regent discreetly left. But Adèle says that

Je dois au Régent la justice de dire qu'il avait les larmes aux yeux en nous faisant
ce récit [...] et qu'elles coulaient le long de ses joues en nous parlant de cette
voix, chantant ces beaux motets de Hændel, et de la violence qu'il avait dû se
faire pour ne pas serrer dans ses bras le vénérable musicien.

[I must do the regent justice to say that he had tears in his eyes when he
told us this story [...] and that the tears ran down his cheeks as he spoke
to us of this voice singing the beautiful motets of Handel and of the self-
restraint that he was forced to exercise on himself to refrain from clasping
the venerable musician in his arms.][26]

As described by Adèle, the reaction of the Prince Regent, who had spent much of his
adult years rebelling against and seeking to annoy his father, perhaps sheds a slightly
more sympathetic light on his character, and the scene pictured is an extremely
moving one and touchingly reminiscent of Fanny's own experience at Kew.

The Kew encounter was not in fact Fanny's last dialogue with the king
about Handel. In the early days of his reign he had acquired a harpsichord that
had belonged to the great man, and Handel's music had always dominated the
frequent concerts of ancient music that he patronized. A bust of Handel also
occupied a prominent position in the Japan Room of the Queen's House at
Greenwich. Fanny records that in May 1790, well after the king's first recovery,
she received a message from him 'desiring to know if I wished to go to Handel's
Commemoration, and if I should like the *Messiah*'.[27] Showing excellent taste, and
not a little tact, she chose the *Messiah*, which was being performed in a series of
concerts of Handel's music at Westminster Abbey.

After the king's recovery, and as court life returned to a more normal state, Fanny became increasingly unhappy and eager to resign her post. She had suffered emotionally from an unfulfilled relationship with a senior courtier, Colonel Digby, and she developed a cough, pains in the side, weakness and sleeplessness. She writes: 'My loss of health was now so notorious that no part of the House could wholly avoid acknowledging it [...] frequent pains in my side forced me 3 or 4 times [...] to creep to my own Room for Hartshorn and for rest.'[28] Eventually she composed a long resignation letter to the queen, which she submitted through Mrs Schwellenberg. To give her credit, Mrs Schwellenberg at last seemed sympathetic and 'behaved with a humanity I had not much reason to expect.'[29] Even so, Mrs Schwellenberg tried at first to persuade her to take back the letter and take temporary sick leave rather than to resign, but with the support at last of her father, who could now recognize the serious threat to his daughter's health, she resisted this and managed to get the letter to the queen herself. It still took several weeks before the queen accepted her departure, and the farewell meeting with the queen, the king and the royal princesses did not take place until 7 July 1791.

It was an emotional occasion. The queen had already indicated that she would grant Fanny from her own private purse a pension of half her salary (that is, £100 a year), and tearful expressions of gratitude and friendship were uttered on all sides. According to Fanny's journal, the queen 'had her handkerchief in her Hand, or at her Eyes the whole time – I was so much moved by her condescending kindness, that as soon as I got out of the Close I nearly sobbed'. The farewell with the king was a curiously but movingly silent one:

The King came into the Room. He immediately advanced to the window, where I stood, to speak to me. I was not then able to comport myself steadily. I was forced to turn my Head away from him. He stood still and silent, for some minutes, waiting to see if I should turn about: but I could not recover myself sufficiently to face him, strange as it was to do otherwise; and perceiving me quite over come, he walked away – and I saw him no more.[30]

This was an anticlimactic but none the less touching farewell between Fanny and her friend the king.

Although in future years Fanny was mindful of the need to maintain her relationship with the queen, and sought to avoid any action that might offend her or, in more practical terms, prejudice the continuation of her pension, she had only limited contact with the royal family. She dedicated *Camilla*, her third novel, to Queen Charlotte and went to Windsor in July 1796 to present specially bound copies to her, to the king and to the princesses. Poor Mr d'Arblay travelled with her and was obliged to carry the very heavy load of books right up to the castle gates, but, as a Frenchman, during a time of war with France, he was not allowed to proceed any further. Fanny, now greeted as a successful author rather than as a court functionary, was admitted to the royal presence, and the queen 'began a conversation – in her old style – upon various things and people, with all her former graciousness of manner, which soon, as she perceived my strong sense of her indulgence, grew into even all its former kindness.'[31] The king later joined the party and soon began a dialogue about whether Fanny had begun or written any part of it when she was working for the queen and asked what Mr Lock and her father thought of it. He also enquired, in his curious but endearing way, who corrected the proofs. When Fanny replied that she had done so herself, the great royal bibliophile commented:

Why some Authors have told me [...] that they are the last to do that work for themselves. They know so well by heart what *ought* to be, that they run on, without seeing what *is*. They have told me, besides, that a mere plodding hand is best and surest for that work – and that the livelier the imagination, the less should be trusted to it.[32]

This was shrewd advice indeed.

Among the last comments on King George III recorded by Fanny were those in a letter to Frederica Lock of 17 February 1820, following the king's death (he had died on 29 January, having lived in seclusion at Windsor for many years).

No one, my dearest friend, can live – and breathe – and think; and dare lament that the so good, so pious, so amiable, and so exemplary *George the Third* should be gone to his great reward – should be relieved from those trammels of Earthly machinery that were no longer informed by the faculties that for so many years guided him to all that was Right – should

have his soul liberated from the malady of his Brain and freed to enjoy
the salubrity of those Regions for which it was fitted, – nevertheless,
no one could have known him as I have known him, in all the private
excellencies of his domestic benevolences, – and have shared as well as
witnessed them – without feelings of depression and sadness that such
a Man is no more.[33]

Even allowing for the floridity of Fanny's prose on this occasion, and a certain
flattery even bordering on obsequiousness, whenever she wrote to or about the
royal family, and notwithstanding that many of the king's political opponents
would have found it hard to endorse her sentiments, this was a fitting tribute by
her to a monarch whom she truly loved and who seemed genuinely fond of her.

As a brief tailpiece to Fanny's association with British kings and queens, it is
worth noting that she lived long enough to see Queen Victoria on the throne.
In her last surviving letter – to Charlotte Barrett, dated 30 July 1839 – she leapt
to the defence of the young queen in the notorious affair of her allegedly pregnant lady-in-waiting, Lady Flora Hastings, who had been required to leave the
court in disgrace, although a subsequent autopsy showed that she had not been
pregnant but suffering from a liver complaint. Loyal as ever to royalty, Fanny
wrote of Victoria:

I am convinced she has been betrayed into a wrong measure from being
deluded into a wrong opinion, and therefore, though not blameless, is
extremely to be pitied: for her hasty order of exile from her presence was
a mere unweighed impulse of *Virtue*. How could she disbelieve a medical
man?[34]

The real culprit was the queen's doctor, Sir James Clark, who had wrongly diagnosed Flora Hastings's condition.

ADÈLE AND THE BRITISH ROYAL FAMILY

Adèle's experience was, of course, mainly of French royalty, but during her
various stays in London she had many opportunities to meet and observe the

British royal family at close quarters too. In addition to the earlier account of the Prince Regent's meeting with his blind and confined father, she wrote a fascinating account of another occasion in London in the spring of 1816. She had just returned to London to join her father and received an invitation to a concert given by the Prince Regent for his mother, Queen Charlotte. Adèle's frank comments on both the queen and the Prince Regent are interesting. The protocol that governed the occasion was nearly as complicated and intimidating as that of the restored Bourbon court in Paris, and Adèle, for all her experience of court procedure, was quite overwhelmed. She says:

> *au moment où j'approchai, la Reine se leva en pied, et les quarante personnes qui l'entouraient imitèrent son mouvement. Ce froufrou, auquel je ne m'attendais pas, commença à m'intimider. La Reine fut très bonne et très gracieuse, je crois; mais, pendant tout le temps qu'elle me parlait, je n'étais occupée que de l'idée de ménager ma retraite.*

> [the queen rose the moment I approached, and the 40 persons who surrounded her followed her example. This general rustle, which I was not expecting, began to intimidate me. The queen was, I believe, very kind and gracious, but during the whole time she talked to me I was preoccupied with the idea of organizing my retreat.]

Adèle concluded her account by admitting that, although no longer young enough to be shy and accustomed to high society, '*il me reste de cette soirée et de cette présentation de faveur un souvenir formidable* [to this day I preserve a dread remembrance of the evening and the presentation]'.[35] It took quite something to reduce the experienced Adèle to this state.

Adèle was not particularly impressed by Queen Charlotte and did not mince her words in describing her:

> *Ce n'est pas que la reine Charlotte fût d'un aspect bien imposant. Qu'on se figure un pain de sucre couvert de brocart d'or, et on aura une idée exacte de sa tournure. Elle n'avait jamais été grande et, depuis quelques années, elle était rapetissée et complètement déformée.*

[It was not that Queen Charlotte was very imposing to look at. Imagine a sugar loaf covered with gold brocade, and you will have a fairly accurate picture of her appearance. She had never been tall, and for some years she had become shrunken and completely deformed.]

However, after this rather cruel portrait Adèle deigned to admit that

elle ne manquait pourtant pas d'une sorte de dignité; elle tenait sa cour à merveille, avec une extrême politesse et des nuances fort variées.

[she was not lacking in a certain dignity; she conducted her court marvellously, with extreme politeness and with a manner that could assume very varied shades of expression.][36]

This was not quite the same affectionate and respectful picture of the queen that Fanny had painted some years previously, and it was a little uncharacteristic of Adèle's normally generous style and approach. She was, however, unusually kind to the Prince Regent, by whose courtesy to his mother she was much taken. She noted that in his behaviour towards her:

Le prince régent donnait l'exemple des égards. Il était très soigneux et très tendre pour elle en particulier. En public, il la comblait d'hommages.

[the Prince Regent was exemplary in his consideration for her. He was very caring and tender towards her in private, and in public he overwhelmed her with respect.][37]

She was especially impressed by the way in which he insisted personally on taking a tray of tea to her and removing her cup after she had finished with it. This was presumably not the sort of familiar behaviour common among the senior royals that she had been used to witnessing at Versailles or at Louis XVIII's court, and her complimentary comments on the Prince Regent on this occasion recall those on his display of affection for his father in the episode at Brighton when he could hardly restrain himself from throwing his arms round the old, blind and deluded monarch.

Contrary to many of his subjects, for whom the prince, both then and later as king, became the personification of gluttony and dissipation and eventually a political irrelevance, Adèle was impressed by his behaviour, and in later comment she spoke admiringly of his openness and generally sociable and approachable manner. She wrote '*Le prince régent menait la vie d'un homme du monde. Il allait dîner chez les particuliers et assistait aux réunions du soir* [The Prince Regent lived the life of a man of the world. He went to dinner with private individuals and attended evening parties].'[38] He was extremely accessible:

Si on écrivait pour obtenir une audience ou qu'on la lui demandât d'avance, il recevait habillé et dans son salon, mais cela dérangeait ses habitudes et le gênait. En se présentant à sa porte sans avoir prévenu, il était rare qu'on ne fût pas admis. Il commençait la conversation par une légère excuse sur le désordre où on le trouvait, mais il en était de meilleure humeur et plus disposé à la causerie.

[If you wrote to him to secure an audience, or asked for one in advance, he would receive the visitor in full dress in his drawing room, but this upset his habits and embarrassed him. If you called at his door without notice, you were usually admitted. He would begin the conversation by some excuse for his untidy state, but he was in the best possible humour and as a result more ready to talk.][39]

She was, however, much less complimentary about the estranged wife of the Prince Regent (by then King George IV), Queen Caroline, and would no doubt have taken his part against her in the unseemly public dispute between them if she had stayed longer in London. Adèle had been far from impressed by her behaviour when she had previously come across her, travelling on the Continent. In the summer of 1820 she was visiting Aix, where she had successfully taken a cure at the spa waters in the previous year, and the carriages of Caroline, who was making a European tour, happened to be passing through at the same time. Adèle was shocked by the stories she heard of her conduct. Curious to learn the truth, she later questioned the owner of an inn at which Caroline was said to have stayed on the way to Aix. After references to '*une orgie perpetuelle* [a perpetual orgy]'[40] on the journey through Switzerland, the hostess told Adèle, '*J'étais honteuse, madame, de ce que je voyais moi-même, et j'avais répugnance à envoyer mes servantes pour la servir* [I was ashamed, madame, of what I saw myself, and I did not even like sending my servants to wait on her].' More than that, the inhabitants of the village were so shocked by Caroline's behaviour that

> *il y eut une explosion de fureur générale. Toute la population y prit part. On la voulait lapider, et elle en courut quelque risque.*

> [there was an explosion of popular anger. The whole population joined in it. They wanted to stone her, and she ran some risk of being so treated.]

Adèle was not normally prudish, censorious or easily shocked, but, for whatever precise reason at the time, the behaviour of Queen Caroline and Lady Hamilton surprised her, to say the least. It is interesting that by contrast she did not speak disparagingly of the Prince Regent's mistress, Mrs Fitzherbert, who was a family friend and had entertained Adèle and her parents when they arrived in England as refugees of the Revolution many years previously.

ADÈLE'S EARLY YEARS AT VERSAILLES

Adèle's experience of French royalty covered an unusually long period, from her childhood years at Versailles to the reign of Louis-Philippe and a little beyond. As she endured the burdensome protocol of Louis XVIII's attempts to restore the old formalities, her mind must often have gone back to those early days at the court of Louis XVI and Marie-Antoinette. Indeed, the importance of recording this for posterity was one of the main reasons for deciding to write her memoirs. Her principal memory – as of Fanny at Windsor – was of the elaborate protocol imposed. Saturday evenings and Sundays were particularly onerous, as both ministers and members of the royal households were required to be in attendance and full court dress was obligatory. Lesser mortals generally dined at a common table, but the higher ranks had an opportunity to dine with the king in his private apartments, known as '*souper dans les cabinets*'. But even this was a curious and aleatory affair. Ladies received invitations either the evening before or on the very morning, but gentlemen had to take their chance by waiting in an ante-room beforehand, while the king, viewing them secretly from an adjacent room, decided which of them were to be admitted. This he did by writing their names on separate pieces of paper, which were handed to an usher who in turn read them out one by one. Once the list was completed and the lucky – or unlucky? – ones had entered the dining room, '*l'huissier repoussait la porte avec une violence d'étiquette* [the usher closed the door with a customary bang]'.[41] Not surprisingly, despite pressure from Mme d'Osmond, Adèle's father found this custom distasteful and seldom attended.

Although Adèle in retrospect found all this overbearing to the point of absurdity, she seems on the whole to have enjoyed a happy childhood and spoke well of both the king and queen, and other members of the inner royal family. She writes that '*Le Roi et la Reine surtout me comblaient de bontés* [The king and queen especially overwhelmed me with kindnesses]'.[42] She spoke highly of Marie-Antoinette, who was '*très aimée et très aimable, et n'était occupée qu'à raccommoder les petites tracasseries qui s'y élevaient* [was loved and loving, and was occupied solely in the task of resolving the little differences that caused her problems]',[43] and she became a great favourite of Mme Adélaïde's, the king's sister, to whom her mother was a lady-in-waiting. Mme Adélaïde allowed her to accompany her on her walks in the gardens and had made for her, at great expense,

> *une magnifique poupée, avec un trousseau, une corbeille, des bijoux, entre autres une montre de Lépine que j'ai encore, et un lit à la duchesse où j'ai couché a l'âge de sept ans.*

> [a magnificent doll, with a complete wardrobe, basket and jewels, including a watch by Lépine [the king's watchmaker], which I have to this day, and a duchesse bed in which I slept at the age of seven.]

The presentation of the doll became '*une fête pour la famille royale* [a special occasion for the royal family]'.[44] The king held Adèle's hand as the doll was produced; the queen and her sister-in-law, Mme Elisabeth, got down on hands and knees to make the bed to put the doll in, and everyone wanted to play with Adèle's new toy.

The king himself, although quite ready to enjoy informal moments with the infant Adèle, was still governed by a formidable set of rules, not least at bedtime, or 'le coucher'. Adèle, with tongue obviously in cheek, describes this in great detail. At half past nine every night, after ritual prayers and much passing of candles and prayer books between the various functionaries on duty, the king stripped to the waist, and the highest ranking person present – usually one of the royal princes, if they were in attendance – was formally presented with a nightshirt which he in turn handed to the king. Then followed the royal dressing gown, while three valets unfastened the king's waist belt and knee breeches, which fell to his feet.

> *Et c'est dans ce costume, ne pouvant guère marcher avec de si ridicules entraves,*
> *qu'il commençait, en traînant les pieds, la tournée du cercle.*

> [And it was in that garb, hardly able to walk with these ridiculous fetters,
> that he would begin to shuffle round the circle of those present.][45]

To complete this almost Chaplinesque scene, the king moved slowly backwards, sank into a waiting chair and raised both his legs so that two pages, down on their knees, could simultaneously pull off his shoes, which they '*laissaient tomber* [...] *avec un bruit qui était d'étiquette* [let fall with a crash, which was a point of etiquette]'.[46] Such was the glory of the Versailles court to which, for Adèle and her parents and all concerned, the Revolution put such an abrupt end.

LOUIS XVIII AND LOUIS-PHILLIPE

After the long interval of the Napoleonic empire and the two restorations, Louis XVIII tried to re-establish the customs of the old court, which the now older and more experienced Adèle found very tedious. Her views on Louis himself were mixed. She was clearly quite fond of him personally, and sympathized with the immense task he faced (who on earth in any case could follow Napoleon?), but she deplored his lack of judgement on a number of issues and occasions. One early example was the needless way in which he snubbed and alienated Tsar Alexander I by his cool, even offensive, reception of him at Compiègne in 1814 before his entry into Paris. The tsar was given inferior quarters, relegated to a place below his imperial status at dinner and was so offended that he left in high dudgeon to return to Paris early. At a time when Louis needed all the friends he could make among the allies, '*cette conduite de l'empereur Alexandre n'a pas peu contribué à amener le retour de l'empereur Napoléon l'année suivante* [this treatment of Emperor Alexander contributed more than a little to the return of the Emperor Napoleon in the following year]'.[47] Adèle relates that on the same occasion the king, by refusing to talk business with him, snubbed Talleyrand, who had played an important part in restoring him to the throne, with the result that Talleyrand also emulated Alexander and, after staying only a few hours, returned to Paris.

Thereafter Alexander showed little liking for the Bourbon house and preferred to associate with members of the Bonaparte family, especially Hortense de Beauharnais. According to Adèle, the tsar

se plaisait à répéter sans cesse que toutes les familles royales de l'Europe avaient prodigué leur sang pour faire remonter celle des Bourbons sur trois trônes, sans qu'aucun d'eux y eût risqué une égratignure.

[delighted in saying repeatedly that all the royal families of Europe had spilled their blood in order to help the Bourbons to recover three thrones, while none of them had risked a single scratch.][48]

There was probably some justice in this, but Adèle's judgement was perhaps not entirely uninfluenced by the commanding appearance of the tall and handsome tsar, in contrast with the now fat, ailing and gouty king, and by her close family friendship with the Russian ambassador, Pozzo di Burgo, and other senior members of Alexander's entourage.

Adèle was nevertheless generous to the king at the time of his death. Summing him up in 1814, she wrote:

Certainement le roi Louis XVIII avait beaucoup d'esprit, un grand sens, peu de passion, point de timidité, grand plaisir à s'écouter parler et le don des mots heureux.

[Certainly King Louis XVIII had plenty of spirit and common sense, if little passion or peace of mind. He took great pleasure in hearing himself speak and had a gift for choosing the right words.][49]

However, the first lady at court in the absence of a queen, Madame la Duchesse d'Angoulême, the daughter of Louis XVI and therefore the king's niece, did not contribute to Bourbon popularity by her frequently stiff and haughty behaviour, which Adèle somewhat ironically attributed to a lack of good breeding (although perhaps it was really a function of the opposite). At a court function she had snubbed Adèle's father, in contrast to the warm welcome he had received from the king. On the same occasion 'Madame' treated her coolly whereas the king welcomed her familiarly, calling her '*sa petite Adèle, me parlant de Bellevue et me disant des douceurs* [his little Adèle, talking about Bellevue [her home] and all kinds of nice things]'.[50]

At the political level, Adèle applauded some of the king's early policies, including the Declaration of Saint-Ouen, which had liberal intentions and was the basis of the subsequent Constitutional Charter. This reaffirmed that, although authority in France remained in the person of the king, it recognized key political gains of the Revolution, including equality before the law, individual freedom and property rights, and the opening of all civil and military posts to everyone. To that extent it rejected, at least in principle, any reversion to the society of the *Ancien Régime*. She also particularly welcomed the king's firm action in preventing Marshal Blücher from vindictively blowing up the Jena bridge and the column in the Place Vendôme. But she perceptively foresaw the end of his reign (politically) as, following the assassination of the Duc de Berry in February 1820, he fell further under the influence of his brother Monsieur le Comte d'Artois, his future successor as Charles X, and the extreme right-wing Ultra-Royalist party led by the Comte de Villèle, whom Charles retained when he became king in September 1824. In the end, Louis XVIII died with dignity, observing the principle that

un roi de France ne se devait aliter que pour mourir. Il s'est montré fidèle à ce principe; car, entre le 25 août et le 16 septembre, dernier jour de sa vie, il a encore paru en public et tenu deux fois sa Cour.

[a king of France should only take to his bed in order to die. He proved himself loyal to this principle, as between 25 August and 16 September, the last day of his life, he still appeared in public and held his court on two occasions.]

Adèle's comment on his end was a kindly one. She wrote with obvious affection, moved by the marked deterioration in his health and physical condition, which shocked her, although at heart she probably felt he was never really adequate for the tasks that he faced. She wrote:

j'avais l'impression que je voyais pour la dernière fois ce vieux monarque dont la sagesse avait été mise à tant d'épreuves et qui aurait peut-être triomphé de toutes les difficultés de sa position si la faiblesse et la maladie ne l'avaient jeté, tout désemparé, entre les mains de ceux contre les folies desquels il luttait depuis trente années.

[I had the impression that I was then seeing for the last time this old monarch, whose wisdom had been put to the test so many times and who would perhaps have triumphed over all the difficulties of his situation had infirmity and illness not made him helpless in the hands of those against whose follies he had struggled for thirty years.][51]

However, just as she did not attend the coronation of his successor, she did not attend his funeral.

It was a different matter with the Duc d'Orléans, who became Louis-Philippe, Roi des Français, as opposed to Roi de France (an important distinction, intended to symbolize the basis of the king's authority in the people), as a result of the July 1830 Revolution, in which Adèle played such an active part. The title of Duc d'Orléans was traditionally given to the king's closest brother, but the house to which the present duc belonged, which descended from Philippe d'Orléans, the only brother of Louis XIV, had been estranged from the main Bourbon line for some years. Louis-Philippe was the son of the so-called Philippe Egalité, who had voted in favour of Louis XVI's execution but was nevertheless imprisoned and guillotined under Robespierre. He had fought in the revolutionary wars, which brought him wide popularity, and had spent much time abroad. Though rich, he nevertheless led an outwardly simple life, had a large family (eight children), and closely and deliberately associated himself with bourgeois society of his day – hence his future description as 'le roi bourgeois'. Louis XVIII had always maintained a severe prejudice against the House of Orléans, which greatly irritated them, and, according to Adèle,

ne perdait pas une occasion d'être désobligeant pour eux. Il cherchait à établir
une différence de traitement entre madame la duchesse d'Orléans, son mari et
sa belle-sœur, fondée en apparence sur le titre d'Altesse Royale qu'elle portait,
mais destiné au fond à choquer les deux derniers qu'il n'aimait pas.

[never lost an opportunity to show them some discourtesy. He tried to
adopt a different mode of behaviour towards the Duchesse d'Orléans,
her husband and her sister-in-law, ostensibly based on the title of Royal
Highness that she bore, but really in order to shock the two latter personages whom he did not like.][52]

His succession to the throne after the July 1830 Revolution was a reaction against
the increasingly illiberal policies of Louis XVIII's successor, Charles X. Charles
started on the political right and went further in that direction as his reign progressed, appointing the hardliner Jules de Polignac as head of government in
August 1829. Matters came to a head with the snap calling of an election and
publication of four authoritarian ordinances on 25 July 1830, culminating in
disturbances in Paris and the abdication of Charles X, who left the country and
sought refuge in Prague. As public tension and dissatisfaction mounted, Adèle
foresaw the end of his reign, and her critical opinion of him was exacerbated
by the fact that he disliked Pasquier, her friend and close companion of later
years, and excluded him from his Council of Ministers. Her judgement when he
abdicated was: '*jamais souverain n'est tombé devant un assentiment plus unanime*
[never was a sovereign overthrown by greater unanimity of popular feeling]'.[53]

Louis-Philippe initially sought to install a parliamentary monarchy resting
on the middle class. He showed himself openly in the streets of Paris, and Fanny
Trollope recorded seeing him strolling down a boulevard with his top hat and
umbrella like an ordinary bourgeois citizen.[54] As with his predecessors, however,
opposition, including serious riots in Paris and industrial disturbances in other
major cities, caused by a combination of economic distress and frustration at
the lack of further political progress on the part of those who had succeeded in
the July 1830 Revolution, pushed Louis-Philippe into more restrictive policies.
In April 1834 a number of citizens were massacred by troops in Paris when barricades were again erected in the Hôtel de Ville district (earning the king another
title – 'le roi des barricades' – as he joined the troops himself), and there were

several attempts on his life in the following years. He too was finally forced to abdicate in February 1848, the year of revolutions right across Europe, and he and Marie-Amélie fled into exile in England. He was in fact the last king in the history of France. Following a period of provisional government, followed by the election under universal suffrage of a majority of moderate republicans to the Assembly, and further serious civil disturbances in Paris, Prince Louis-Napoléon, the nephew of Napoleon I, was elected President of the Republic in December 1848 and established an essentially conservative government. He soon, however, succeeded in extending his presidential powers and, following a plebiscite in November 1852, announced the re-establishment of the empire, taking the imperial reins himself as Emperor Napoleon III in December 1852. The imperial wheel had come full circle.

This was really the end of political life for Adèle. She remained loyal to the House of Orléans and maintained contact with the former king and queen during their years of exile in England. She had backed them in 1830 and remained very close and supportive to them during the nearly 20 years of their reign. Before they had acceded to the throne she was a frequent visitor at the Orléans residence, the Palais Royal, where regular dinners and receptions were held, for which

> *on avait soin que les invitations fussent toujours suffisamment mélangées pour que toutes les opinions se trouvassent représentées et qu'il n'y eût repoussement pour aucune.*

> [care was taken that the invitations were sufficiently mixed to ensure that all shades of opinion were represented, to the exclusion of no particular party.][55]

The duc was carefully building up a broad political constituency. Adèle greatly admired his all-round capabilities:

> *Monsieur le duc d'Orléans se tenait au courant de tout ce qui paraissait de nouveau soit dans les arts, soit dans les sciences. Les savants lui communiquaient leurs découvertes; celles qui étaient de nature à intéresser les princesses étaient produites et démonstrées au salon. Les artistes qui passaient y étaient entendus et y apportaient une variété qui le rendait fort agréable aux habitués.*

[The Duc d'Orléans kept himself familiar with every novelty in the arts or in science. Scientific men communicated their discoveries to him, and those that were likely to interest the princesses were displayed in the salon. Artists who came in were listened to, and they introduced an element of variety that was much appreciated by regular guests.][56]

There is almost something of the first Napoleon in this. He too encouraged the arts and science, not least in his otherwise ill-fated Egyptian campaign of 1798, when the large assemblage of scientists, scholars and archaeologists he took with him effectively founded the modern science of Egyptology.

Adèle's principal affection, however, was for her oldest friend, Louis-Phillipe's wife, the Duchesse d'Orléans, Marie-Amélie. She was a true blue-blooded royal, being the daughter of King Ferdinand IV of the Two Sicilies (another Bourbon) and of the Archduchess Maria Carolina, Marie-Antoinette's sister. Adèle could not speak too highly of the support she gave to her husband and to her family. She wrote:

Je ne saurais assez exprimer la profonde vénération et le tendre dévouement que j'éprouve pour madame la duchesse d'Orléans. Adorée par son mari, par ses enfants, par tout ce qui l'entoure, le degré d'affection, de vénération qu'elle inspire est en proportion des occasions qu'on a de l'approcher. La tendre délicatesse de son cœur n'altère ni l'élévation de ses sentiments, ni la force de son caractère. Elle sait merveilleusement allier la mère de famille à la princesse.

[I could not possibly express well enough the deep veneration and tender devotion that I feel for the Duchesse d'Orléans. She was adored by her husband, by her children and by all around her, and the more often anyone came into contact with her, the deeper was the veneration and affection that she inspired. The tender and sympathetic nature of her heart in no way altered the loftiness of her sentiment or the strength of her character. The roles of mother of a family and princess were wonderfully combined in one.][57]

This was affection and adoration of a high order and helps to explain why Adèle, acting as an intermediary between the Charles X and Orléans camps, had done so much to encourage the duchesse publicly to support her husband and to urge him to grasp the power that was his for the taking in the final crucial stages of the

July Revolution. There is a truly triumphant note in her lively account of those dramatic days when she was here, there and everywhere, using her influential contacts, both French and Russian, to further the Orléanses' cause. She was so proud that in evicting Charles X and putting her friend Louis-Philippe on the throne,

> *la France s'est levée comme un seul homme et, s'étant faite géant par l'unité de sa volonté, elle a secoué les pygmées qui prétendaient l'asservir.*

> [France rose as one man and, becoming a giant by the unity of her resolve, she shook off the pygmies who attempted to enslave her.][58]

Once Louis-Philippe was on the throne, Adèle had access to the inner circles of the court and the royal family, and, although she continued to deny that she was really interested in politics, she was able to enjoy being at the heart of political and social events for the next two decades. But on a personal level nothing seemed to have given her greater pleasure than a tour by the king of the newly restored Palace of Versailles, which must have revived so many memories of her childhood. It was in a sense sad that she lived to see the end of the Bourgeois reign in 1848 and the irony of another Napoleon on an imperial throne.

This selection of experiences shows how close Fanny and Adèle were at different times to their respective monarchies – in Adèle's case to the British as well as the French – and provides some intimate pictures of life, albeit often of trivial details, at court. While Adèle's perspective was both personal and political, and Fanny's comments were almost exclusively on personal matters, there were many similarities, not least in their observations on and portrayals of court protocol and etiquette. But apart from the period after 1830 under the Bourgeois King, when court life was less formal, the impression they leave is that the protocol of the Bourbon court was more severe than that at Windsor under George III, despite the rigours of Fanny's daily routine as Second Keeper of the Robes to Queen Charlotte. As the child of an aristocratic family, Adèle was petted by Louis XVI and Marie-Antoinette at Versailles, almost as one of the family, and she later enjoyed an intimate relationship with Louis-Philippe and Marie-Amélie. It is difficult, however, to imagine that as an adult she could have developed quite as warm, touching and affectionate a relationship with any of the Bourbon kings as Fanny did with George III, both in his healthy prime and during his tragic illness.

SIX

ACTORS, ARTISTS & INTELLECTUALS

W hile both Fanny and Adèle consorted closely with kings, queens, princes and princesses, they also counted among their friends and acquaintances some of the pre-eminent intellectual, artistic and cultural luminaries of their day. Fanny's introduction was largely through her father's household in London and later as a result of the patronage of Mrs Thrale at Streatham. Adèle's contacts came more from the political world than Fanny's, but through her own salon, and those of others in Paris, she became intimate with such great society intellectuals as Mesdames de Staël and Récamier, Benjamin Constant and Chateaubriand. There was also some overlap with Fanny, who was introduced to Mme de Staël in 1793 when she was a member of the Juniper Hall colony in Surrey. This chapter will present a more intimate picture of some of these personalities as they emerge from the journals and memoirs of Fanny and Adèle.

When Charles Burney moved, at the urging of his friends, from King's Lynn to Poland Street in Westminster in early 1760, Fanny was not yet eight years old, and so far had received no formal education. As her father's reputation as a music teacher grew, the young Fanny was exposed to a constant stream of celebrated actors, writers and artists who visited the Burney household, such as David Garrick, Sarah Siddons, Joshua Reynolds and his sister Frances, Oliver Goldsmith, Richard Brinsley Sheridan and Edmund Burke. The most famous of them was probably Dr Samuel Johnson, with whom Charles Burney had already corresponded from King's Lynn as a young man, although Fanny's main contact with him was to come later when she was admitted to the Thrale circle. It is perhaps surprising that, although musical evenings were frequently held at the Burneys' and her sister Hetty often performed before the assembled company, fewer musicians seem to feature among the guests described in Fanny's journals. Perhaps this reflects Fanny's own literary interests and preferences. She loved the theatre and, despite her subsequent triumph as a novelist, she always wanted to become a success as a playwright, especially of comedies, but sadly never managed to produce a play that was a real success. The visitor who made the greatest early impression on the young Fanny was the famous actor–manager David Garrick. Even at this early age, the observant Fanny must have been thinking about writing down her experiences of this remarkable personality. She often attended performances at Drury Lane Theatre, where Garrick made his box available to her father and other members of the family.

GARRICK AND THE THEATRICAL SET

Garrick seems to have been the life and soul of the party, both on and off the stage. He was in his early forties when the Burneys moved to London, and came from Huguenot stock, his grandfather having fled to London in 1685 when the Edict of Nantes was abolished, revoking the rights of Protestants in France. He was brought up in Lichfield and after attending the local grammar school, he became a pupil of Dr Johnson's, who remained a lifelong champion and friend, and moved to London in 1840. After various acting engagements, both in and out of London, he took over the Drury Lane Theatre in April 1740 and remained its manager and most celebrated performer – the Laurence Olivier of his day – until his retirement in 1776. He was best known, not only in England but also on the Continent, for his interpretation of the main Shakespearian roles.

One of Fanny's earliest references to him was in her journal entry of 30 May 1772, when she described a visit to Drury Lane to see him perform in perhaps his most famous role, that of Richard III. In her words:

> Garrick was sublimely horrible! – how he made me shudder where ever he appeared! It is inconceivable, how terribly great he is in this Character. I will never see him so disfigured again – he seemed so truly the monster he performed, that I felt myself glow with indignation every time I saw him.[1]

From then on he was a frequent visitor to her father's house, and she was able to get to know the man beneath the greasepaint and the exotic stage costumes. According to Fanny, he was 'the most entertaining of mortals',[2] and a particularly amusing account is contained in a journal entry of March 1775, describing his whirlwind descent on the house one day in the early morning. Mr Burney was in the process of having his hair dressed, 'surrounded by Books and Papers innumerable'; Charlotte, Fanny's younger sister, was reading a newspaper and Fanny herself, always busy and useful, was making the breakfast. Garrick, 'who was himself in a most odious scratch wig', burst in on them and completely disrupted this cosy domestic scene. He put on a look 'in the Abel Drugger style' – a role played by him in Ben Jonson's *The Alchemist* – asked if the hairdresser could touch up 'his frightful scratch', impersonated several other Burney friends, including Boswell, Johnson and Charles Burney's former music master Thomas Arne, rushed into the library to survey the books there, shot down the stairs, frightened the maid and, finally, 'in this sportive manner he continued till the Door was shut'. Fanny obviously loved him and the fact that, at five foot four inches, he only just overtopped her probably endeared him all the more to her.

There are many subsequent references to Garrick in Fanny's journals, all affectionate on Fanny's part. She was as stout a defender of him in face of any criticism, as Dr Johnson, of whom Sir Joshua Reynolds said, according to Boswell, that, 'Johnson considered him to be as it were his property.'[3] A particularly interesting account is in a letter to Daddy Crisp of 27–8 March 1775, which relates an appearance by Garrick before the king, queen and the royal family at Windsor. Garrick read 'in different Voices, and Theatrically'[4] his own adaptation of *Lethe*, a farce that he himself had written. It was apparently not a success. Garrick, who was used to the noisy and enthusiastic, if often ribald, reactions of the audiences at Drury Lane, 'was extremely hurt at the coolness of the King's applause, and did not find his reception such as he expected'.[5] The royal family were apparently not amused.

Garrick's friends were more philosophical about this. Mr Seward, another member of Mrs Thrale's circle, said, 'He has been so long accustomed [...] to the Thundering approbation of the Theatre, that a mere *very well*, must necessarily and naturally disappoint him'; while Dr Johnson added:

> he should not, in a Royal apartment, expect the hallowing and clamour of the one shilling gallery. The King, I doubt not, gave him as much applause as was rationally his due: and, indeed, great and uncommon as is the merit of Mr Garrick, no man will be bold enough to assert that he has not had his just proportion both of Fame and Profit: he has long reigned the unequalled favourite of the public, – and therefore nobody will mourn his hard fate if the King, and the Royal Family, were not transported into rapture, upon hearing him read *Lethe*.[6]

However, having made due obeisance to the judgement of the king, Johnson then went on to mount a lengthy and vigorous defence of Garrick's character, particularly against accusations of vanity and meanness, although he admitted that Garrick was an attention-seeker.

> Garrick never enters a Room, but he regards himself as the object of general attention, from whom the Entertainment of the Company is expected, – and true it is, that he seldom disappoints them; for he has infinite humour, a very just proportion of Wit, and more convivial pleasantry than almost any other man living.[7]

Judging by the detail in which Fanny remembered and recorded Johnson's remarks, she thoroughly agreed with him. But Garrick was clearly an enormous showman, who loved his audiences, bathed in attention, always sought to steal the show and expected as warm and enthusiastic a reception at performances before the king and queen at Windsor as at Drury Lane. Indeed, his reputation travelled across the Channel into Continental Europe, and we know that his final performance as Hamlet at Drury Lane on 27 April 1776 was attended by a theatre party from Paris that included Mme Necker, the mother of Mme de Staël.

SARAH SIDDONS

The Burney household was also favoured by the leading actress of the day, Mrs Sarah Siddons. She was slightly younger than Fanny, having been born in 1755, and after an acting career in the provinces she made her London debut at Drury Lane in 1782, becoming particularly famous for her portrayal of Lady Macbeth. In a long letter to Susanna in January 1783 Fanny expressed great admiration for her, with the following tribute: 'She is certainly by far the *best* Actress we have, and as to her not fulfilling all my ideas, nobody, after Garrick, I suppose ever could.'[8] This comparison, almost putting her on the same level as Garrick, was praise indeed from Fanny. She became quite a favourite of the king's and the royal family's, often being invited to give readings at the Queen's House at Windsor and, in a journal letter of December 1785 Fanny also described George III's views of Mrs Siddons. In the course of a more general discussion about players and plays, she reported him as saying: 'I am an *Enthusiast* for her, cried the King, quite an Enthusiast; I think there was never *any* player, in my time, so excellent, not Garrick himself.'[9] If Garrick could have heard this he would no doubt have been rather irritated at being given second place to Mrs Siddons, particularly after his somewhat cool reception at Windsor. He would have been comforted, however, by Fanny's later remarks, which indicated that she disagreed with the king but kept her mouth shut since 'to enter into an argument was quite impossible'.[10]

That Mrs Siddons came second to Garrick in Fanny's estimation is confirmed by other earlier comments on her in her journals. When asked to write down her overall assessment of Mrs Siddons in December 1782 she wrote, in what she described as a 'very honest opinion':

I must confess my admiration of Mrs Siddons does not keep pace with that of the Town; yet I think her a pleasing and elegant actress. Her Countenance is intelligent, and full of sensibility, her voice is penetrating and affecting, her attitudes, upon striking occasions, are very noble, though, in general, her arms are awkward. I think her neither *great* nor *astonishing*; her manner seems to me monotonous, her Walk mean, her air wants spirit, and her dignity is studied. Upon the whole, I think she has much merit and but few defects yet, altogether, something through-out, is wanting to produce upon me much effect.[11]

For one who was generally enthusiastic about Mrs Siddons, this was pretty faint, if not damning, praise and at odds with the opinion she expressed to Susanna only a few weeks later. One wonders if at the time there had been some personal friction between them. Fanny's more critical view was, however, echoed in a much later assessment in a letter to Susanna of August 1787, commenting on an appearance by Mrs Siddons at Windsor, like Garrick earlier, to read a play to the royal family – her own royal-command performance. Fanny was required to receive and look after her on arrival, and 'was perfectly well inclined to reap some pleasure from the meeting'. But she went on to declare: 'I was much disappointed in my expectations.' Contrasting Mrs Siddons's appearances on the stage as the 'Heroine of a Tragedy – sublime, elevated and solemn' with her rather shallow and uninteresting conversation, she concluded: 'Whether Fame and success have spoiled her, – in making her imagine That to *speak* alone is enough, from Her, to *charm*, or whether she only possesses the skill of representing and embellishing materials with which she is furnished by others, I know not. But still I remain disappointed.'[12] If this criticism was merited, Mrs Siddons will not have been the first actor to disappoint when the make-up and stage setting are removed and the person underneath is revealed at closer quarters.

Even if Fanny had reservations about Mrs Siddons, she scored highly in the estimation of Adèle, who had presumably seen her performing on the stage in London during one of her periods of residence there. In a chapter of her memoirs about events in the late 1820s during the reign of Charles X, she lamented the death of François-Joseph Talma, the great classical French actor, who became a close friend of both Napoleon Bonaparte's and his court painter Jacques-Louis David's, with whose works Fanny also became familiar when she lived in Paris. For many years he dominated the Comédie-Française in the same way as David Garrick had dominated Drury Lane. In referring to his great acting talent Adèle drew a comparison with Mrs Siddons in the following terms:

Talma en France et mistress Siddons en Angleterre m'ont paru ce qu'il pouvait y avoir de plus parfait au théâtre, car ils se transformaient complètement dans le personnage qu'ils représentaient; et, de plus, l'un et l'autre étaient si beaux et si gracieux, leur voix était si harmonieuse, que chacune de leurs poses composait un tableau aussi agréable à l'œil que leurs accents étaient flatteurs pour l'oreille [...] Ainsi j'aurais grande joie à entendre un acteur ou une actrice qui me fissent autant de plaisir que Talma et mistress Siddons; mais je doute que cela se rencontre de mon temps.

[Talma in France and Mrs Siddons in England have always seemed to me to be absolutely perfect on the stage, because they completely identified themselves with the character they portrayed. What is more, both of them were so handsome and graceful, and their voices so harmonious, that their attitude formed a picture as agreeable to the eye as their words were charming to the ear [...] I should thus have great joy in hearing an actor or actress who could give me as much pleasure as Talma or Mrs Siddons, but I doubt if any such will be found in our times.][13]

Adèle could not, of course, make any comparison with the acting of David Garrick, since he had retired from Drury Lane some years before she first went into exile with her parents to live in London, but it is interesting that during her time at Juniper Hall in 1793, Adèle's friend Mme de Staël saw Mrs Siddons perform in London and was immensely impressed by the force and vitality of her acting, which was so different from the formality of French classical theatrical convention.

SIR JOSHUA REYNOLDS

Of the other regular visitors to the Burney household with whom Fanny formed a close friendship, the most notable was Joshua Reynolds, who became Sir Joshua when he received a knighthood from George III in 1769. Born in 1723, and therefore nearly 30 years older than Fanny, Reynolds rose from relatively humble origins in Devon to become the most celebrated British portrait painter of his day. Together with Thomas Gainsborough, he was a founder of the Royal Academy, of which he became the first president and continued in that role until his death in February 1792. He enjoyed great commercial success, and it was said that in the late 1750s he had four or five sittings a day, allocating about an hour to each one of them. He was also a founder member of the famous 'Club', which included Garrick, Boswell, Sheridan, Edmund Burke and, most notably, Dr Johnson, and met for dinner and conversation every Monday evening at the Turk's Head in Gerrard Street (once a fortnight while Parliament was sitting). This was virtually the same set that frequented the Burney house.

Reynolds was a close friend of Dr Burney's and a familiar face at Burney household gatherings, so that Fanny would have met him at an early age. Since he was in 1784 appointed 'Principal Painter in Ordinary to the King' (to his disgust at the reduced salary of £38 a year, which was less than a fifth of Fanny's subsequent salary as Second Keeper of the Robes), she may also have come across him from time to time at court during the late 1780s. Her first reference to his paintings occurs in an account of a visit in February 1775 with her mother and sister Susanna to an exhibition of his work, of which she said: 'We were very much delighted; the ease and elegance of this Painter seem unrivalled among English Artists.'[14] Her acquaintance thereafter became a closer and more personal one, and in a letter to Susanna of 11 June 1779 she described a long and ban-tering conversation among very grand company at Sir Joshua's house, at which both he and the up-and-coming playwright Richard Brinsley Sheridan praised her writing – Evelina had only been published in the previous year – and urged her father to ensure that she continued it. She was particularly impressed when Sheridan, who was roughly her own age and whom she much admired, turned to Reynolds and said, 'Sir Joshua I have been telling Miss Burney that she must not suffer her Pen to lie idle; – ought she?' To which he replied, 'No, indeed, ought she not.'[15] They then went on to encourage her, on the basis of the talent for dialogue she had shown in Evelina, to write a comedy for the stage, alas, with the not very successful results already referred to.

The young Fanny must have been very flattered and excited to be praised and encouraged by such figures as the leading portrait painter of the day and the rising playwright Sheridan, who was already renowned for The Rivals and The School for Scandal. Her association with the older Reynolds continued throughout the rest of his life and she was obviously extremely fond of him. In October 1779 she visited Knole Park, the country house and estate of the Duke of Dorset, where, among assorted old masters, several paintings by Reynolds were on display. These included portraits of Dr Johnson and Oliver Goldsmith, whom Fanny, of course, knew well in real life. Commenting on Reynolds' paintings, Fanny wrote: 'though mixed in with those of the best old Painters, they are so bewitching, and finished in a style of Taste, Colouring, and expression so like their Companions, that it is not, at first view, easy to distinguish the New from the Old.'[16] Reynolds clearly reciprocated Fanny's affection, and in a letter of 3 November 1779 to Susanna there is a nice reference to a remark by the Revd Dr John Delap, a regular guest at the Thrale household, who, hearing some criticism of Reynolds in Fanny's presence, interjected: 'You must not run down Sir Joshua Reynolds because he is Miss Burney's friend.'[17]

As he grew older, Reynolds's health deteriorated. He had always suffered from deafness, notoriously causing him to use an ear trumpet, and in August 1789 he lost the sight of his left eye, which led him to retire from active painting in 1791 at the age of 68. Fanny was distressed by his ailments, and in a letter of November 1791 she described in touching terms a visit to him with her father:

> He had a bandage over one eye, and the other shaded with a green half-bonnet. He seemed serious even to sadness, though extremely kind. 'I am very glad,' he said, in a meek voice and dejected accent, 'to see you again, and I wish I could see you better but I have only one eye now, – and hardly that.'[18]

Fanny added that she was quite moved and hardly knew how to express her concern for his altered situation. It is a great pity that Reynolds, who painted her father and a number of their friends (many of which were on display in a gallery at the Thrale house in Streatham), never painted a portrait of Fanny, although it would have had to be extremely good to compete with the magnificent one by Edward Francis Burney, which is on the cover of this book. Reynolds died in February 1792, and Fanny wrote in her journal: 'He was always peculiarly kind and sweet to me – and he worked at my deliverance from a life he conceived to be too laborious for me, as if I had been his own daughter'[19] (the reference was to the help Reynolds gave in extricating her from her job as Second Keeper of the Robes at court).

MRS THRALE, THE STREATHAM CIRCLE
AND SAMUEL JOHNSON

As we have seen earlier, Fanny's big social breakthrough came when she was introduced to, and taken up by, Mrs Thrale. Hester Lynch Thrale was born on 16 January 1741 in Caenarfonshire in Wales into the Salusbury family, one of the great land-owning families of the Georgian period, and received an excellent early education, although, on her own admission, 'education was a word then unknown as applied to females'.[20] After her father John Salusbury had gone bankrupt, she married in October 1763 a rich brewer, Henry Thrale (who had inherited the business at Southwark from his father), bore him 12 children and lived with him in a grand three-storey house at Streatham Park, set in grounds of about 100 acres and at that time in the countryside about eight miles outside London. With the financial and other resources now available to her, she established a literary group, known as the Streatham Circle, which enabled her to indulge her own literary and cultural interests.

In a similar way to the great Parisian salons of the late eighteenth and early nineteenth centuries, the Streatham Circle attracted a range of the London cultural elite of the day, both men and women, including many who also frequented the Burney household. Hester Thrale was never in the first rank of poets and writers herself, or perhaps even in the top second class, despite aspirations to be so; however, there is no doubt that she was not just a fashionable hostess but an attractive, highly cultured and intelligent woman, who more than held her own in the circle's debates. This is also true of her husband who, although perhaps sometimes thought of as just a successful brewer and tradesman, had been educated at Eton and Oxford, became a Member of Parliament and was greatly respected by the star of Mrs Thrale's circle, Dr Samuel Johnson. Johnson admired and felt great affection for him, and Boswell wrote of their relationship: 'Johnson had a very sincere esteem for Mr Thrale, as a man of excellent principles, a good scholar, well skilled in trade, of sound understanding, and of manners such as presented the character of a plain independent English Squire.'[21] Such praise was a good deal more than many of Dr Johnson's other acquaintances ever received.

Fanny's very first meeting with both Mrs Thrale and Dr Johnson in fact occurred at her father's house in St Martins Street in 1777, before she had published *Evelina* and been revealed as its author. From that time onwards we owe to Fanny's journals some of the most immediate, lively and revealing portraits of both of them on record. In a letter to Daddy Crisp of 28–9 March in that year, she described Hester Thrale as follows: 'Mrs Thrale is a very pretty woman still, – she is extremely lively and chatty, – has no supercilious or pedantic airs, and is really gay and agreeable.'[22] The fact that Mrs Thrale was only four foot seven inches tall, so that even the diminutive Fanny could almost tower over her, perhaps was a cause of endearment to Fanny too. As she was invariably referred to by Fanny as 'Mrs Thrale' (or later, after her second marriage, as 'Mrs Piozzi'), we perhaps tend to forget that she was only 11 years older than Fanny, who may have regarded her, despite her married state and continual pregnancies, more like an older sister than a maternal figure.

As for her first sight of Dr Johnson, she was intrigued to meet this shambling and almost mythical celebrity, whom she described in the same letter as follows:

He is indeed, very ill favoured, – he is tall; and stout, but stoops terribly – he is almost bent in double. His mouth is almost constantly opening and shutting, as if he was chewing; – he has a strange method of frequently twirling his Fingers and twisting his Hands; – his Body is in continual agitation, *see sawing* up and down; his Feet are never a moment quiet, – and, in short, his whole person is in perpetual motion.[23]

The letter then went on to describe his dress, his short-sightedness, which meant that when music was being played he '*poked his Nose* over the keys of the Harpsichord, till the Duet was finished', his deafness and his habit, when visiting anyone's house, of making for the library and poring over the books 'shelf by shelf, almost brushing the backs of them, with his Eye lashes, as he read their Titles'.[24] Fanny also commented that after Dr Johnson had been induced to leave the library and return to the dining room, he 'entered freely and most cleverly into conversation; though it is remarkable, that he never speaks at all, but when spoken to; nor does he ever *start*, though he so admirably *supports* any subject'.[25] This last observation seems rather surprising, even implausible, and perhaps not an opinion that Fanny would have held to as she got to know him better.

After this first meeting with Mrs Thrale and Dr Johnson on home territory, Fanny was soon invited into the Thrale circle at Streatham, first with her father and then increasingly in her own right as the newly revealed and celebrated author of *Evelina*, the literary sensation of the day. She became a favourite of Mrs Thrale's, who delighted in showing her off to her friends, many of whom could not believe that the hitherto unknown Fanny – such a young woman and from such a respectable household – could possibly be the author of such a worldly wise, sophisticated and even racy novel. Between 1778 and 1784, when their friendship was broken as a result of Mrs Thrale's marriage to Gabriel Piozzi, Fanny often stayed at Streatham and travelled with Mr and Mrs Thrale to such fashionable places as Bath and Brighton. This meant, of course, that she also spent much time in the company of Dr Johnson, who by this time had become a regular house guest both at Southwark and at Streatham, and often accompanied the Thrales on their travels too, not only in Britain but also in France and elsewhere on the Continent. Like Fanny later from Queen Charlotte, Dr Johnson was granted a royal pension of £300 a year from George III, but until he received a very large advance for his great dictionary project (£1,575, which is roughly the equivalent of over £135,000 today), which assured him of a decent income for the future, he was generally short of ready cash. He was, nevertheless, always generous in handing spare cash out to waifs, strays and down-and-outs whom he came across in the streets, some of whom he collected and took back to live in his house at Bolt Court. Thus one of the reasons for his rupture with Mrs Thrale over the Piozzi marriage was that he feared that the patronage and hospitality he had enjoyed while his beloved and respected friend Henry Thrale was still alive would cease to be available. It is clear from Boswell's comments that he was genuinely afraid that he would no longer enjoy the Thrale comforts, although until the marriage rupture he tactfully 'continued to show a kind attention to his widow'.[26]

One of Fanny's most striking portraits of Johnson, which reinforces her description of him at their first meeting at her father's house, is in a journal entry of August 1778 regarding her first visit with her father to Streatham. After Mrs Thrale had welcomed her, and in a tactful but rather roundabout way made an oblique and sensitive reference to *Evelina* – of which Fanny later saw a copy discreetly displayed on a reading table in the library – and then introduced her to Mr Thrale, to whom she took an instant liking, Dr Johnson arrived for dinner and was placed next to Fanny. Her account of the occasion is worth quoting in full:

Soon after we were seated, this great man entered. I have so true a veneration for him, that the very sight of him inspires me with delight and reverence, notwithstanding the cruel infirmities to which he is subject, for he has almost perpetual convulsive movements, either of his Hands, lips, Feet, knees, and sometimes of all together. However, the sight of them can never excite ridicule, or, indeed, any other than melancholy reflections upon the imperfections of Human Nature; for this man, who is the acknowledged first Literary man in this kingdom, and who has the most extensive knowledge, the clearest understanding, and the greatest abilities of any Living author, – has a Face the most ugly, a Person the most awkward, and manners the most singular, that ever were, or ever can be seen. But all that is unfortunate in his *exterior*, is so greatly compensated for in his *interior*, that I can only, like Desdemona to Othello, '*see his Visage in his mind*'. His Conversation is so replete with instruction and entertainment, his Wit is so ready, and his Language at once so original and so comprehensive, that I hardly know any satisfaction I can receive, that is equal to listening to him.[27]

Fanny was utterly won over by him, and they had an extensive conversation about her book, which he discreetly but greatly praised, and about mutual friends, notably David Garrick, of whose virtues and merits Dr Johnson spoke at great length, defending him vigorously from suggestions by Mrs Thrale that, as an actor, he was past his best. She was also overwhelmed by the reception she received from the Thrales and in particular the tactful way in which both they and Dr Johnson had referred to her book without embarrassing her ('indeed, the delicacy I met with from him and all the Thrales was yet *more* flattering to me than all the praise which I have *heard* they have Honoured my Book').[28] Mrs Thrale made it clear that she hoped Fanny would visit Streatham frequently and from time to time stay there, and from then onwards many of Fanny's letters are dated from Streatham or such fashionable places as Bath and Brighton, which she visited with them. Dr Johnson was unfailingly supportive and affectionate towards Fanny, and a letter of late June 1779 to Susanna told how, in an argument about female writers, which he had with fellow guest Sir Philip Jennings, Johnson said, referring to Fanny, '"So extraordinary, Sir," answered he, "that I know none like her, – nor do I believe there *is*, or there ever *was* a *man* who could write *such* a

Book so young.'"[29] This was high praise indeed from a man well known for his cautious views on young women, whose company he enjoyed, but not if they showed themselves to be too clever.

According to Mrs Thrale, in her *Anecdotes of Samuel Johnson* (which was written after her husband's death), at the age of two he had been taken by his mother to London

> to be touched by Queen Anne for the scrophulous evil, which terribly afflicted his childhood, and left such marks as greatly disfigured a coun-tenance naturally harsh and rugged, besides doing irreparable damage to the auricular organs, which never could perform their functions since I knew him; and it was owing to that horrible disorder, too, that one eye was perfectly useless to him.[30]

Whether or not scrofula, which is an ulceration of the lymph node infected with tuberculosis and commonly caused by drinking untreated cows' milk, was the cause of these particular problems is not certain, but Johnson's sight and hear-ing were certainly seriously affected – the former perhaps also by conjunctivitis, for which there was no effective cure at the time. He partly grew out of this in his youth, and in his middle years he became proud of his fitness, strength and athleticism, often seeking to show it off. But his increased bulk and swollen legs (probably affected by dropsy) impeded his mobility with age, and his sight and hearing deteriorated. There is an amusing account in the *Anecdotes* of his sensi-tivity to this in an argument between him and Sir Joshua Reynolds. Dr Johnson objected to the way in which Reynolds, in painting his portrait, had depicted him as looking into the 'slit' of his pen and holding it very close to his eye. Mrs Thrale tried to smooth the situation over by pointing out that a picture of the partially deaf Reynolds himself showed him 'holding his ear in his hand to catch the sound'. But Johnson would have none of it, and riposted, 'He may paint himself as deaf as he chooses; but I will not be *blinking* Sam.'[31]

'Blinking Sam' or not, Dr Johnson's worsening condition caused Fanny great concern. Several of her letters refer to it and in one of 19 June 1783 to Susanna she described how, on hearing he had been taken ill, she and her father immediately went to visit him. She says, 'He had earnestly desired me, when we lived so much together at Streatham, *to see him frequently if he should be ill*.'[32]

In fact, because the doctors and others were with him, and his bedroom was so crowded, Fanny was unable to get to him, 'but he sent me down a most kind message, that he thanked me for calling, and when he *was* better, should hope to see me *often*'. During his final illness in late November 1784 she was allowed to visit him alone on his sickbed and reported with relief that 'I had a longer and more satisfactory conversation with him than I have had for many months. He was in rather better spirits, too, than I have lately seen him.'[33] She was, however, greatly distressed when she was not permitted to go up to his room again to see him shortly before he died, although she was very moved to know that only a day or two earlier he had asked her father 'How *Fanny did*? I hope *Fanny* did not take it amiss that I did not see her? I was very bad'; and had also requested that Fanny should pray for him. Fanny's response was: 'O that I had been present to have answered it!' and 'Ah, Dear Dr Johnson! – might I but have *Your* prayers!'[34] When eventually the news of his death on 13 December was confirmed to her she was utterly grief-stricken and told Susanna that she would never go back to Bolt Court, Johnson's home, again.

This was an extremely stressful period for Fanny. She had lost her Chessington mentor, Daddy Crisp, two years earlier; together with her father she was worried about Susanna, who after her marriage had been taken away by her husband Captain Phillips to live in lodgings in Boulogne; her friendship with Mrs Thrale had been broken following the latter's marriage to Gabriel Piozzi. She became ill herself with a nervous fever and a cough, so much so that in January 1785 her alarmed father sent for one of the king's doctors, Sir Richard Jebb, to attend to her. Her condition was probably as much psychological as physical, but it was several months before she began to recover and move freely again in society.

It is a great shame that Adèle was never able to meet Dr Johnson, as she would surely have been intrigued by him. When he died she was not yet four years old, and his visit to Versailles with the Thrales, where they obtained permission to observe the king and queen at breakfast and the latter remarked on Queeney Thrale, took place a few years before she was born. He had a reputation as a misogynist, especially as the author of the often repeated remark that 'a woman's preaching is like a dog walking on hind legs',[35] and of other similar derogatory comments on the female sex. He was certainly wary of extremely talented and independent women such as Mary Wollstonecraft, and perhaps, as Kate Chisholm in her fascinating study *Wits and Wives: Dr Johnson in the Company of Women* put it in *Animal Farm*-like terms, he wanted women to be equal, but not too equal.[36] He did, however, form friendships with a large number of women, admittedly mainly much younger ones, and frequently sought and enjoyed their company. He had also, of course, although it was a very complex relationship, doted on his much older wife, Elizabeth 'Tetty' Jervis, who had done much to support him when he was establishing a reputation and building a career in his earlier years. His bark, especially in old age, when he tended to become irritable and somewhat overbearing in company and needed to show off, was much worse than his bite. Among the young women he took to were Sir Joshua Reynolds's sister Frances – a very talented painter herself – the writers Elizabeth Parker, Charlotte Lennox and Hannah More, and, of course, Fanny Burney and Hester Thrale – the sort of clever young people who featured in Sir Richard Samuel's celebrated painting, *Nine Living Muses*.

Adèle admittedly had the disadvantage from Johnson's point of view of being French, about whom he was usually very rude, dismissing them once as frog-eaters. However, after a little further acquaintance and inspection I suspect he would have respected her formidable intellect, her extraordinary experience of both her own country and of England, her political nous and wide range of distinguished acquaintances and her witty but shrewd judgement. It is possible that he might have been put on the defensive because Adèle's spoken English would have been so much better than his French, which he tended to avoid speaking, certainly to Frenchmen. But she could probably have got by in Latin, which would have much pleased him. For her part, Adèle would have found him intellectually stimulating, if physically rather repulsive, but she was used to dealing with intellectuals and people of great pretensions, and, being rather more worldly wise than Fanny, she would probably have dealt with him robustly and seen off a good deal of his bantering nonsense.

MME DE STAËL AND THE JUNIPER COLONY

Although Adèle never met Dr Johnson, she did become a close friend and admirer of the next real intellectual star in Fanny's firmament, Mme Germaine de Staël.

When Fanny first met her at Juniper Hall early in early 1793, de Staël was only 26 years old, some 14 years younger than Fanny, but in many ways much more experienced in the world – certainly in the world of politics – in spite of Fanny's five years' hard labour with Queen Charlotte at court. She was still to produce her most celebrated literary and historical works, but had already published a best-selling novel, *Sophie*, and several political dissertations. As the daughter of the rich banker Jacques Necker, who had been Louis XVI's finance minister and had on dismissal retired with a full purse to the Château de Coppet on Lake Geneva in Switzerland, she already had a place in society and had established her famous salon both at Coppet and in Paris. She was a strong opponent of Napoleon and during the imperial era was watched closely by Napoleon's police and for much of the time obliged to remain in exile outside France, only visiting Paris from time to time at great personal risk.

At the age of 20, she had, like Adèle, contracted a marriage of convenience with an older man, in her case Baron Erik Magnus Staël de Holstein, a Swedish diplomat who was appointed Swedish ambassador in Paris, although, unlike Adèle, she took many lovers. A great advantage of her marriage was that, as ambassadress, she held a much higher place in Parisian society than if she had married other than a very high-ranking French nobleman; the diplomatic protection it afforded enabled her not only to get away from Paris herself during the massacres of the Revolution in 1792 but also to help other aristocratic friends to escape. Notable among those whom she hid and saved were several members of the Juniper colony, including the Comte de Narbonne, the former Minister of War, who was now her lover and had taken refuge in her house before she was able to smuggle him out with a false passport and arrange his passage to England, and the erstwhile cleric and great European statesman-to-be Talleyrand, by whom Fanny was later immensely impressed. Mme de Staël joined them at Juniper Hall at the end of January 1793, having narrowly escaped imprisonment and execution herself when she was brought before Robespierre and the Committee of Public Safety at the Hôtel de Ville in Paris, where she only extricated herself by forcibly asserting her rights of immunity as the wife of the Swedish ambassador and threatening a serious diplomatic rift between Sweden and France if anything happened to her.

Fanny had been briefed in advance about the Juniper set by her sister Susanna and the Locks. She was intrigued by the reports she had heard about the brilliant conversations held in the Juniper Hall drawing room and was clearly anxious to be introduced to them. At the same time she was apprehensive about meeting

Mme de Staël, who had rapidly established herself, in Fanny's words, as 'head of the little French Colony in this neighbourhood'.[37] This was partly because of her, in local eyes, scandalous and immoral relationship with the Comte de Narbonne and partly because the Juniper set, as French 'constitutionalists', who in principle favoured the ideals of the Revolution, but not its excesses, were thought to be politically unsound, and association with them might prejudice her relationship with the royal family and thus her pension from Queen Charlotte. Fanny's father, for example, regarded Mme de Staël as a dangerous democrat.

It is a matter of speculation whether, if left to herself, Fanny would have ignored these considerations, particularly given her blossoming relationship with d'Arblay, who was helping Mme de Staël with the copying of the book *De l'influence des passions sur le bonheur des individus et des nations* (*The Influence of the Passions on the Happiness of Individuals and Nations*) that she was currently writing at Juniper Hall. Her good friends the Locks shared none of her concerns and even invited Mme de Staël to stay with them in their house in London. Her sister Susanna also felt quite free to associate with her. But they were not under the same pressure as she was from her father and other London friends to keep her distance from the Juniper set, especially Mme de Staël. This led her into embarrassing and rather ill-mannered behaviour both at Juniper and later in Paris.

Fanny's nervousness and uncertainty are well displayed by her contact with Mme de Staël some three weeks after the latter arrived, which is described in letters to Frederica Lock and her father between 14 and 19 February 1793.[38] Mme de Staël sent her two friendly English notes and although, according to Fanny, they were 'quite beautiful in *ideas*, and not very reprehensible in idiom', she sought a way of avoiding any commitment in replying to them. She did not want to incur what she described as 'the wrath of John Bull'. She was, however, up against a persistent and extremely clever opponent: 'Mme de Staël however will not easily be parried, and how I may finally arrange I know not. Certainly I will not offend or hurt her, – but *otherwise*, I had rather be a visitor than a guest.'

It is sad that Fanny fell – or was forced – into this situation, since she clearly admired Mme de Staël, who reciprocated that respect, once describing Fanny while at Juniper as '*la première femme d'Angleterre*'.[39] Fanny's admiration was revealed in an extraordinarily enthusiastic description of her in another letter from Mickleham of the same time, in which she wrote:

She is a woman of the first abilities, I think, I have ever seen. She is more in the style of Mrs Thrale than of any other celebrated Character; but she has infinitely more depth, and seems an even *profound* politician and metaphysician. She has suffered us to hear some of her works in mss, which are truly wonderful, for powers both of thinking and expression. She adores her Father – but is much alarmed at having had no news of him since he heard of the massacre of the martyred Louis – and who can wonder if it should have overpowered him.[40]

The reference to Mme de Staël's admiration for her father would further have endeared her to Fanny. Fanny went on later in the same letter to describe how Mme de Staël had been pressing her urgently to spend some time with her before she returned to London and that, despite her misgivings, she found this 'impossible to resist'. Again she drew a parallel with Mrs Thrale in terms of 'the ardour and warmth of her temper and partialities'.

She was, however, still under strong pressure from her father and friends to limit, if not terminate, the acquaintance and wrote to Susanna from Chessington in May, soon after Mme de Staël had left Juniper:

I have regretted excessively the finishing so miserably an acquaintance begun with so much spirit and pleasure, and the *dépit* I feel Mme de Staël must have experienced. I wish The World would take more care of itself and less of its neighbours. I should have been *very safe*, I trust, without such flights, and distances, and breaches! – But there seemed an absolute resolution to crush this acquaintance, and compel me to appear its wilful renouncer. All I did, also, to clear the matter, and soften to Mme de Staël any pique or displeasure, unfortunately served only to increase both [...] I am vexed, however, – very much vexed at the whole business. I hope she left Norbury Park with full satisfaction in its steady and more *comfortable* connection? I fear mine will pass for only a *fashionable* one.[41]

This shows that Fanny's behaviour went against her own better inclination, but, alas, it did not prevent her from getting into a similar tangle when she next came across Mme de Staël in Paris a decade or so later. For the moment, however,

Mme de Staël did not seem to be too deterred or upset, and asked Susanna to assure Fanny that she still loved her sincerely and bore no grudge against her.

Soon after she reached Paris with her husband and young son Alex in the spring of 1802, Fanny wrote in a letter to Frederica Lock that the moment Mme de Staël had heard of her arrival, she sent her (Fanny) a note, expecting that she would respond and call on her. Then followed an embarrassing and almost farcical game of protocol hide-and-seek. Mme de Staël, surprised to receive no response to her note, asked a friend whether she should take the initiative in calling on Fanny, even though 'it is not the Custom of *les dames françaises* to make the first visit'.[42] Fanny maintained a low profile, 'my whole mind being strongly bent, as you will know, against renewing an acquaintance which had already cost me so much pain and difficulty'. Mme de Staël was puzzled, asking a friend: '*Croyez vous que Mme D'Arblay me recevra avec amitié?* [Do you think Mme d'Arblay will receive me with friendship?]' She remained, however, determined to see her and, after putting out further feelers, sent another letter, in French this time, saying:

Je voudrais vous témoigner mon empressement, Madame, et je crains d'être indiscrète; j'espère que vous aurez le bonté de me faire dire quand vous serez assez remise de fatigues de votre voyage pour que je puisse avoir l'honneur de vous voir sans vous importuner.

[I should like to show you my eagerness, Madam, but I do not want to be indiscreet. I hope you will be good enough to let me know when you have recovered sufficiently from the fatigue of your journey so that I might have the honour of seeing you without troubling you.]

This was a very difficult approach to resist, particularly since it surely proved that Mme de Staël had a genuine regard for Fanny, despite the discourtesy that she appeared to be receiving. But Fanny still believed it necessary to avoid a meeting, perhaps also now because her husband felt that overt association with Mme de Staël ran the risk of falling foul of Napoleon, with whom she was *persona non grata*. This might even threaten his own modest job at the ministry. She therefore consulted him and sent the following rather cold and stiff reply in French, which he drafted:

Mme d'Arblay ne peut qu'être infiniment flatté de l'extrême bonté de Mme la comtesse de Staël. Elle aura certainement l'honneur de se présenter chez Mme de Staël – aussitôt que possible.

[Mme d'Arblay cannot but be infinitely flattered by the extreme kindness of Mme la comtesse de Staël. She will certainly have the honour of visiting Mme de Staël – as soon as possible.][43]

Fanny still intended to do nothing, but, to her surprise, Mme de Staël was undeterred and a few days later, contrary to all normal rules of etiquette, called at the d'Arblays' house and asked for Fanny. The position was now desperate. The only recourse was outright deception. Fanny sent down a note saying that she was not available as little Alex was ill, and Mr d'Arblay excused himself by saying that he was '*en déshabillé* [not formally dressed]'[44] and therefore also could not receive her. They were, however, ashamed of what they had done and decided that 'to return the visit was indispensable', or at least to call and leave their names. Steeling themselves to it, a few days later they took a cab to Mme de Staël's address, and as Fanny gave her hand to her husband – 'who was nearly as much disturbed as myself' – in order to step down from the cab, 'a person came out to say that Madame, though still in Paris, was just gone out'. To their great relief they were, therefore, saved by the bell, and Fanny says that they 'escaped as fast as possible'. To their further relief they heard the next day that Mme de Staël had left Paris and was thus out of the way for the time being.

It was an unfortunate episode and Fanny was rightly regretful and ashamed of it. She concluded in her letter to Frederica Lock:

Thus ends, in nothing thank Heaven, a little history that menaced me so much pain, embarrassment, unjust judgements from others, and cruel feelings in myself [...] You will I am sure, more than any one, conceive how irksome to myself has been the seemingly, ungrateful, Nay, insolent part I have appeared to act, towards one whom all the world admires, and whom we have All – once – been so disposed to love.[45]

The painful memory of it stuck with Fanny for a very long time. In a letter of 26 August 1813 to her friend Georgina Waddington, who had recently seen

Mme de Staël, she rehearsed again at length the details of the affair. While it was 'too long and difficult to write upon', she explained that she could not help what she had done because

> none of my friends, at that time, would suffer me to keep up the intercourse! I had messages – remonstrances – entreaties – representations Letters and Conferences, till I could resist no longer, though I had found her so charming, that I fought the hardest battle I dared fight against almost all my best connexions! – She is now received by all mankind – but that, indeed, she always was – all womankind, I should say, with distinction and pleasure.[46]

Although we may regret that Fanny could not fight just a little harder – after all, she was now an older and more mature woman than when she first met Mme de Staël at Juniper Hall – this contrite account, with her revelation of the acute pressures placed on her, perhaps excuses her behaviour, and it is to be hoped that Mme de Staël herself had some inkling of the reasons for it. Apart from anything else, it has deprived us of what could have been many more fascinating stories of her relationship with that remarkable woman.

ADÈLE AND MMES DE STAËL AND RÉCAMIER

There was none of these embarrassing complications in the relationship between Adèle and Mmes de Staël and Récamier, both of whom were pre-eminent figures in Parisian social, intellectual and salon society in the early nineteenth century. So far as marriage is concerned, Mme Récamier followed the same pattern of marrying a much older man as both Adèle and Mme de Staël. Eleven years younger than de Staël, she married even earlier, at the age of 15, a rich banker, Jacques-Rose Récamier, who was nearly 30 years her senior; the marriage was a loveless one – some reports say it was never consummated and that she remained technically a virgin all her life. Like Mme de Staël, however, she had many admirers, if not actual lovers, including such intellectual luminaries as Benjamin Constant, who for years had unsuccessfully sought to marry Mme de Staël, and Adèle's friend Chateaubriand. Again, like Mme de Staël, she was a strong opponent of Napoleon and hostess of a salon that attracted other distinguished political dissidents. As a result, she was, like de Staël, eventually exiled from France by the emperor, and took refuge in Rome and Naples (where she was on good terms with the king, Napoleon's former marshal Joachim Murat and his wife Caroline Bonaparte, who were then plotting against Napoleon), but eventually returned to Paris after Napoleon's defeat and established her famous salon in her apartment at L'Abbaye-aux-Bois in the Rue de Sèvres.

Adèle's first meeting with Mme de Staël occurred in 1806 and was quite a dramatic one. She was staying at the Hôtel d'Europe in Lyons, en route to her husband's house in Savoie, and received a note informing her that Mme de Staël was in the hotel and asking to see her. A few moments later Mme de Staël entered her room, followed by a train of admirers including her current suitor Benjamin Constant and the great actor François-Joseph Talma, whom Adèle had compared to Mrs Siddons. The reason for Mme de Staël's visit to Lyons, which was a dangerous breach of her conditions of exile, was to see Talma perform in the Lyons theatre that evening. Although she says that Mme de Staël quickly put her at her ease, Adèle was overwhelmed by this visitation and records that Mme de Staël 'resta toute la matinée dans ma chambre y recevant ses visites, m'enchantant par sa brillante conversation [stayed all morning in my room, receiving callers and enchanting me with her brilliant conversation]'.[47] They later dined together and Adèle accompanied them to the theatre.

Although not physically very attractive, Germaine de Staël obviously possessed an extraordinary magnetism and charisma, which quickly fascinated and won over anyone she met – even to the extent of being able to descend like a meteor (as Adèle put it) and take over the hotel room of a comparative stranger for the day and use it to receive her own visitors. Adèle's description of her on this occasion must be one of the frankest, freshest and most revealing on record, and is worth quoting at length:

> Au premier abord, elle m'avait semblé laide et ridicule. Une grosse figure rouge, sans fraîcheur, coiffée de cheveux qu'elle appelait pittoresquement arrangés, c'est-à-dire mal peignés; point de fichu, une tunique de mousseline blanche fort décolletée, les bras et les épaules nus, ni châle, ni écharpe, ni voile d'aucune espèce: tout cela faisait une singulière apparition dans une chambre d'auberge à midi. Elle tenait un petit rameau de feuillage qu'elle tournait constamment entre ses doigts. Il était destiné, je crois, à faire remarquer une très belle main,

mais il achevait l'étrangeté de son costume. Au bout d'une heure, j'étais sous le charme et, pendant son intelligente jouissance du débit de Talma, en examinant le jeu de sa physionomie, je me surpris à la trouver presque belle. Je ne sais si elle devina mes impressions, mais elle a toujours été parfaitement bonne, aimable et charmante pour moi.

[At first she seemed to me ugly and ridiculous. A big red face, a complexion lacking in freshness and her hair arranged in a manner she called picturesque – in other words, badly done. She had no fichu, a white muslin blouse that was very low cut, arms and shoulders bare, no shawl or scarf or veil of any kind, all of which formed a strange apparition in a hotel room at midday. She held a small leafy twig which she was constantly twiddling in her fingers with the object, I believe, of showing off a very beautiful hand, though it was the finishing touch to the eccentricity of her costume. At the end of an hour I was completely under her charm, and throughout her intelligent enjoyment of Talma's performance I watched the play of her features and was surprised to find her almost beautiful. I do not know if she divined my impressions, but she was always good, amiable and charming to me.][48]

Adèle's portrait of her in her memoirs continued with an eyewitness description of what she this time called '*de scènes bien déplorables* [very deplorable scenes]'[49] between Mme de Staël and her suitor Benjamin Constant the following year at Aix in Savoie. Constant had long tried to persuade her to marry him, but she had many admirers and although '*elle en avait le goût le plus vif pour son esprit* [she had a very real taste for his intellect]' and wanted to '*le retenir à son char* [keep him tied to her chariot]', she did not want to be yoked to him permanently. Adèle also thought that social snobbery played a part in this, since '*elle tenait beaucoup trop aux distinctions sociales pour échanger le nom de Staël-Holstein pour celui de Constant* [she attached too much significance to social distinctions to exchange the name of Staël-Holstein for that of Constant]'. Adèle's rather severe conclusion, bearing in mind her sometimes excessive consciousness of her own aristocratic pedigree, was on this occasion: '*Jamais personne n'a été plus esclave de toutes les plus puériles idées aristocratiques que la très libérale madame de Staël* [no one has ever been such a slave to the most childish aristocratic ideas than the very liberal Mme de Staël].'

The friction between Constant and Mme de Staël increased in intensity. It turned out that in frustration Constant had secretly married a German countess – the Countess of Magnoz – who was so jealous of Mme de Staël that she took a drug that made her vomit and threatened to poison herself once and for all unless Constant gave up Mme de Staël and announced his marriage to her publicly. The result at Aix was that '*les matinées se passaient en scènes horribles, en reproches, en imprécations, en attaques de nerfs* [the mornings were spent in horrible scenes, in reproaches, imprecations and nervous attacks]'.[50] But, as Adèle realized, it was all a '*comédie*' and, gradually, over dinner, '*les parties belligérantes se calmaient* [the warring parties calmed down]'. A compromise was eventually agreed under which Mme de Staël would write to the new Mme Constant to recognize the marriage, but Constant would delay any public announcement of it until she (de Staël) had departed on a planned visit to America. In the event she did not set off for America, and Adèle, seeing through the comedy, commented that she thought Mme de Staël

> *avait eu le désir de se ménager la plus puissante distraction dont lui était l'esprit de monsieur Constant, et de l'emmener en Amérique.*

> [had a desire to engineer a continuation of the amusement and pleasure that she derived from the mind of Mr Constant and wanted to take him to America.]

Obviously the scenes at Aix were quite as entertaining to Adèle as the theatre at Lyons.

Following these events at Aix, Mme de Staël returned to her father's house at Coppet, where she hoped to escape from Napoleon's spying agents. Adèle again paints an amusingly colourful picture of the bohemian, almost hippy, mode of life at Coppet, but now with a more serious edge:

> *La vie de Coppet était étrange. Elle paraissait aussi oisive que décousue; rien n'y était réglé: personne ne savait où on devait se trouver, se tenir, se réunir. Il n'y avait de lieu attribué spécialement à aucune heure de la journée. Toutes les chambres des uns et des autres étaient ouvertes. Là où la conversation prenait, on plantait ses tentes et on y restait des heures, des journées, sans qu'aucune des*

habitudes ordinaires de la vie intervînt pour l'interrompre. Causer semblait la
première affaire de chacun.

[Life at Coppet was strange. It seemed as idle as it was disconnected.
Nothing was regulated and no one knew whether he should be anywhere
or do anything at any special time. There was no special meeting place for
any particular hour of the day, and every single room was always open.
Wherever a conversation began tents were pitched, and you stayed there
for hours and days, uninterrupted by any of the ordinary things of life.
Talking seemed to be everyone's first duty.][51]

Life at Coppet, in the safe environment of Switzerland, flowed colourfully on
in this vein. Conversation flourished and visitors came and went, but Mme de
Staël, after rejecting Benjamin Constant, had now fallen into a relationship with
a young army officer, Albert de Rocca, who was 23 years her junior and had
returned from the war in Spain badly wounded. He amused her and she was
flattered by the attentions of such a young man. Unfortunately he fell violently in
love with her and she became pregnant by him and concealed it, not only from
her children, who thought she was suffering from dropsy, but from Napoleon's
spies who would have loved to exploit it in order to discredit her. She remained
at home to visitors as usual, merely saying as necessary that she was unwell, and
after the birth of the child – a boy – she left Coppet. Rocca followed her, but she
was now tired of him and he died, reputedly of grief, six months later.

Adèle was neither shocked by nor really critical of her behaviour – Fanny certainly would have been – since she understood the acute pressures that de Staël
had been under as a result of her exile and constant harassment by Napoleon's
agents. Nor did she believe de Staël ever really loved Rocca. She wrote perceptively of de Staël's actions at that time:

*Elle était d'autant plus charmée d'inspirer un grand sentiment à l'âge qu'elle
avait atteint que sa laideur lui avait toujours été une cause de vif chagrin. Elle
avait pour cette faiblesse un singulier ménagement; jamais elle n'a dit qu'une
femme était laide ou jolie. Elle était selon elle, privée ou douée d'avantages
extérieurs. C'était la locution qu'elle avait adoptée, et on ne pouvait dire, devant
elle, qu'une personne était laide sans lui causer une impression désagréable.*

1 *Fanny Burney, by Edward Francisco Burney*

2 *Adèle de Boigne, from a miniature by Isabey*

3 *Charles Burney, by Joshua Reynolds*

4 *Susanna Phillips (née Burney),*
   by Edward F. Burney

5 *Hester Lynch Piozzi*
   (Mrs Thrale), by unknown artist

6 *Samuel Johnson,*
by Joshua Reynolds

7 *Sarah Siddons,*
by Gilbert Stuart

8 *Richard Brinsley Sheridan,*
by John Russell

9 *Sir Warren*
Hastings, by
Joshua Reynolds

10 *King George III, Studio
of Allan Ramsay*

11 *Queen Charlotte, Studio
of Allan Ramsay*

12 *George III and family, by Johan Zoffany*

13 *The Esplanade, by James Gillray*

14 *George IV ('A voluptuary under the horror of digestion'), by Gillray*

15 *Louis XVI, King of France, by Joseph Boze*

18 *Maria Letizia Bonaparte (Napoleon's mother), by Achille Devéria*

16 *Marie Antoinette, by Emile Desmaisons*

17 *Napoleon Bonaparte on horseback, by Jacques-Louis David*

20 *General de Boigne, by P.E. Moreau, a pupil of David*

19 *Arthur Wellesley, 1st Duke of Wellington, by Thomas Heaphy*

21 *Juniper Hall in the 18th century. Watercolour, possibly by Alexandre d'Arblay*

22 *Juniper Hall today*

23 *Stained glass window in Juniper Hall, with Fanny, d'Arblay and others*

24 *Mickleham Church, where Fanny Burney and Alexandre d'Arblay were married*

[She was all the more delighted to be able to inspire a deep devotion at her age, as her plainness had always been a cause of acute grief to her. Her way of dealing with this weakness was unusual. She never said that a woman was plain or pretty, but merely that she possessed or lacked *external advantages*. This was her habitual phrase, and one could not say in her presence that a person was plain without hurting her feelings.][52]

These were very understanding, even touching, comments. Adèle herself had never pretended to be a great beauty and she knew how much the attentions of a handsome young officer must have meant to the ageing Germaine de Staël, however reprehensibly by conventional standards she behaved in the end.

Mme de Staël died in July 1817 after several years of travelling in Austria, Germany, Finland, Sweden and Russia. She returned to France after the defeat of Napoleon, and re-established her salon in Paris, where she developed a friendship with the Duke of Wellington and used her influence on him (more effectively than Adèle had been able to) to accelerate the departure of the occupying troops from France – an issue on which his reluctance to take action had so angered Adèle. She was also a prolific publisher, both of successful novels and the important political history (published posthumously) entitled *Considérations sur les principaux événements de la Révolution française, depuis son origine jusques et compris le 8 juillet 1815* (*Considerations on the Principal Events of the French Revolution since its Beginning up to and Including 8 July 1815*). Adèle thought that this book had a damaging effect on subsequent political attitudes, and declared:

Je crois que cet ouvrage posthume de madame de Staël a été un funeste présent fait au pays et n'a pas laissé de contribuer à réhabiliter cet esprit révolutionnaire dans lequel la jeunesse s'est retrempée depuis et dont nous voyons les funestes effets.

[I believe this posthumous work of Mme de Staël's was a fatal gift to the country and has contributed to reviving that revolutionary spirit which afterwards took hold of the younger generation and whose fatal results we now see.][53]

This was a curiously harsh judgement by Adèle, given her generally liberal views and her own later role in the July 1830 Revolution.

Her final comment on her friend occurred in the sections of her memoirs covering her time in London between 1816 and 1820. Adèle wrote the following comments on the occasion of her death, which she said caused her sincere, if not heartrending, grief:

Il y avait une trop grande différence d'âge et assurément de mérite entre nous pour que je puisse me vanter d'une liaison proprement dite avec madame de Staël, mais elle était extrêmement bonne pour moi et j'en étais très flattée. Le mouvement qu'elle mettait dans la société était précisément du genre qui me plaisait le plus, parce qu'il accordait parfaitement avec mes goûts de paresses.

[There was too big an age gap and certainly one of merit between us to enable me to boast of a friendship in the true sense of the word with Mme de Staël, but she was extremely kind to me and I was greatly flattered. The manner in which she enlivened society was exactly that which especially pleased me, because it was perfectly in accordance with my own lazy inclinations.][54]

This was a slightly curious and also rather self-deprecating epitaph. There is no doubt that Adèle, who was certainly not a lazy person, admired and respected Germaine de Staël, but perhaps she saw into her flamboyantly brilliant but flawed character more deeply than some of her other critics or admirers.

Unlike Mme de Staël, Juliette Récamier was not only clever but also very physically beautiful. Indeed, in her biography of Adèle, Françoise Wagener neatly described the pair as '*d'un côté, la plus jolie femme de son temps, et, de l'autre, la plus intelligente* [on one hand the prettiest woman in the world and on the other the most intelligent]'[55] – though this is parhaps a little hard on Mme Récamier's intelligence. Adèle first met her at a ball in Paris in 1805, soon after Napoleon's self-coronation in December of the previous year. She heard that she was present and sought her out because '*J'étais anxieuse de voir madame Récamier* [I was anxious to see Mme Récamier]',[56] of whom she had heard so much. She was not disappointed:

je vis en effet qu'une figure qui m'avait peu frappée était parfaitement belle. C'était le caractère définitif de cette beauté, qu'on peut appeler fameuse, de le paraître toujours d'avantage chaque fois qu'on la voyait. Elle se retrouvera probablement sous ma plume; notre liaison a commencé bientôt après et dure encore très intime.

[I saw in fact that a face that had impressed me only a little was absolutely beautiful. It was the special feature of this beauty, which can be called famous, to appear to greater advantage every time it was seen. She will probably reappear in my memoirs, as our relationship began soon afterwards and is still intimate.]

Adèle was true to her prediction and Mme Récamier appears frequently in her memoirs from that time onwards. Soon after the above occasion she came to stay with Adèle for a few days at Beauregard, the house near Paris that her husband General de Boigne had made available to her. This was soon after the curious incident described earlier, when she had been persuaded to send to the Empress Josephine some exotic heron plumes that her husband had brought from India and given her. At this stage her relationship with Mme Récamier was no more than a polite social one, but this visit seems to have cemented it into a close and lasting friendship. Adèle was completely charmed by her guest, as the following extracts from her account of that visit show:

Je la trouvai si calme, si noble, si simple dans cette circonstance, l'élévation de son caractère dominait de si haut les habitudes de sa vie que j'en fus extrêmement frappée. De ce moment date l'affection vive que je lui porte et que tous les événements que nous avons traversés ensemble n'ont fait que confirmer.

[I found her so calm, so noble, so simple in this situation, and the loftiness of her character stood so high above the ordinary habits of her life as to impress me very greatly. From that moment dates the keen affection that I bear towards her, which has only been confirmed by all the various events that we have been through together.][57]

Adèle had now found a soul mate and her memoirs continue with fulsome praise. She wrote, for example, on the same occasion:

On a fait bien des portraits de madame Récamier sans qu'aucun, selon moi, ait rendu les véritables traits de son caractère; cela est d'autant plus excusable qu'elle est très mobile. Madame Récamier est le véritable type de la femme telle qu'elle est sortie de la main du Créateur pour le bonheur de l'homme. Elle en a tous les charmes, toutes les vertus, toutes les inconséquences, toutes les faiblesses. Si elle avait été épouse et mère, sa destinée aurait été complète.

[Many portraits have been made of Mme Récamier, but none, in my opinion, has reproduced the real features of her character, which is all the more excusable since they are so variable. Mme Récamier is the true type of womanhood as made by the hand of the Creator for the happiness of man. She had all the charms, all the virtues, all the inconsistencies and all the weaknesses. If she had been a wife and mother her destiny would have been complete.]

This was almost adoration rather than just friendship, and the remark about motherhood is an interesting confirmation of the belief that Mme Récamier was unable to consummate her marriage. Adèle remained childless, too, and was no doubt particularly sensitive to this point.

Mme Récamier retained her beauty as she grew older and had famous affairs with Benjamin Constant, who chased her (as he had not too long previously chased Mme de Staël), and Chateaubriand, whom she in turn pursued for some 15 years. Aspects of both these relationships feature regularly in Adèle's memoirs. Writing of her in 1814, when she returned to Paris after Napoleon's first abdication, Adèle said:

Madame Récamier avait trouvé dans son exil la fontaine de Jouvance. Elle était revenue d'Italie, en 1814, presque aussi belle et beaucoup plus aimable que dans sa première jeunesse. Benjamin Constant la voyait familièrement depuis nombre d'années, mais tout à coup il s'enflamma pour elle d'une passion extravagante.

[Mme Récamier had discovered the fountain of youth during her exile. She had returned from Italy in 1814 almost as beautiful and much more lovable than in her early youth. Benjamin Constant had associated with her familiarly for a number of years, but he suddenly became inflamed with an extravagant passion for her.][58]

I think there is perhaps a trace of envy in Adèle's remarks.

Although she rejected his advances, Mme Récamier continued to exercise a powerful influence over Constant. With Napoleon safely domiciled – apparently – as sovereign of Elba, she persuaded him in 1814 to write a scathing lampoon on him, which was widely distributed in Paris. When Napoleon returned from Elba a few months later, Constant was terrified and feared the worst when he was summoned by the dreaded police minister, Fouché, to appear before the emperor. To his astonishment and relief, Napoleon told him that he wanted to harness all the talents available and asked Constant to help draft a new liberal constitution. This saved Constant's immediate bacon, but on the other hand Adèle tells us that he was now suspected by the imperialists, who never forgave him for his lampoon on Napoleon, and detested by the royalists, who hated him for his recantation, so that he became a general figure of contempt. He sought comfort with Mme Récamier, who 'le traitait avec douceur et bonté [treated him with sweetness and kindness]'.[59] Adèle greatly admired her conduct and summed her up in the following words:

Je n'ai jamais connu personne qui sût, autant que madame Récamier, compatir à tous les maux et tenir compte de ceux qui naissent, des faiblesses humaines sans en éprouver d'irritation. Elle ne sait pas plus mauvais gré à un homme vaniteux de se laisser aller à un acte inconséquent, pas plus à un homme peureux de faire une lâcheté qu'à un goutteux d'avoir la goutte, ou à un boiteux de ne pas marcher droit. Les infirmités morales lui inspirent autant et peut-être plus de pitié que les infirmités physiques. Elle les soignait d'une main légère et habile qui lui a concilié la vive et tendre reconnaissance de bien des malheureux.

[I have never known anyone who was as able as Mme Récamier to sympathize with every misfortune and to understand the weaknesses that arise in human nature without showing any irritation. She would no

more show irritation with a vain man who let himself be drawn into some
inconsistency or a frightened man who committed some act of cowardice
than with a gouty man for having the gout or a lame man for not walking
properly. Moral weaknesses inspired her with as much and perhaps even
more pity than physical weaknesses. She tended them with a light and
gentle touch that secured her the keen and tender recognition of many
unhappy people.][60]

This was almost a picture of a saint, and Mme Récamier no doubt needed all
these qualities in dealing with Benjamin Constant.

The friendship between Adèle and Mme Récamier continued over the following decades, when both played an active part in Parisian politics, not least during
the July 1830 Revolution when Mme Récamier strongly supported Adèle in her
efforts to put the Duc d'Orléans on the throne. They were both closely linked to
Chateaubriand, who was constantly frustrated at not achieving the high position
in government that he thought he deserved, and they conferred closely on how
the farcical attempt by the Duchesse de Berry in 1832 to create an insurrection
in the Vendée should be handled. Sadly Mme Récamier, who, despite Adèle's
efforts to console her, had been deeply affected by the death of Chateaubriand in
the previous year, was struck with cholera and died in May 1849, when she was
71 and Adèle 68 years old. It had been, to use the phrase of Françoise Wagener,
'une amitié primordiale [a primordial friendship]', such that, to quote Wagener
again, 'Si Mme de Boigne eût eu une sœur, sans conteste, elle l'eût voulue à l'image
de la belle Juliette [If Madam de Boigne had had a sister, she would without any
doubt have wanted her to be in the image of the beautiful Juliette]'.[61]

The pictures painted by Fanny and Adèle of the celebrated artistic and intellectual contemporaries they came to know are not definitive. There have been
many other exhaustive and scholarly works devoted to the persons involved – in
the case of Samuel Johnson, of course, Boswell's great biography. But there are
few more vivid and intimate glimpses of aspects of their lives than those we find
in these diaries, journals and memoirs. The descriptions of Garrick, shouting
and storming through the Burney household while Fanny was preparing the
breakfast, upsetting the family and frightening the servants, of Johnson, with
his mouth constantly opening and shutting as if he were chewing, and poking
the volumes on the Thrales' book shelves and the keys of the harpsichord

with his nose because of his short sightedness, of de Staël, ruling the roost over the Juniper Hall set, taking over Adèle's bedroom in the hotel at Lyons, on first acquaintance and without so much as a by-your-leave, and presiding over the disorderly bohemian chaos of her salon at Coppet, and of the beautiful Juliette Récamier, seducing Benjamin Constant into writing a dangerous lampoon of Napoleon, while resisting his advances yet still keeping him tied to her chariot – all add a vividness and dimension to their characters that we do not find elsewhere.

SEVEN

VIEWS ACROSS THE CHANNEL

F anny and Adèle spent similarly long periods in each other's country. Fanny
lived in Paris from April 1802, when she was nearly 50, to August 1812,
and again for a few months from May 1814, before fleeing to Brussels at
the start of Napoleon's Hundred Days in March of the following year. Adèle lived
as a child, an adolescent and then as a young woman in England with her parents
from February 1794 to September 1804, initially for two years in Yorkshire and
Westmoreland, but for the rest of the time in London. She later returned at the
age of 35 to live in London again with her father, then the French ambassador,
from January 1816 to early 1819. Both developed close friendships – in Fanny's
case, a marriage – with nationals from the other country, so that they had more
than enough experience to observe and comment on life and manners on the
other side of the Channel. This chapter will relate some of those observations.

The experiences of them both fell essentially into two parts. Until she was introduced to the Juniper Hall colony in early 1793, Fanny's experience of France and French people was relatively limited. After her mother died in 1762, when Fanny was only 10 years old, to her great regret she was kept at home by her father instead of, like her sisters Hetty and Susanna, being sent to school in Paris and having an opportunity to learn not just to read and understand, but also to speak French fluently. Although she sought to teach herself French and Italian at home by reading such authors as Voltaire, Dante and Petrarch, she remained very nervous and diffident about speaking French, particularly in front of strangers. It was not, therefore, surprising that when she met Alexandre d'Arblay at Juniper Hall, and was immediately romantically attracted by him, she readily agreed to his suggestion that they should become each other's tutor in their respective languages. They wrote compositions, or '*thèmes*' as they called them, for each other, which they corrected before returning them. That this meant so much to Fanny is evidenced by the fact that she preserved them for her grandchildren in a bundle of papers, tied and labelled as 'Some Original Thèmes in French and in English that passed between General d'Arblay and F Burney [...] to the month of April when the Thèmes were changed happily! happily For reciprocated Letters, till F Burney became the thrice blest wife of the most amiable and Honourable of men'.[1]

Before her exposure to the Juniper Hall set, Fanny's view of France and the French, who were after all at that time England's mortal enemy, probably reflected that of many of her contemporaries. She may also have absorbed a little of the francophobia of her great friend Dr Johnson. According to Boswell, 'he had an unjust contempt for foreigners',[2] especially the French; and in her *Anecdotes of Dr Johnson* Mrs Thrale says he referred to them as 'fellows that eat frogs',[3] and in a literary argument dismissed the French playwright Pierre Corneille as 'like a clipped hedge to a forest'[4] in comparison with Shakespeare. The popular caricature of the excitable, emotional, frequently immoral Frenchman, speaking rapidly in an incomprehensible language, perhaps finds some expression in Fanny's depiction of the rather vulgar French grandmother, Mme Duval, in *Evelina*, and her companion, the rather quieter M. Du Bois. With her frequent cries of 'ma foi' and 'pardie', the 'old Beldame' – or 'old Madame French', as the equally vulgar Captain Mirvan called her – was often ridiculed and placed in the most undignified of circumstances. When she suggested to the captain that he would benefit from spending some time in Paris, his response was: 'What, I suppose you'd have me learn to cut capers? – and dress like a monkey? – and palaver in French gibber-ish.'[5] Although Fanny was no doubt also satirizing the ignorant attitude of many of her compatriots towards the French, his crude overreaction was perhaps not a million miles from her own amused, though much kindlier, reaction when she met a group of stranded French travellers in Winchester in August 1791.

Writing to her father on 13 August, she described how, while staying in Winchester en route to Sidmouth in Devon,[6] she met for the first time a party of refugees from the Revolution, who were trying to find accommodation at the same inn at which she was staying. While feeling sorry for them, she was amused by what obviously appeared to her as typically excitable French behaviour, as they rushed around trying unsuccessfully to obtain a room for the night. At first, she and her companions, like 'good Daughters of John Bull', pretended to take little overt notice of them, but when they came across them again later in the day, and saw that 'the poor French Travellers' had still been unable to find 'Horses, Beds, or even one Room to sit in', they decided to 'shake off a part of the John Bullism that had encrusted us', and 'ask them to our sitting Room, to drink Tea'. Fanny, the only one in her party who apparently could speak a little French, was asked to put this invitation to them, but, still very diffident about her proficiency in spoken French, she declined, and in the end they asked a waiter to carry the invitation to the travellers for them.

Whether the French party would have welcomed some strong coffee, or even a glass of wine, rather than a cup of English tea is not recorded, but they were immensely grateful for the invitation and 'a shower of French was poured upon us, *vehicling* thanks and compliments'. One of the French ladies 'spoke English toler-ably, though comically' – as French people do! – but another, whose language skills were rather less proficient, 'seemed exactly a French Character drawn by an English Author'. I wonder if Fanny was thinking back to Mme Duval when she wrote this...

Nevertheless, aided by Fanny's tentative French, they went on to have a long conversation about the horrors of the Revolution and Fanny, now feeling genu-inely sorry for them, concluded that 'I should much like to see them again'. But she was probably not too impressed by a remark of the French spokeswoman that 'I find London so little pretty to Paris! – Have the goodness to excuse me – there is no comparison.' It was to be another decade before Fanny could test this for herself, but she was pleased on this occasion that eventually the good waiter found a sitting room in the inn for the French group.

All this was prior to Fanny's introduction to the very superior group of aristocratic French refugees at Juniper Hall in early 1793. She was overwhelmed by their intellectual brilliance and the scintillating conversations that took place among the group, but was disconcerted by what she regarded as the immoral relationship between Mme de Staël and her lover the Comte de Narbonne. This, together with Mme de Staël's radical politics and the pressures from her father and other friends caused the regrettable complications in Fanny's future relationship with her. Fanny went on, of course, to marry one of their number – the handsome, gentle, cultured and certainly not politically radical Alexandre d'Arblay – but her real experience of France and French life did not begin until she accompanied her husband in April 1802 to spend what she later described as 'my Ten years seclusion in France'.[7]

Adèle's early formative years in England, during which she became bilingual, had an immense influence on her, so much so that in 1804, on returning to the Continent en route to Paris after her many years in London, she wrote of herself: 'Quant à moi, je ne sais trop ce que j'étais, anglaise je crois, mais certainement pas française [As for me, I don't really know what I was; English, I think, but certainly not French].'[8] She always retained her admiration for the English political system, with its constitutional monarchy and equality before the law, but her allegiance shifted gradually back to France over the years as her patriotic instincts were revived by the ultimate defeat of the French armies, the prolonged occupation of Paris by allied troops and the infliction of substantial war indemnities on France. Writing of her views in 1814, after Napoleon's abdication and the first restoration of Louis XVIII by allied troops, she said:

> J'avais perdu en grande partie mon anglomanie; j'étais redevenue française, si ce n'est pas politiquement, du moins socialement; et [...] le cri des sentinelles ennemies m'avait plus affectée que le bruit de leur canon. J'avais éprouvé un mouvement très patriotique, mais fugitif.

> [I had for the most part lost my anglomania; I had become French again, at least socially, if not politically, and [...] the challenge of enemy sentries had affected me more than the noise of their cannon. I had experienced a sensation of patriotism, transitory as it was.][9]

The references to enemy sentries in Paris, whose presence particularly offended her, and the distinction between her political and social views on life in England are both revealing. She expanded her views on the latter in a later passage, which is worth quoting at length:

> *Les combinaisons de la société politique en Angleterre n'ont jamais cessé de me paraître ce qu'il y a de plus parfait dans le monde. L'égalité complète et réelle devant la loi qui, en assurant à chaque homme son indépendance, lui inspire le respect de soi-même, d'une part, et, de l'autre, les grandes existences sociales qui créent des défenseurs aux libertés publiques et font de ces patriciens les chefs naturels du peuple lequel leur rend en hommage ce qu'il en reçoit en protection, voilà ce que j'aurais désiré pour mon pays; car je ne conçois pas la liberté, sans licence, qu'avec une forte aristocratie.*

[The organization of political life in England has always seemed to me the most perfect in the world. On the one hand there is complete and genuine equality before the law, which assures to every man his independence and inspires him with self-respect; on the other hand there are great social distinctions, which create defenders of public liberties and make the patricians the natural leaders of the people, who return in homage what they receive by way of protection. This is what I would have wished for my own country, for I can only conceive of liberty, as opposed to licence, based upon a strong aristocracy.][10]

Leaving aside Adèle's views on the virtue of a strong patrician class that recognized its responsibilities – she never forgot her own ancestry – this is a startling, if rather idealized, tribute to the English political and constitutional system, at least such as it was supposed to operate in principle. It is hard to find in the journals of the much less politically conscious Fanny any similar expression of political or constitutional opinion, but there is a fascinating passage in her long account of the trial of Warren Hastings in February 1788 in Westminster Hall, which perhaps serves to epitomize the virtues of the English system of equality under the law that Adèle was extolling.

Fanny had been given by Queen Charlotte one of the much sought-after tickets of admittance to the trial and, no doubt aided later by newspaper and other accounts of the day, she recorded in detail, 'to the best of my power from memory',[11] large sections of the trial proceedings. The passage here in question is part of the opening speech by the chancellor, Lord Thurlow, who read out the charges and invited Hastings to 'Bring forth your Answers and defence with that seriousness, respect and truth, due to Accusers so respectable'. He proceeded to outline the time and facilities, including bail, that would be available to the defendant 'for the better forwarding your defence' and concluded by saying: 'This is not granted you as any indulgence; it is entirely your due; it is the privilege which every British subject has a right to claim, – and which is due to every one who is brought before this high Tribunal.' Fanny adds that the speech had 'an effect upon every Hearer of producing the most respectful attention'. Hastings's response was equally dignified: 'My Lords, – Impressed, – deeply impressed – I come before your Lordships – equally confident in my own integrity, and in the Justice of the Court before which I am to clear it.'

If Adèle, who had witnessed at firsthand the breakdown of law and order in France and the horrors of the Revolution, which had resulted in many of her family's friends being arbitrarily executed without any semblance of a fair trial, and later the despotic nature of Napoleon's manipulation of the law, could have heard or read this account, she would have regarded it as a classical statement of what she most admired in the English political and constitutional system. As for Fanny herself, whose direct political utterances were few, she wrote: '*Impressed*, and *deeply* impressed too, was my mind by this short, yet comprehensive speech: and all my best wishes for his clearance and redress, rose warmer than ever in my Heart.'

Although Fanny had, after her marriage to d'Arblay in July 1793, nearly a decade in which to adjust to French ways, her arrival in Paris with her small son Alex in April 1802, for what was to become an involuntary 10-year stay there, was quite a novelty, if not a shock, to her. She was leaving Britain for the first time, abandoning a relaxed and peaceful retired life in their little Camilla cottage at rural West Humble, where she could quietly pursue her writing, for an unpredictable future in a strange city, with no assured home or income apart from her royal pension, which in the event she was unable to access in France. She had also had a terrible first sea journey from Dover to Calais. She wrote in her journal:

My voyage was cruelly long, from a dead calm, which kept the vessel motionless for 8 Hours, just after we had sailed from the Port of Dover. We were a whole Day, and a whole Night at sea, and I was sick nearly without intermission all the time, and quite terrified for my poor Alexander who was so ill, and so pale and exhausted, I thought he would have been demolished.[12]

With the comforts and speed of modern travel, we tend to forget that every voyage of this kind made by both Fanny and Adèle was a hazardous and often extremely unpleasant experience.

However, she perked up a bit at Calais where, to her surprise, she heard a band strike up 'God Save the King' and observed with pleasure the colourful variety of costumes and ornaments worn by the children and women in the streets. She was also reassured by the words of an English gentleman who told her that 'Calais was so long in the possession of the English that our race must still subsist in it.'[13] Her Christian conscience was also reconciled as they proceeded by diligence from Calais to Paris: 'I found the people quite enchanted throughout the whole Country from Calais to Paris, by the restoration of The Dimanche.'[14] This was a result of Napoleon's concordat of 8 April with the Pope, which restored Catholicism in France and decreed that Sunday was to be kept as a day of religious rest.

Fanny was, however, less impressed with Paris itself, which in her view bore no comparison to London. The streets were too narrow, the houses too tall and the pavements no more than muddy paths.[15] But she was pleased with the apartment in Rue Miroménil that her husband had found and prepared for her,

which, though up two pairs of stairs, is really very pretty, and just new papered and furnished. The view from the window is very pleasant, open to the Country, and airy and healthy. I have a good sized (*for me*) little neat Drawing room, a small ante-room which we make our Dining Parlour, a tidy Bed Chamber, and a closet within it for Alexander. This, with a kitchen and a bit of a bed-room for my Maid, all on the same floor, comprise my habitation.[16]

As well as designing and building a cottage from scratch in Surrey, d'Arblay was obviously no slouch at decorating and furnishing an apartment in Paris.

Fanny's initial reaction to Paris was not unlike that of another distinguished literary Fanny, the indomitable Mrs Fanny Trollope – the mother of Anthony Trollope – when she stayed for a few months in Paris some 32 years later. In her travel book *Paris and the Parisians*, published in 1835, although she found the view from the top of Notre-Dame less polluted than that from a similar vantage point in London (because of the 'impenetrable mass of dire, dull smoke'[17] hanging over London – a feature to which Adèle was to refer later), she was horrified by that 'monstrous barbarism, a gutter in the middle of the street, expressly formed for the reception of filth, which is still permitted to deform the greater portion of this beautiful city'.[18] In contrast with the by now macadamized streets of London, the still almost medieval Paris suffered from the fact that 'almost the only thing in the world which other men do, but which Frenchmen cannot, is the making of sewers and drains'.[19] This theme recurs throughout the fastidious Fanny Trollope's book, and she attributed the 'dreadful smell', which permeated Paris and much of the rest of France, partly to the 'comparative poverty of the people' in relation to England, partly to a certain 'deficiency of refinement',[20] but above all to the sheer inability of the French to construct drains and sewers. Obsession with cleanliness and public hygiene was a characteristic of Fanny Trollope's travel writings, as she had shown even more forcefully in her earlier best-selling *Domestic Manners of the Americans*, which caused such offence in that country but earned her a great deal of fame and money. But it does seem that sanitary conditions in Paris had not improved much since Fanny Burney's arrival there over 30 years earlier. It must be said also that Fanny Trollope was from the start more than a little biased in favour of London. She compared Notre-Dame unfavourably with Westminster Abbey and thought the Pantheon decidedly inferior to King's College, Cambridge.

When Adèle returned to England to join her father in 1816, her reactions to London were in most ways the opposite of Fanny's to Paris. She was going back to a country she knew well:

je rentrais dans la patrie de ma première jeunesse; chaque détail m'était familier et pourtant suffisamment éloigné de ma pensée journalière pour avoir acquis le piquant de la nouveauté. C'était un vieil ami, revenu de loin, qu'on retrouve avec joie et qui rappelle agréablement le temps jadis.

[I re-entered the country of my early youth; each detail was familiar to me and yet sufficiently far from my everyday thoughts to have acquired the attraction of novelty. It was an old friend, returned from afar, whom one finds again with joy, and who brings back the memory of past times.][21]

Adèle was also '*très frappée de l'immense prospérité du pays* [struck by the immense prosperity of the country]'.[22] In the following long and affectionate description she also became absolutely lyrical about the state of the countryside:

Ces chemins si bien soignés, sur lesquels des chevaux de poste, tenus comme nos plus élégants attelages, vous font rouler si agréablement, cette multitude de voitures publiques et privées, toutes charmantes, ces innombrables établissements qui ornent la campagne et donnent l'idée de l'aisance dans toutes les classes de la société, depuis la cabane du paysan jusqu'au château du seigneur, ces fenêtres de la plus petite boutique offrant aux rares rayons du soleil des vitres dont l'éclat n'est jamais terni par une légère souillure, ces populations si propres se transportant d'un village à un autre par des sentiers que nous envierions dans nos jardins, ces beaux enfants si bien tenus et prenant leurs ébats dans une liberté qui contraste avec le maintien réservé du reste de la famille, tout cela m'était familier et pourtant me frappait peut-être plus vivement que si c'eût été la première fois que j'en étais témoin.

[There were the well-maintained roads, along which the post horses, maintained like our most elegant carriages, conveyed you very agreeably; the multitude of public and private carriages, all delightful, the innumerable country residences that decorate the countryside and give an impression of comfort in every class of society, from the cottage of the peasant to the country seat of the lord, the windows of the smallest shop which present to the rare rays of sunshine a glass that is never tarnished by the slightest stain, the neatly dressed country folk travelling from one village to another on paths that we would envy in our gardens, the handsome and well-turned-out children amusing themselves with a freedom that contrasts with the reserve of the rest of the family – all those things were familiar to me and impressed me perhaps more vividly than if I had been witnessing them for the first time.][23]

This was again an extremely romantic and idealized picture, but in essence it reflected the superior economy, based on developing industry and more productive agriculture, with which Britain had emerged from the Napoleonic wars and which caused Adèle to ask why France could not emulate it. Commenting on what she saw while travelling from Dover to London (admittedly on a fine Sunday), she wrote:

> Il s'y mêlait de temps en temps un secret sentiment d'envie pour ma patrie. Le Ciel lui a été au moins aussi favorable; pourquoi n'a-t-elle pas acquis le même degré de prospérité que ses voisins insulaires?

> [From time to time a secret feeling of jealousy for my own country came into my mind. Heaven had been just as kind to France; why could she not acquire the same degree of prosperity as her island neighbours?][24]

It is just the kind of question sometimes asked about the relative economic performance of less successful member states in the Councils of the European Union at present, although it is unlikely that any representative of France would now be prepared to speak of the United Kingdom in quite the same terms as Adèle did. It is worth adding, however, that true to her pride in the gastronomic superiority of her country, she still flew the French flag by observing somewhat contemptuously, with reference to the eating habits of the refugee Duc de Bourbon in London, that the 'boutique de côtelettes', or 'Chop House', in which he chose to dine 'ne mérite pas le nom de restaurateur [does not deserve the name of a proper restaurant owner]'.[25]

As the passage in her memoirs just quoted shows, the aspect of Britain that made the strongest impression on Adèle was the countryside. She drew, however, a sharp contrast between the freshness and clear air of the countryside and that of London, where 'l'atmosphère lourde et enfumée de cette grande ville me pesa sur la tête [the heavy and smoky atmosphere of this great town hung above my head]'.[26] Whereas Paris lacked sewers, drains and proper pavements, London had no clean air policy, with the result that

> le nuage orange, strié de noir, de brun, de gris, saturé de suie, qui semble un vaste éteignoir placé sur la ville, influe sur le moral de la population et agisse sur les dispositions.

[the orange cloud, streaked with black, brown and grey, permeated with soot, which resembles a vast extinguisher placed above the town, influences the morals and affects the dispositions of the population.]

A more specific consequence noted by Adèle was that

La robe blanche, mise le matin, porte avant la fin de la journée des traces de souillure qu'une semaine ne lui infligerait pas à Paris.

[A white dress, put on in the morning, will be soiled before the end of the day with more dirt than a week would cause in Paris.]

This is precisely the same observation as that made by Fanny Trollope some 20 years later, showing that, like Paris with its lack of sewers and drains, London had still made little progress in combating the smog, which was to continue to be a health hazard, and a dirtier of clothes, well into the twentieth century.

One particular and perceptive observation by Adèle has an interesting bearing on London planning in more recent times. She wrote:

La Tamise, aussi bien que son immense mouvement qui attacherait un caractère particulier à cette capitale du monde britannique, est soigneusement caché de toute part. Il faut une volonté assez intelligente pour parvenir à l'apercevoir, même en l'allant chercher.

[The Thames, together with its immense traffic, which would give a special character to this capital of the British world, is carefully hidden on every side. A special effort of intelligence is needed to perceive its existence, even if you set out to look for it.][27]

It has taken many years for London to absorb this lesson. Despite the building of embankments in the nineteenth century, only in the relatively recent past have cultural and other developments on the South Bank, such as the South Bank Arts Centre, the Globe Theatre, the London Eye, the Tate Modern and the Millenium Bridge made the Thames a central feature of tourist London, as opposed to the boundary demarcating a territory on the south side where previously only southern commuters and few tourists dared to venture.

As time went on, Adèle's view of London and England inevitably became less rose-tinted. This was partly because of her resentment of the continuing occupation of Paris by British and other allied troops under Wellington's command and partly because she was now beginning to lose many of the old friends she had known in London in former days. She wrote rather sadly:

> Je me retrouvai à peu près étrangère dans le monde anglais; la société s'était presque entièrement renouvelée. La mort y avait fait sa cruelle récolte; beaucoup de mes anciennes amies avaient succombé. Un assez grand nombre voyageaient sur le continent que la paix avait enfin rouvert à l'humeur vagabonde des insulaires britanniques.

> [I found myself nearly a total stranger in an English world that had almost entirely changed. Death had reaped its cruel harvest, carrying away many of my former friends. A considerable number of them were travelling on the Continent, which peace had at last opened again to the vagabond instincts of the British islanders.][28]

Adèle followed these nostalgic comments with a long disquisition on the upbringing of English young ladies compared with their counterparts in France and in particular on 'la chasse à mari [the hunt for a husband]'.[29] As so many Georgian and Victorian novelists made clear, not least Anthony Trollope a little later in the nineteenth century, English upper-class mothers were always desperately hard at work, looking for good matches for their unmarried daughters. Adèle described them as 'les suivant à la piste [tracking them like hounds]' and moving heaven and earth to secure suitable introductions to eligible suitors. Nevertheless, despite all this laborious scheming and manoeuvring, an English girl was 'toujours censé se marier par amour [always supposed to marry for love]', as opposed to the system in France, at least among the upper classes, where marriages were generally arranged by agreement between the parents concerned – as Adèle knew only too well from her own experience, although in this case she had been as much the arranger as the arranged. In Adèle's view, this left English wives ill-prepared for the later years of marriage when the fires of love had died down, the children had grown up and they were no longer preoccupied, as in their first married days, with all the practical problems of setting up a new household. To Adèle they seemed to have few interests of their own, and tended to be left alone at home while '*le mari a pris l'habitude de passer sa vie au club* [the husband has taken up the habit of spending his life at the club]'. She concluded, therefore, that '*Nos demoiselles françaises ne doivent pas trop envier à leurs jeunes compagnes anglaises la liberté dont elles jouissent et leurs mariages soi-disant d'inclination* [Our French girls should not be too envious of the freedom that their English counterparts enjoy in their so-called marriages of inclination]'. This examination of the marriage market reinforced her overall conclusion that, although England might be materially better off, when it came to social life France was superior. What she did not add was that the marriage arrangements among girls in France also provided more excuse, and perhaps opportunity, for extramarital liaisons at a later stage, of the kind that disconcerted Fanny when she met such people as Mme de Staël.

These considerations, however, did not prevent Adèle from continuing to admire the fundamental English commitment to the rule of law. She followed her critical analysis of social customs with an encomium of '*le noble caractère, l'esprit public qui distingue la nation* [the noble character and public spirit that distinguishes the nation]'.[30] Like a good but liberal aristocrat, she was pleased to note that the Englishman, '*malgré son indépendance personnelle, reconnaît la hiérarchie des classes* [despite his personal independence, recognizes class distinctions]'. But at the same time,

> *ce même homme n'admet point de supérieur là où son droit légal lui paraît atteint. Il a également recours à la loi contre le premier seigneur du comté par lequel il se pense molesté et contre le voisin avec lequel il a une querelle de cabaret. C'est sur cette confiance qu'elle le protège dans toutes les occurrences de la vie qu'est fondé le sentiment d'indépendance d'où naît ce respect de lui-même, cachet des hommes libres.*

[this same man will never admit any superior to himself on a point where he believes his legal rights are concerned. He can apply for the same legal protection against the first lord of the county by whom he may think himself injured as against a neighbour with whom he has quarrelled in a tavern. This confidence that the law will protect him in every aspect of his life forms the basis of that feeling of independence, from which is born the self-respect that marks the free man.]

This is a further eloquent, if somewhat idealized, tribute by Adèle to the rule of law in England, which she found so lacking in France and which was epitomized in the speeches recorded in Fanny's account of the chancellor's opening speech in the Warren Hastings trial.

One of Adèle's most endearing and entertaining habits in her memoirs is, from time to time, to divert from her narrative to give the reader a snippet of fascinating information on something not always central to her main theme. It is thus we learn about 'l'usage du shake-hand [the custom of hand-shaking]',[31] which the Duc de Berry was said to have introduced to Parisian society, and of Adèle's own pioneering of sea bathing at Boulogne, to the wonder and puzzlement of admiring onlookers. On the subject of swimming, she also recorded how the duc's colourful widow, the Duchesse de Berry, an intrepid traveller who sometimes dressed like a man, with a pistol in her belt, 's'aventurait à nager dans la mer lorsque la vague était assez grosse pour effrayer les matelots eux-mêmes [dared to swim in the sea when the waves were rough enough to frighten the sailors themselves]'.[32] She related too, en passant, how the duchesse managed to get herself invited to the historic opening of the Manchester to Liverpool railway in November 1830 and climbed up to take her seat in the first wagon.[33] If this report is true, the duchesse would also have met the Duke of Wellington, who attended the opening as prime minister and was also in the first coach. The event was marred by the horrific death of the Member of Parliament for Liverpool, William Huskisson, a former minister and political opponent of the duke's, and coincidentally grandson of a fellow prisoner under threat of the guillotine with Grace Elliott during the Terror in 1793. He was struck by the Rocket on an adjacent rail when trying to clamber into the duke's coach and had his thigh crushed; he died in agony a few hours later. With her penchant for death scenes, it is odd that Adèle did not mention this.

In this section of her memoirs, during the discourse on young ladies and the marriage market described above, she also, for no particular reason, suddenly informs us that 'en 1816 aucune demoiselle anglaise ne valsait [in 1816 no young English woman danced the waltz]'.[34] According to her, it was introduced to London by the Duke of Devonshire, following a visit to Germany. He announced at a grand ball one evening that '*une femme n'était complètement à son avantage qu'en valsant* [a woman was never seen to better advantage than when waltzing]'. The immediate effect of this was that '*au bal prochain, toutes les demoiselles valsaient* [at the next ball, all the young ladies were waltzing]'. Unfortunately the duke then spoiled the story by declaring to the Duchess of Richmond that, for his part, he would never marry a lady who waltzed. The word quickly got around and most people stopped waltzing, except for '*quelques jeunes filles plus fières* [a few young ladies of a prouder disposition]'.

After she left Paris in 1819 at the end of her father's tour as French ambassador, Adèle spent no further time in London and became totally devoted to French society and politics, and to her growing friendship with Chancellor Pasquier. Elements of her English heritage continued, however, to influence her, so much so that early in 1827, when Charles X caused a draft law on the right of primogeniture to be introduced, with her pride in her ancestry also coming to the fore, she wrote: '*il plaisait assez à mes idées anglaises et à mes goûts aristocratiques* [it really pleased my English ideas and my aristocratic tastes]'.[35] In the event the legislation was rejected by the House of Peers, which increased their popularity at the expense of the king's.

In the autumn of 1846 Adèle recorded her disapproval of the intervention of the British government, on an initiative by Lord Palmerston, in a dispute over an attempt by Catholic and aristocratic cantons in Switzerland to form a new union, to be known as the Sonderbund, to oppose the growing Swiss Protestant and revolutionary parties. The French government, who supported the Sonderbund, unfortunately left it too late to influence the outcome. The president of the ministerial council, François Guizot, though wanting to thwart his old rival Lord Palmerston, delayed French intervention, and in the meantime Palmerston sent Mr Peel as an emissary to Berne with a large cash bribe that galvanized the Protestants into action and secured the dissolution of the Sonderbund. Adèle, who had previously spoken of the 'entente cordiale' between England and France (this must be one of the earliest literary references to this phrase, which did not come into official usage until the agreement between Britain and France signed in London on 8 April 1904), wrote ruefully that '*ce fut un grand échec pour notre gouvernement* [this was a great setback for our government]'.[36]

She became more disenchanted with Britain as she moved further into old age. Writing about the fall of Louis-Philippe in 1848 – the Year of Revolutions – and

musing on the fact that she had seen three powerful governments collapse –
the Napoleonic empire as a result of tyranny and defeat in war, the House of
Bourbon through incompetence and unintelligent pretensions to legitimacy,
and Louis-Philippe through fear of upsetting the Paris bourgeoisie – she spoke
about England in the following terms:

> *L'Angleterre, après nous avoir fait dévorer, succombera à son tour à son cruel
> et perfide égoïsme. Mais elle résistera plus longtemps, grâce à cet esprit public
> que l'Anglais puise dans son île et porte avec lui aux extrémités de la terre, sans
> jamais en rien perdre.*

> [England, after having devoured us, will succumb in its turn to its cruel
> and perfidious egoism. But it will hold out much longer, thanks to this
> sense of public spirit that the Englishman draws on in his island and car-
> ries with him to the extremes of the earth, without ever losing any of it.][37]

These comments still reflected some of her old admiration for the English character and public spirit, but the English were definitely now on the other side as
far as she was concerned. The comments were written at a time when she was
increasingly infirm – 'Mon âge et l'affaiblissement de ma santé m'autorisaient à
renoncer au grande monde [My age and declining health permitted me to stop
going out into society]'[38] – and she was saddened by the deaths of many old
friends, including most recently one of the closest of them all, Mme Adélaïde,
the sister of Louis-Philippe. It is perhaps sad but not surprising then that, on the
fall of Louis-Philippe, when she and her companion M. Pasquier – who were
both living near Trouville – were contemplating leaving France and going into
exile, she wrote:

> *Nous hésitions entre Pau, pour lequel son doux climat et le voisinage de l'Espagne
> militaient, et Jersey, donnant une sécurité plus positive. Je ne pensais pas à
> l'Angleterre, malgré mes relations intimes et de famille.*

> [We hesitated between Pau, which was favoured for its mild climate and
> proximity to Spain, and Jersey, which offered greater security. I did not
> think of England, in spite of my intimate connections and family.]'[39]

To be fair, she added that in any case M. Pasquier would not have liked to live in any country where they did not speak French, but it is sad that towards the end of her life she no longer wanted to return to the country in which she and her parents had found refuge and happiness so many years before. She would in any case have been too late to meet Fanny Burney, who had died eight years earlier.

EIGHT

BLOOD & DEATH

D espite the horrors of war, famine and natural disasters, which have
been brought right into our living rooms on a daily basis via televi-
sion screens in the twentieth and twenty-first centuries, the actual
experience of death was probably closer to most ordinary people in everyday life
in Europe in the eighteenth and nineteenth centuries than it is now. Life expec-
tancy was much lower and child mortality rates higher. In the mid nineteenth
century the number of child deaths within the first year was between 150 and
160 per 1,000 inhabitants in England and Wales, compared with about half a
dozen in the early twenty-first century. It was not untypical, particularly with
the wide incidence of syphilis and other sexually transmitted diseases, for more
progeny in a family to die at birth or in early childhood than to survive. Fanny
Burney's friend, Mrs Thrale, endured 14 years of almost continual pregnancy,
during which she gave birth to 12 children, of whom only four (all girls) survived
into adulthood. She also suffered two late-term miscarriages. The majority of

the children who died did so in infancy. By the time Fanny was eight years old, she had already lost three male siblings: Charles, at 16 months, when she was only four months old; a second Charles, about a year later; and another boy, Henry Edward, who died only a few months old three years later. Adèle did not suffer such immediate family tragedies, but as a child she was old enough to be aware of the murderous excesses of the Revolution and the execution by Mme Guillotine of many of her mother's and father's aristocratic friends. Indeed, if they had not succeeded in fleeing from France and finding refuge, first in Italy and then in England, they might well have suffered the same fate themselves. Later in life Adèle also witnessed at firsthand the bloodshed at the barricades in the Revolution of 1830, heard a close eyewitness account of the gory assassination of the Duc de Berry on the steps of the opera in Paris and witnessed directly the ravages of the cholera epidemic that caused nearly 20,000 deaths over a few months in Paris in 1832.

Against this background a literary tradition developed in England in the late eighteenth and early nineteenth centuries which, though historically set in a medieval context, specialized in tales of the macabre, fantastic and supernatural, often set in graveyards, haunted castles or wild and desolate landscapes. Principal exponents of the English Gothic novel, contemporaneous with Fanny and Adèle, were Ann Radcliffe, Maria Edgeworth, William Beckford, and 'Monk' Lewis. Jane Austen satirized the genre in *Northanger Abbey*, and the tradition continued through Mary Shelley and the Brontës into the works of many later nineteenth-century novelists, the pre-eminent being Charles Dickens and Wilkie Collins. It is not surprising, therefore, that blood and death get a fair airing in the journals, diaries and memoirs of Fanny and Adèle, and this chapter will select and discuss some of the most interesting and spectacular passages.

In her memoirs Adèle gives us several graphic descriptions of death scenes, with no shortage of blood and suffering. With one major exception, Fanny's journal entries are much more restrained, although in *Cecilia* we are presented with the shocking suicide of Mr Harrel in Vauxhall Gardens, whom Cecilia herself discovers covered in blood after he has shot himself in the head with a pistol. More blood then flows, when Mortimer Delville, Cecilia's lover, tells his mother that he is resolved to marry Cecilia, and she becomes so angry that she collapses with a burst blood vessel, blood flowing from her mouth and nose. It says a great deal for Fanny's creative imagination that she was able to conjure up scenes of this sort, given her otherwise rather sheltered upbringing. Generally, however, Fanny's death scenes are recorded in a more sober, poignant and moving way, as we would expect when the subjects are usually dear and close relatives or personal friends, rather than, as is the case mostly with Adèle, leading political figures or other personalities, the recording of whose deaths is of particular historical interest.

We have already seen how distressed Fanny was not to be able to visit Dr Johnson on his deathbed shortly before he died. Her description of the events leading up to his death, after a long period of deteriorating health, was restrained and redolent of deep affection and concern. She wrote to Susanna in December 1784:

> I hear from everyone he is now perfectly resigned to his approaching fate, and no longer in terror of Death. I am thankfully happy in hearing that. He speaks himself now of the change his mind has undergone from its dark hour, and says he feels the irradiation of Hope! – Good and pious and excellent Christian, who shall feel it if not he?[1]

These sentiments preceded Fanny's grief at her inability to gain access to him on the very eve of his death, which was only partially assuaged by being told by Mr Bennett Langton, Johnson's close friend, that 'he is very sorry not to see you, – but he desired me to come and speak to you myself, and tell You he hopes you will excuse him, for he feels himself too weak for such an interview'.[2]

Fanny wrote about the deaths of Daddy Crisp, her father, her husband and her son Alex, the people dearest to her in her life after the death of her sister Susanna, in similarly restrained terms. When her father died in April 1814, a week before his 88th birthday, she wrote to her friend Georgina Waddington:

> Be not uneasy for me, my tender friend – My affliction is heavy, but not acute: my beloved Father had been spared to us something beyond the verge of the prayer for his preservation which you must have read – for already his sufferings had far surpassed his enjoyments! I could not have wished him so to linger! – though I indulged almost to the last hour a hope he might yet recover, and live to comfort. – I last of all gave him up! – but never wished his duration such as I saw him on the last few days. Dear blessed Parent! How blest am I that I came over to him while he was yet

susceptible of pleasure – of happiness! – Many thoughts I had given to years more to his life! – alas! – my best comfort in my grief – in his loss – is that I watched by his revered side the last night – and hovered over him 2 hours after he breathed no more.[3]

The account of her beloved husband's death in May 1818 at their home in Bath is, if rather fuller and longer, similarly restrained. In a journal entry of 2–3 May she described his last tranquil night and his gentle passage towards death in the course of the following day. She wrote: 'On Sunday Morning – fatal – fatal – to me for-ever wretched Sunday 3rd May, 1818! – my Patient was still cheerful, and frequently took saline Draughts, always prepared by our dear Alex; after which, he composed himself tranquilly to rest, and, now slept often, but not long'.[4] As the day progressed, he rallied a little, called for a cup of cocoa and, supported by pillows,

he bent forward, and taking my hand, and holding it between both his hands, with a smile celestial, a look composed, serene, benign, – even radiant, he impressively said: *'Je ne sais si ce sera le dernier mot – mais, ce sera la dernière pensée – Notre Réunion!* [I don't know if this will be the last word – but it will be the last thought – Our Reunion!]'[5]

These were the last words he addressed directly to Fanny, except that when in the evening, after their maid had left the room, Alex helped him to sit up by raising his pillows, he said to him *'Bien* [...] *Vous le faites Presque – aussi bien qu'elle* [Well done [...] You do it almost as well as she does].'[6] These were his very last words before he fell peacefully into the sleep of death.

Fanny was overwhelmed by grief and wrote that 'I had certainly a partial derangement' and could not recollect 'with truth or consistency what occurred during the succeeding hours'. The room was a blur to her, 'with a medley of silent and strange figures grouped against the Wall just opposite to me', but, after begging the doctor to allow her to remain for an hour, 'telling him I had solemnly engaged myself to pass it at his side',[7] she in fact maintained a vigil beside her departed loved one for the following two hours.

The death of her only son Alex, nearly 20 years later, must have been an even greater blow to Fanny. Despite showing precocious talent, especially in mathematics, as a schoolboy in France and gaining a scholarship to Caius College, Cambridge, he never fulfilled his early promise. After moving to Christ's College, following a misunderstanding about the course that his scholarship at Caius obliged him to follow, he took a first, was elected a fellow and was ordained into the Church of England. He then spent a somewhat wandering and purposeless life. He travelled to Switzerland with two Cambridge friends who were to gain great distinction in later life – Charles Babbage, the father of the computer, and William Herschel, the astronomer – but soon left them and continued on his own. In 1834 he was made curate of the new Camden Chapel in the parish of St Pancras, but, though reputedly a fine preacher, he neglected his charge and only lasted there for two years until, after another short stay at Cambridge, on the recommendation of one of Fanny's old friends, he was offered the living of St Etheldreda's in Ely Place, Holborn. This was a damp and semi-derelict building that had been closed for some years, and it was hoped that Alex would be able to revive it both spiritually and physically. Sadly, while preaching there, he caught a cold, which turned into serious influenza, and he died at his mother's house at the age of 42 on 19 January 1837. He had for some time kept a relationship with Mary Ann Smith and had become engaged to her, but he never married her as he felt he had so little to offer her. Before he died, however, he asked her in the event of his death to take care of his mother, a task that she fulfilled loyally by moving in to live with her as her companion until the end of Fanny's life.

Fanny was now in her 85th year and once more overcome with grief. But she bore it well, sustained by the support of Mary Ann and by moving letters of condolence from some of her surviving friends. Only when left alone did she give way to her real grief at Alex's death. In a letter to her nephew Charles Parr Burney (her brother Charles's son) some two months later, she confessed: 'My heart is lead. I cannot describe the chasm of my present existence – so lost in grief – so awake to Resignation – so inert to all that is proffered – so ever and ever retrograding to all that is desolate! – I am a non-entity.'[8] Nevertheless, though very deaf and nearly blind in both eyes, she still had the spirit and energy to move to a new apartment at 112 Mount Street, off Park Lane, where she still received visitors, including Sir Walter Scott, and lived with Mary Ann until her death some three years later.

FANNY'S OPERATION

Starkly contrasting with these patient accounts of death and bereavement was Fanny's account of her own most blood-curdling experience: the mastectomy operation in Paris in 1811, referred to previously in Chapter One. The operation took place on the last day of September, and Fanny's long account of it, in a letter to her sister Hetty, was dated 22 March 1812 on the first sheet, but was not completed until June.[9] It is astonishing that at so early a date she was able to bring herself to relive and write down the appalling details of the occasion. Reports of the operation had reached certain friends in England, so that Fanny wanted her sister Hetty to know the truth, but she was desperately anxious that news of it should not at that stage reach her father. Indeed, in the final paragraphs of her letter she wrote: 'My dearest father and my dearest Mrs Locke live so little in the world, that I flatter myself that they will never hear of this adventure. I earnestly desire it may never reach them.' Throughout the whole of this affair Fanny always seemed as much, if not more, concerned to protect her husband, her son and her father from sharing or knowing the dreadful details of what had happened to her as she was with her own suffering.

In August 1810 Fanny had suffered from a small pain in her breast, which gradually got worse. She initially rejected her husband's advice to consult a doctor, but eventually agreed to consult Antoine Dubois, a distinguished Paris physician who was then attending as accoucheur the pregnant empress, Marie-Louise. After seeing Fanny, he concluded 'that a small operation would be necessary to avert evil consequences', but the 'confounded and stupefied' Fanny deferred a decision, convincing herself that her condition was getting better and that an operation would be unnecessary. Over time, however, the pains worsened and d'Arblay finally persuaded her to let him call in the great Baron Dominique-Jean Larrey, the most celebrated military surgeon of his day. Larrey accompanied Napoleon on many of his major military campaigns, including both the disastrous invasion of Russia in 1812 and the Battle of Waterloo in 1815, and made important advances in battlefield surgery and care. As Napoleon lay dying on St Helena in 1821, he made several despairing but abortive appeals for the services of Larrey.

Larrey agreed to treat her but suggested also calling in a colleague, Dr François Ribes (called 'Ribe' throughout Fanny's account), another eminent anatomist and surgeon. After meeting her, though without giving her any intimate physical examination – this was normal with upper-class ladies at that time – their joint recommendation was firmly in favour of an operation. With great courage, Fanny finally gave her consent to it. She tried to persuade herself that it was still unnecessary, but in her heart, she wrote:

> I felt the evil to be deep, so deep, that I often thought if it could not be dissolved, it could only with life be extirpated. I called up, however, all the reason I possessed, or could assume, and told them that – if they saw no other alternative, I would not resist their opinion and experience.

The actual description of the ensuing operation is more horrific than anything written or imagined by Mary Shelley, Victor Hugo or any of the English Gothic novelists, and almost unbearable to read. D'Arblay arranged for Fanny to be moved from their current apartment, which was up three flights of stairs, to a ground-floor one on the Rue Miroménil, but she then had to endure a further agonizing wait of three weeks until preparations for the operation were completed, with both Larrey and Dubois chosen to officiate. During this time she made her will but concealed it from her husband and arranged for it to be lodged with a lawyer.

The awful day of the operation was 30 September 1811. She was only informed of this early that very morning but immediately sent a letter to her husband's chef de division at the Ministry of the Interior, asking him to set him sufficient work 'to detain him till all should be over'. She then suffered several further hours of unimaginable suspense until all the practical arrangements were completed and the necessary bandages, compresses, sponges and lint assembled. After being given no more than a wine cordial, she was led to her bedroom, where to her surprise a bedstead had been covered with two old mattresses and an old sheet – she had expected the operation to take place in an armchair! She rang for her maid and nurses, but 'before I could speak to them, my room, without previous message, was entered by 7 Men in black', that is, Larrey, Dubois, Ribes and four other doctors. A cambric handkerchief was spread over her face to prevent her seeing what was happening, but she says that she could see through it and witness all the ensuing operation. She resisted any attempt to secure her to the bed and wrote: 'I refused to be held; but when, Bright through the cambric, I saw the glitter of polished Steel – I closed my Eyes. I would not trust to convulsive fear the sight of the terrible incision.'

The whole operation lasted for 20 minutes – a hellish eternity in such circumstances. It was more radical than Larrey had intended, and as he physically tired, he had to change hands and cut deeper, while Fanny herself, incredibly, held her own breast so that he could get at it. It is impossible to imagine the excruciating pain that Fanny had to endure. Even she could not restrain screaming in agony. She wrote:

> when the dreadful steel was plunged into the breast – cutting through veins – arteries – nerves – I needed no injunction to restrain my cries. I began a scream that lasted unintermittingly during the whole time of the incision – and I almost marvel that it rings not in my Ears still! So excruciating was the agony.

And this was not the end.

> Oh no! presently the terrible cutting was renewed – and worse than ever, to separate the bottom, the foundation of this dreadful gland from the parts to which it adhered – Again, all description would be baffled – yet again all was not over, – Dr Larrey rested but his own hand and – Oh Heaven! – I then felt the Knife rackling against the breast bone – scraping it! – This performed, while I yet remained in utterly speechless torture.

How Fanny, who had never seemed to be strong physically, and had often shown signs of hypochondria, survived this awful operation and could even bring herself so soon afterwards to write about it is beyond any belief. As she said herself in her letter to Hetty:

> not for days, not for Weeks, but for Months I could not speak of this terrible business without nearly going through it! [...] even now, 9 months after it is over, I have a headache from going on with the account! And this miserable account, which I began 3 Months ago, at least, I dare not revise, nor read, the recollection is still so painful.

But survive it she did, and lived for nearly another 29 years, which, awful to suggest, perhaps indicates that it was not cancer she was suffering from and that in fact the operation was unnecessary. We shall never know. After it was over she had been put to bed, while Larrey, who had seen more bloody mutilation and had probably amputated more limbs on the battlefield than any other surgeon of his time, was left 'pale nearly as myself, his face streaked with blood, and its expression depicting grief, apprehension, and almost horror'. Afterwards her husband and Alex were finally called and admitted to her bedside. If ever anyone is ever tempted to criticize Fanny for lack of physical or moral courage in any other aspect of her life, they should remember her conduct through this terrifying ordeal.

Although Adèle suffered various periods of illness and became involved in some extremely dangerous situations right from her infancy at Versailles, she never experienced anything remotely resembling the horror of Fanny's operation. But she did witness or hear first-hand accounts of many dramatic death scenes or other bloody incidents. A particularly fascinating case in point is the death of Lord Castlereagh and the circumstances that preceded it.

THE DEATH OF CASTLEREAGH

Castlereagh, who became Lord Londonderry when his father died in 1821, was the British foreign secretary from 1812 to 1822 and, together with the Duke of Wellington, played a leading role in the Congress of Vienna in 1814–15 and in subsequent conferences involving the great European powers, although Adèle always regarded him as being outmanoeuvred by Metternich, his Austrian opposite number. In domestic politics he took much of the blame for many of the illiberal policies of the government of Lord Liverpool and he was not universally lamented when he died. Adèle got to know both him and Lady Castlereagh very well during her father's ambassadorship in London from 1816 to 1819, and they sometimes visited the couple at their modest three-bedroomed house at North Cray Place in Kent.

Adèle's terse account of his death by suicide on 12 July 1822 is as follows:

Un matin, il sortit à son heure accoutumée du lit conjugal, entra dans son cabinet, fit une partie de sa toilette, puis revint dans la chambre de sa femme chercher les pilules qu'il prenait journellement, les avala, et, en retournant dans son cabinet, se coupa, avec un très petit canif, l'artère jugulaire si artistement qu'une blessure de fort peu de lignes le fit tomber mort presqu'immédiatement. Lady Londonderry entendit sa chute et se précipita vers lui, mais tous les secours étaient déjà inutiles.

[One morning, he got out of the conjugal bed at the usual hour, went into his own private room, completed part of his toilet, then returned to his wife's bedroom to look for the pills that he took daily, swallowed them, and, returning to his own room, with a very small knife slit his main jugular artery so artistically that a wound that was hardly visible made him fall down dead almost at once. Lady Londonderry heard him fall and rushed towards him, but any help was now quite useless.][10]

There was much speculation about the reasons for his suicide. Some people alleged that it was related to his being blackmailed for having a homosexual affair. Adèle's explanation was more straightforward. She dismissed '*des causes politiques* [political reasons]' on the grounds that he was '*d'un caractère froid et calme, peu propre à s'émouvoir de pareilles considérations* [a cool and calm character, most unlikely to be swayed by such considerations]' and judged that '*sa mort ne peut s'attribuer qu'à un accès de folie, maladie héréditaire dans sa famille* [his death can only be attributed to a fit of madness, which was a hereditary disease in his family]'.

Adèle's conclusion should not be dismissed. Most interestingly, at the time when she and her father first saw him regularly, she observed of Castlereagh that '*il ne donnait aucun signe de la fatale maladie héréditaire qui l'a porté au suicide* [he showed no signs of the fatal hereditary disease that drove him to suicide]'. But she noticed that Lady Castlereagh used to keep an exceptionally close watch on her husband, never leaving him, following him to both town and country and accompanying him on every journey. Adèle began to ask herself:

Avait-elle découvert quelque signe de cette malaise qu'une si affreuse catastrophe a révélée au monde, et voulait-elle être présente pour en surveiller les occasions et en atténuer les effets? Je l'ai quelquefois pensé depuis.

[Had she discovered some sign of this illness that such an appalling catastrophe revealed to the world, and did she want to remain with him in order to keep a close eye on the opportunities and to mitigate their effects? I have sometimes thought so since then.]

We know also that shortly before he died, Castlereagh behaved in such a bizarre manner at an audience with George IV that the king advised him to go to his house in the country and consult his doctors.

It is somewhat ironic that Lady Castlereagh's almost obsessional care did not extend to giving her husband the benefit when it became a choice between him and her favourite dog. Again, Adèle tells us the story. Lady Castlereagh had a powerful bulldog, and when one day it attacked a little spaniel, Lord Castlereagh tried to intervene and separate them. Alas,

Il fut cruellement mordu à la jambe et surtout à la main. Il fallut du secours pour faire lâcher prise au bull-dog *qui écumait de colère. Lady Castlereagh survint; son premier soin fut de caresser le chien, de le calmer.*

[He was cruelly bitten in the leg and more seriously in the hand. Help was required to force the bulldog, which was foaming at the mouth with anger, to release its grip. Lady Castlereagh arrived on the scene, but her first concern was to stroke the dog, and to calm it.]

The bites were extremely serious.

Ce n'est qu'au bout de quatre mois, quand Lord Castlereagh fut complètement guéri, que, d'elle-même, elle se débarrassa du chien que jusque-là elle avait comblé de soins et de caresses.

[It was only four months later, when Lord Castlereagh had fully recovered, that she got rid of the dog, which until then she had covered with concern and caresses.]

This must rank high, certainly among French shaggy dog stories, as one of the most remarkable tales of mad dogs and Englishmen – or should it be mad Englishmen and dogs?

THE ASSASSINATION OF THE DUC DE BERRY

Adèle's bloodiest and most dramatic death story is probably the assassination in 1820 at the Paris opera of the Duc de Berry, the son of the Comte d'Artois, the future Charles X, and therefore in line to be the future king. The assassination was not a political one, but carried out by Louis Pierre Louvel, a saddler employed in the imperial saddlery, who appeared to have some personal grievance against the duc and had been pursuing him for some time. Indeed, Adèle expresses surprise that something like this had not happened before as

> la vie irrégulière de monsieur le duc de Berry le menait presque journellement et sans aucune escorte dans les lieux où il semblait bien autrement facile de l'atteindre.

> [the irregular life of the Duc de Berry brought him almost daily and without any escort into places where it seemed much easier to attack him.][11]

Louvel was subsequently tried and found guilty of the murder; he was executed in June 1820.

Adèle did not actually witness the assault but was attending a social gathering nearby to which the news of it was first brought, and she heard eyewitness accounts as they arrived throughout the ensuing night. As the reports were so dramatic as to be difficult to credit on first hearing, she sought to allay any disbelief on the part of her future readers by declaring:

> Les récits qui m'en ont été faits sont de la plus scrupuleuse exactitude. Ils me sont revenus par trop de bouches pour que j'en puisse douter un instant.

> [The reports that I received are scrupulously correct, and have been confirmed by too many mouths for me to doubt them for an instant.]

I think we can trust Adèle on this.

Using her great skill as a reporter and storyteller, she prefaced her account by telling how, only the day before the assassination, the Duchesse de Berry had been at a performance of Salieri's opera Les Danaïdes, at the theatre of the

Porte St Martin. She had become involved in a humorous argument with the principal actor, who in the opera had given daggers to his daughters with which to kill their husbands, regarding where exactly the heart should be stabbed. Adèle, who was present, saw the Duchess eventually leave the theatre with one of the stage daggers in her hand, and in her account prepared the reader for the ensuing assassination drama by saying: '*Hélas! vingt-quatre heures ne s'étaient pas écoulées qu'un couteau plus formidable était enfoncé dans ce cœur qu'on lui conseillait de toucher* [Alas! Twenty-four hours had hardly passed by before a more deadly knife had been plunged in that heart she had been advised to strike].'

The account of the actual attack is a mixture of tragedy and black comedy. Adèle was at a party at the nearby house of a friend, Mme de Briche, when news was brought to them that the duc had been stabbed as he was returning to the opera to see the last item of a ballet performance. At first it was thought that it was not too serious, and that he had been taken back to the Elysée Palace. Gradually, however, reports of the horrific truth began to filter in. As the duc was entering the opera house, despite the attendance of two aides-de-camp and two sentries stationed at the entrance, a man pushed past them to the duc, placed one hand on his shoulder and with the other

enfonce, par-dessous l'épaule, un énorme couteau qu'il lui laisse dans la poitrine et prend fuite sans que personne, dans tout ce nombreux entourage, ait le temps de prévenir son action.

[drove into his breast, below the shoulder, an enormous knife, which he left in the wound, and fled, before anyone in the numerous escort had time to prevent his action.]

The duc, almost as if performing a role on the stage, cried out: '*Cet homme m'a frappé* [This man has struck me]', thinking at first that he had simply struck him with his fist. But then: '*Ah! c'est un poignard; je suis mort* [Ah! It's a dagger; I am dead].'

There was then confused chaos. Attendants managed to carry the duc to a small room adjacent to his box, but then went off to seek further help, leaving him, with the knife still protruding from his chest, with the duchesse and a companion, Mme de Béthisy. Having failed to pull the knife out himself, the duc, in agony, begged one of them to do so, and Mme de Béthisy eventually steeled herself to do this, with the result that '*Le sang alors jaillit avec abondance; sa robe et celle de madame la duchesse de Berry en furent inondées* [the blood then spurted out profusely: her dress and that of the Duchesse de Berry were covered in it]'. Meanwhile, bizarrely, the ballet performance still continued in the background and, when the poor women opened the door of the room, '*les applaudissements du parterre, venaient faire un contraste épouvantable à la scène qu'elles avaient sous les yeux* [the applause of the pit made a dreadful contrast with the scene before their eyes]'. There could not have been a more melodramatic scene on the stage itself.

Eventually doctors arrived, followed by the duc's father, the Comte d'Artois, the Duc d'Orléans and other members of the royal family, including finally even the old king himself, Louis XVIII, who slowly dragged himself along the corridors of the opera house. The Duc de Berry, however, was not going to waste his death scene. Although no doubt in agony, and bleeding to death, he had time and the presence of mind to ask the Duc d'Orléans to take care of his wife, who was pregnant, and also commended to his wife's care two English girls, who were his daughters by a certain Mrs Brown; he also commended to his brother, the Duc d'Angoulême, a child he had recently fathered by a young dancer, Virginie, at the Paris Opera.

Adèle's comments on this extraordinary scene are superb. On the one hand, '*la mort de monsieur le duc de Berry a été celle d'un héros, et d'un héros chrétien* [the death of the Duc de Berry was that of a hero, and a Christian hero]. Moreover, she thought that

> *si monsieur le duc de Berry avait été élevé par des personnes raisonnables, si on lui avait appris à vaincre la fougue de ses passions, à compter avec les autres hommes, à sacrifier ses fantaisies aux convenances, il y avait en lui de l'étoffe pour faire un prince accompli.*

[if the Duc de Berry had been brought up by reasonable people, and if he had been taught to conquer his more extreme passions, to consider public opinion and to sacrifice his whims to social conventions, he would have had it in him to become an accomplished prince.]

On the other hand, although at the personal level she sincerely regretted his death, Adèle concluded, somewhat dismissively: '*Tel qu'il était, sa mort n'était pas une perte ni pour son fils, ni pour sa famille, ni pour son pays* [Such as it was, his death was no loss either for his son, or for his family, or for his country].' This was a pretty tough verdict, but no doubt a realistic one politically in the circumstances. The country and the Bourbon monarchy survived the loss of the second in line to the throne, for a few years at any rate, although the affair did lead to the resignation of King Louis' first minister, Elie Decazes, who was sent away to be ambassador in London. But the duchesse duly bore a son and thereafter took on a new lease of life, even if it ended in her farcical and abortive attempt to raise the Vendée.

In the middle of this exciting narrative, Adèle still found space to drop in another of those fascinating snippets of information that are incidental to the central theme, but nevertheless interesting in their own right. Digressing from the main story, she tells us, of the Duc de Berry, that

> *On ne sait pas assez qu'il a le premier introduit, en France, les caisses d'épargne. Il en avait fondé une pour sa maison et, pour encourager ses gens à y mettre, lorsqu'un d'eux avait économisé cinq cent francs, il doublait la somme. Il s'occupait lui-même de ces détails. Si un de ses domestiques avait besoin de reprendre l'argent placé, il s'informait de la nature de ses nécessités et, lorsqu'elles étaient réelles et honorables, y suppléait.*

> [People do not know well enough that he was the first to introduce savings banks in France. He had founded one of them for his own household, and in order to encourage them to make use of it, when anyone had saved five hundred francs, he doubled it. He took personal charge of the details of the business. If one of his servants needed to withdraw some of the money he had deposited, he enquired into the nature of his needs, and supplied the money when they were real and honourable.]

If a rather paternalistic approach, it was nonetheless a sound one (except for the generous rate of interest that the duc in effect paid!) and, as Adèle suspected of her readers at the time, his initiative is probably still unknown even to most historians of the banking sector in the present day.

Living as she did in such exalted circles, Adèle's accounts of deaths were generally of the highest figures in the land. Even when she was not present herself, there were usually well-placed friends to give her first-hand accounts. Thus she was able to write in kindly terms about the death in 1824 of the ailing Louis XVIII, who was a stickler for protocol to the end, even a few hours from his death correcting a mistake by the royal almoner in reading the prayer for those *in extremis*. She also described with sadness[12] the death of Tsar Alexander I in 1825 at Taganrog, on the shores of the Sea of Azov, as a result of a fever. She had greatly admired him – a charismatic figure, whom she distinguished from the other allied leaders – when he was in command of the Russian troops in Paris after Napoleon's defeat, and was distressed at his lapse into 'monomanie' and deep suspicion of everyone around him – a condition that she suspected was hereditary. She had, however, already described in her memoirs early signs of his eccentric behaviour in Paris in 1815, when he fell under the influence of a religious mystic, Baroness von Krüdener, who developed such a hold over him that she even persuaded him to spend eight hours kneeling in prayer in her private oratory and became attached to him as a close spiritual and political adviser. Most akin, however, to the bloody death of the Duc de Berry was the fatal accident that happened to the Duc d'Orléans, the eldest son and heir of King Louis-Philippe, in 1842.

DEATH OF THE DUC D'ORLÉANS

The year 1842 was for Adèle a disastrous year, marked by '*les accidents fatals, les inondations, les incendies de villes entières, les tremblements de terre* [fatal accidents, floods, entire towns being burned down, and earthquakes]'.[13] But the event that for her was the most serious was '*sans contredit la mort de monsieur le duc d'Orléans* [unquestionably the death of the Duc d'Orléans]', who was '*ce brilliant héritier de la Couronne* [the brilliant heir to the crown]'. Again, Adèle did not actually witness his death, and there were some contradictory accounts of it, but she was satisfied that her trusted method of sticking to what she had seen or heard from reliable sources and believed to be true would produce the best account. One of her sources was the queen herself.

The story of the accident, as told to Adèle, is in brief as follows.[14] The Duc d'Orléans, wishing to travel from the Tuileries Palace to Neuilly for an engagement as quickly as possible, was offered a light open carriage, pulled by '*deux jeunes bêtes fort ardentes* [two young and very spirited horses]' because all the other carriages had already been pre-empted by other members of the royal family. The duc tried at first to change the carriage, since he never normally went out in a carriage without doors, except for short rides in the Paris parks, but as time was scarce he finally accepted the open carriage and set off through the city and on the road to Neuilly. As the carriage gathered speed, he stood up to give instructions to the young groom, who was sitting behind him – probably to urge him to speed up – but lost his balance and fell backwards from the carriage onto the road. Adèle thinks that the carriage may have hit a bump or rut in the road.

It took some time for the postilion in front to realize what had happened, and by the time he had gained control of the horses and turned back, he found the duc being carried into a crude roadside dwelling belonging to a local greengrocer. The dwelling consisted of a small shop at the front, a small square unfurnished room within, with no light except that from a neighbouring courtyard containing a dung heap, and a third chamber opening onto the same courtyard. The injured duc lay here for an hour until he finally expired, '*entouré de toutes les grandeurs de l'Etat, dans cette misérable habitation* [surrounded by all the grandeurs of State, in this miserable dwelling]'. The 'grandeurs de l'Etat' consisted of the other members of the royal family, who had abandoned their engagements and rushed to the scene as soon as news of the accident had reached them. The king had cancelled a cabinet meeting he was due to hold at the Tuileries. He was the first to arrive and initially came out of the dwelling to tell the queen that it was nothing serious: the duc had been bled, and although he was still unconscious, that was normal following such a fall – after all, he himself had once suffered a very bad fall from his horse and had been unconscious for seven hours, but had recovered by the next day.

The queen was far from convinced and later told Adèle that she had had no illusions about the seriousness of her son's condition. The doctors who arrived applied cupping glasses, which seemed to give some relief, and the duc appeared for a moment to rally. But they had failed to spot a serious fracture to the back of his skull, and after sitting up for a moment, and calling in German for the door to be opened to let in some fresh air (as if talking to his Saxon valet), the duc expired with a final loud cry. The distraught queen, falling to her knees in that dirty hovel, invoked in a loud voice the mercy of God on '*son bien aimé, son premier-né* [her beloved, her first-born son]', while other members of the royal family, including Mme Adélaïde, the young princesses, and the duc's brother, the Prince de Joinville, gathered round too. It must have been an astonishing scene, with the stark contrast between the assembled royal family, their deceased son, and the meanness of the crude roadside dwelling in which he lay.

The king tried to take the queen away, but she would not leave without her son and cried: '*Je ne partirai pas sans Chartres; je veux l'emmener avec moi* [I will not leave without Chartres [her son]; I wish to take him with me].' She had her way, and the corpse was placed on a stretcher, covered with a black cloth, and taken on the road to Neuilly, where it was placed in the chapel. The queen followed him and '*s'était jetée à genoux, et restait prosternée sur le parquet, la face contre terre* [threw herself on her knees and stayed prostrate on the floor with her face to the ground]'. The king joined her and covered his dead son with tears and caresses. Adèle herself travelled to Neuilly on the following day, along a route full of mourners, both in carriages and on foot, but was unable, despite their very intimate friendship, to see the queen because '*elle était la plus malheureuse femme qu'il y eût au monde* [she was the most unhappy woman that there was in the world]'. She was, however, given a full account of all that had happened at Neuilly by an old valet of the queen's, who said of the duc: '*Ah! Madame la comtesse, c'était un si bon garçon!* [Ah, madam Countess! He was such a good fellow!]' Adèle returned to her house at Chatenay '*très souffrante dans ce moment, je sentais le besoin d'un peu de repos* [suffering greatly at this moment, I felt the need of a little rest]'.

Adèle's account continued with a moving description of the continuing grief of the royal family, the virtues of the departed Prince, who was '*surtout adoré* [...] *à l'armée* [above all adored in the army]', and the funeral at Notre-Dame, where the mourning was even greater than that at the funerals of Louis XVIII and the Duc de Berry. Her account of the whole tragedy is more sensitive and less melodramatic than the description of the assassination of the Duc de Berry, probably because the family were so close to her and she genuinely shared their grief. It is difficult to believe that it could have been written with greater understanding and affection.

THE DEATH OF TALLEYRAND

The death of Talleyrand, however, was quite a different story – no blood, but plenty of drama. He was unique among the subjects of this chapter in that both

Fanny and Adèle knew him. Fanny's acquaintance with him was admittedly only cursory, when in early 1793 he was a member of the party of French refugees at Juniper Hall, but during that period she came to admire him greatly. For Adèle he was a long-standing acquaintance, as is fitting for one who bestrode the French political scene throughout most of her lifetime and, more remarkably, survived. In a sense he was a high-level Vicar of Bray, changing parties and allegiance through the Revolution, the empire, the Bourbon restoration and the reign of Louis-Philippe. He served his government well when negotiating for them on the Treaty of Paris in 1814 and at the subsequent Congress of Vienna; after serving Napoleon he was highly influential in putting Louis XVIII back on the throne, but he did not scruple to intrigue against the government when it seemed to him more expedient. Napoleon both loved and hated him, but could never fully trust him.

He was born in 1854, being thus a couple of years younger than Fanny but some 30 years older than Adèle, and suffered from birth from a congenital club-foot condition, which caused him perpetual pain and obliged him to wear a specially supported boot all his life. He began his career in the Church, and after becoming Agent-General of the clergy at the age of 26, a very influential position for one so young (it was roughly the equivalent of general secretary of the clerical trades union), he was appointed Bishop of Autun (where Napoleon attended military school) at the age of 35. He then blotted his copybook with the Catholic Church by pressing strongly for Church reform, in effect a form of nationalization, which required priests to swear allegiance to the constitution rather than to Rome. This became one of the major obstacles to his reconciliation with the Church in later years. After he had laid aside his bishop's mitre – he was struck off the list as Bishop of Autun in 1802 – he occupied almost every conceivable high office of state, including that of prime minister, until near his death in 1838.

When Fanny met him at Juniper Hall in February 1793 he had fled to London, for the second time, in fear of his life, after refusing to agree to the overthrow of Louis XVI. For temporary refuge he joined Mme de Staël, who had once been his mistress, and the rest of the émigré party at Juniper Hall, and Fanny was enormously impressed with him. In a letter to Frederica Lock she wrote: 'It is inconceivable what a convert M. de Talleyrand has made of me; I think him now one of the first members, and one of the most charming, of this exquisite set. Susanna is completely a proselyte. His powers of entertainment are astonishing in information and in raillery.'[15] In a letter to her father a few days later she also noted that Talleyrand 'is a man of admirable conversation, quick, terse, *fin*, and yet deep'.[16] While recognizing that here was a man out of the ordinary, little did Fanny realize what a major figure in the history of both France and Europe he would become. Unfortunately the acquaintance at Juniper did not last for very long as Talleyrand returned to London and, in January 1794, after unsuccessfully fighting against the decision, was expelled from the country by Pitt under the Aliens Bill and in March went to live in America for the next two and a half years.

References to Talleyrand abound in Adèle's memoirs and, as with those episodes that she wrote separately, such as the July 1830 Revolution, the Duchesse de Berry's expedition, and the deaths of the Duc d'Orléans and Mme Adélaïde, she dedicated a separate 'fragment' to the death of Talleyrand.[17] The main interest in it here is the extraordinary efforts he made to achieve reconciliation with the Pope and the Catholic Church before he died.

Although he remained active in public life and society until nearly the end of his life, Talleyrand began to feel the hand of mortality not many years before the end. He was French ambassador in London for four years from September 1830, having, like Adèle, played an important part in urging Louis-Philippe to seize the throne. His supreme achievement during the tenure of that post was to bring France into the Quadruple Alliance with England, Spain and Portugal in April 1834, which, on paper at any rate, proscribed war with England for evermore – it was his last great diplomatic triumph. His health, however, was deteriorating and he had already received warnings from his doctors before he went to London. He had, for example, been taken seriously ill at a whist party in Paris in 1827 and, according to Adèle, this caused him to start thinking about an absolution before he died. She wrote:

> *cet avertissement ne fut pas perdu, et c'est de cette époque qu'on peut dater l'anxiété qui saisit monsieur de Talleyrand au sujet de ses funérailles et qui ne l'a plus quitté.*

> [this warning was not lost, and it is from this time that one can date the anxiety that seized Talleyrand with regard to his funeral and that has stayed with him.][18]

In Paris, only the archbishop, with the assent of the Pope, could authorize his absolution and readmission to the Catholic Church. Intensive negotiations were accordingly set in train, with the Duchesse de Dino, a very close friend, who had acted as his ambassadress in London, serving as his intermediary. Though far from well, he maintained a full and active social life and even, against medical advice, in March 1838 delivered an encomium at the Académie on behalf of an old friend, Charles-Frédéric Reinhard, of which he was inordinately proud. A few weeks later, however, he suffered a heavy fall when leaving the dinner table at the British embassy in Paris, apparently stumbling against a corner of the carpet. After he had with difficulty been taken back to his apartment, '*il passa quelques jours dans un état cruel* [he spent several days in a cruel condition]'.[19] Worse was to come, however. On 10 May he was '*pris à table d'un horrible frisson* [seized at the table with a dreadful shudder]', and the next day '*une énorme tumeur se déclara à la cuisse* [an enormous tumour appeared on his thigh]'.[20] It was clear now that his time was approaching and that the negotiations with the Pope needed to be accelerated.

The last few days were typical of the life of this supreme diplomat and negotiator. When pressed to sign the documents that had been exchanged and crawled over so many times by his intermediaries, he procrastinated, no doubt hoping to squeeze out one more last-minute concession from the Pope. Finally, after a visit by his doctor, who urged him to waste no time, he agreed to sign them at 4 a.m. on the following morning. He resisted further entreaties to sign later in the evening, telling his daughter Pauline, '*Je n'ai jamais rien su faire vite et pourtant je suis toujours arrivé à temps* [I have never learned to do things quickly, and yet I have always arrived on time]'.[21] Finally, however, precisely at 4 a.m. the next morning, in the presence of the appropriate witnesses,

il signa d'une main ferme: CHARLES MAURICE, PRINCE DE TALLEYRAND, en présence de l'abbé Dupanloup, de ses gens et de son médecin Cruveilhier dont je tiens ces détails

[he signed with a firm hand: CHARLES MAURICE, PRINCE DE TALLEYRAND, in the presence of Abbot Dupanloup, of his own people and of his doctor, Cruveilhier, from whom I know these details].[22]

He was leaving nothing to chance at the end. He wanted to make absolutely sure that reputable witnesses could verify that there was no '*affaiblissement moral dans ses facultés au moment où il avait tracé la déclaration et qu'elle était l'œuvre de sa propre volonté* [no moral weakness of his faculties at the moment he had signed the declaration, and that it was the work of his own free will]'.[23]

After a visit from King Louis-Philippe, for which he rallied for a moment and, a stickler for detail to the last, gave instructions as to the proper protocol with which to receive him, he died at four o'clock in the afternoon on 17 May 1838. Adèle, who had known him for so long, summed him up in the following somewhat double-edged terms:

> *Malgré sa figure blafarde, sa tournure disgracieuse, à travers les vicissitudes d'une vie orageuse qui l'a poussé dans les voies où il n'a ni rencontré ni mérité l'estime, monsieur de Talleyrand s'est toujours montré grand seigneur.*

> [In spite of his pallid appearance and the awkward bearing that through the vicissitudes of a stormy life pushed him into paths where he neither received nor deserved people's esteem, Talleyrand always showed himself to be a great nobleman.][24]

She even thought that the defrocked bishop might actually be a true believer, saying: '*Qui oserait affirmer qu'à ce moment suprême le sceptique ne fût pas un instant le croyant?* [Who would dare to claim that at this supreme moment the sceptic was not for an instant a true believer?]'[25] I suspect, however, that, as he had always done in his political and diplomatic career, Talleyrand was hedging his bets for the afterlife and that, if he had come face to face with his maker, he would have been ready to negotiate with him too. His powers of negotiation and persuasion were legendary. The Marquise de La Tour du Pin said that despite his faults and immorality he possessed a charm that she had not met in any other man and that '*il vous séduisait* [...] *comme l'oiseau qui est fasciné par le regard du serpent* [he seduced you like a bird fascinated by the look of a snake]'.[26] In fact, on this occasion his recantation nearly came adrift. At first the Pope refused to accept it, and the Cour de Rome reprimanded the Archbishop of Paris for having endorsed it. But fortunately the French chargé d'affaires in Rome persuaded the Cour de Rome eventually to accept it, no doubt armed with a brief that the old survivor had prepared for him in advance, just in case. Adèle says that she subsequently read it and that its terms were general and vague. It is perhaps not surprising that the court did not publish it.

Perhaps the last word on Talleyrand in this chapter ought to rest with Fanny. During her brief stay in Paris in July 1815, after returning from Trier with her injured husband, and while Talleyrand was temporarily head of Louis XVIII's government, she found herself in the same room with him at a reception. When he did not seem to remember her – it was over 22 years since their Juniper Hall days – she went up to him and said in French, '*M. de Talleyrand m'a oubliée; mais on n'oublie pas M. de Talleyrand* [M. de Talleyrand has forgotten me; but one does not forget M. de Talleyrand].' According to Fanny, he started, and she saw 'a movement of surprise by no means unpleasant break over the habitual placidity, of the nearly imperturbable composure of his general – and certainly *made up* countenance'.[27] As Talleyrand himself famously once said of the Duc de Richelieu, Louis XVIII's chief minister, after he died suddenly from a fever in 1822 that had been contracted as a result of travelling in a carriage with the windows down (another excellent deathbed story), '*C'était quelqu'un!* [He was somebody!]'[28]

NINE

FANNY & ADÈLE: A COMPARISON

Although they came from very different backgrounds, Fanny and Adèle lived rich and varied lives in both England and France and shared many of the same kind of experiences. Brought up in an intellectual middle-class home and launched into London's musical, literary and artistic society as a tyro best-selling novelist, Fanny suffered five years of exhausting service in the royal household, before being taken by her husband to spend ten years as an alien in Napoleon's Paris and later as a refugee in Brussels during the anxious days of the Waterloo campaign. Adèle was raised at the royal court of Versailles, spent many years as a refugee from the Revolution in exile in Italy and England, acted as unofficial ambassadress for her father in Turin and London, managed to co-exist with Napoleon and yet remained intimate with successive French royal families, particularly that of Louis-Philippe. If there had been a

French Who's Who of leading political and society personalities of her day, she would have known nearly everyone in it personally (and probably most of those in any English equivalent too).

Fanny's father came from relatively modest origins, but his rapidly growing reputation as a music teacher and musicologist brought him into contact with the elite of London cultural society of his day. Fanny grew up in this stimulating atmosphere and, although she became close to the king and queen and the high personages of the court, it was essentially as an employee and celebrity novelist. By contrast, despite her liberal 'constitutional' political views, Adèle was a true-blue aristocrat and never let herself or others forget it. She was also, in terms of formal education, much better equipped than Fanny. She had private tutors from a very early age, learned English, Italian and Latin, read remarkably widely, in both English and French, and benefited from the undivided attention that her parents were able to give to her education during their long exile in England in the 1790s. Fanny had little formal education during her childhood and was said not to be able to read properly at the age of eight. She had to teach herself both to read and to write and did not learn to speak French with any confidence until after the age of 40, when she married Alexandre d'Arblay. But both of them were exposed to such an array of great writers, artists and intellectuals – and, in Adèle's case, political figures – that their education by osmosis in the 'school of life' went far beyond anything that any more formal or institutional instruction could have given them.

They both grew up loving music – hardly surprising in Fanny's case, given her father's professional occupation and the frequent concerts held at their house, in which her talented older sister Hetty often performed. For Adèle, 'la musique est l'un des axes de son existence [music is a central strand of her existence],'[1] as Françoise Wagener put it. She loved attending the opera, both in London and in Paris, had a fine voice and, though not entirely without nerves, was quite ready to perform before company, even singing in duet with the great Italian diva Giuseppina Grassini, the mistress of both Napoleon and Wellington. The shy Fanny, on the other hand, was most reluctant to perform, either musically or in amateur dramatics. In an entry in her journal of April 1777 she described her absolute terror, even within the family, at taking a minor role in an amateur performance of a comedy by Arthur Murphy, The Way to Keep Him, at Barborne Lodge, the home of the Worcester branch of the Burney family. She wrote:

At length came *my* scene; I was discovered Drinking Tea; – to tell you how *infinitely*, how *beyond measure* I was terrified at my situation, I really cannot, – but my fright was nearly such as I should have suffered upon a public Theatre [...] I am sure, *without flattery*, I looked like a most egregious fool.[2]

After a long description of the rest of the performance, she concluded: 'So that, in short, I am totally, wholly, and entirely – dissatisfied with myself in the whole performance. Not once could I command my voice to any steadiness, – or look about me with any ease or pleasure.'[3] This is a very modest account of her own performance, but it leaves the reader in no doubt that Fanny was genuinely terrified of performing before other people at that age.

A common feature of both their lives was the profound influence their respective fathers had on them. In Fanny's case this was probably intensified by the fact that her mother died when she was only 10 years old; she never developed the same affection for her stepmother, whom her father married five years later. Although she was not the eldest daughter, Fanny was progressively employed by her father as his amanuensis, and she remained unmarried until she was 41, while her siblings married and moved away – brother James, the sailor, literally to the other side of the world with Captain Cook. She was at serious risk of becoming an old maid, tied to her father in perpetuity, like Milton's daughters. She bore it with great love and patience, even though, as she reported in a letter to Susanna and Mrs Lock in October 1791, 'The Day is never long enough, and I could employ two pens almost incessantly in merely scribbling what will not be repressed.'[4] But the result was that, prior to her marriage in 1793, the only times when she really got relief from working for her father for very long were either when she escaped to Daddy Crisp's house at Chessington, or when Dr Burney was travelling on the continent, collecting material for his history of music, as for example in the summer of 1770 when he made a solo tour of France and Italy. She did, of course, get away from him for five years serving as Second Keeper of the Robes to Queen Charlotte, but that period brought its own severe pressures and gave her little time to get on with writing other than letters.

Her career undoubtedly suffered in a number of ways as a result of her father's demands. The time she needed to develop her novel-writing further was restricted, as she was so busy copying or making notes for him. She was also dissuaded by him from persevering, as she would have wished, in her ambition to become a successful playwright, and the unfortunate embarrassments both in England and in Paris in her relationship with Mme de Staël were largely the result of his disapproval of association with her. Her decision to complete and publish *Evelina* without her father's prior knowledge was a very bold stroke, but the crucial assertion of independence was her decision to marry d'Arblay in face of her father's strong opposition. His pressure on this occasion was intense. In a letter of 23 July 1793 to her brother Charles just before her marriage she said that 'from prudential scruples' her father was 'coldly averse to this transaction', which had made her heart 'heavy from his evident ill will to it'.[5] Her father's refusal to attend the wedding was an unkind repayment for her years of dedication to him, but if she had yielded to him on this she might well have found it very difficult indeed not to remain tied to him as an unpaid literary factotum until the day he died.

This is not to say that she did not still sincerely love him and desperately wish to win his approval in whatever she did. Her nervousness about his reactions to *Evelina*, the steps she took to conceal her authorship from him until it was published and her extreme joy when he eventually praised it are all evidence of this. After her marriage she even generously forgave him for his opposition, accepting that it had been primarily due to genuine concern for the smallness of their joint income, which, as a result of d'Arblay's virtually penniless condition, was only likely to amount to some £120 a year, unless she could augment it by her writing. Her reluctant agreement to accept the post at court with Queen Charlotte had also been due in large part to the hope that it could lead to preferment for him and her brothers.

Her ultimate respect for her father was shown in her laborious editing and publication of his papers, which she began in the summer of 1817 at the age of 55, some 14 years after his death. This was an immense task, as he had left some 12 notebooks of unfinished memoirs in addition to a mass of other unsorted material. It took her several years to complete, and in the process she edited them ruthlessly. She was clearly disturbed by some of the details of her father's early life that she found in his papers and were previously unknown to her, particularly in relation to his treatment of her mother; she wished to remove anything that might bring discredit on his public reputation. She then spent the next 12 years writing her own account of his life, which was published in 1832 as *Memoirs of Doctor Burney, arranged from his own manuscripts, from family papers, and from personal recollections, by his daughter, Madame d'Arblay.*[6] Although some initial reviews of this were favourable, the critic John Croker wrote a long and very hostile article in the *Quarterly Review* of April 1833, severely criticizing Fanny for so expurgating her father's papers – in his view, in order to enhance her own reputation. But the fact that Fanny spent so many years on seeking to perpetuate her father's reputation in a favourable light must be testimony to the dominant role he played in her life and to her affection for him.

Adèle's relationship with her father was equally profound, but in many ways less complicated and more equal. Unlike Fanny, who in her earlier life was financially dependent on her father, Adèle by her marriage in effect made her mother and father financially dependent on her. However, although she was now married, she followed her father throughout his career, but she did so largely of her own volition and always retained her independence. Her decision to marry the rich and much older General de Boigne at the age of 17 had been entirely her own and was motivated by the wish to guarantee her father and mother a sufficient and independent income in perpetuity. She not only secured that income but often, throughout her marriage, invited them to live with her in considerable comfort at one or other of the grand houses provided for her at her husband's expense. She also voluntarily accompanied her father to his diplomatic posts in Piedmont in 1814–15, during Napoleon's exile on Elba, and in London from 1816 to 1819, after the second Bourbon restoration. This can partly be explained by the fact that her mother was often unwell and unable to perform fully the duties of an ambassadress, but it primarily reflected Adèle's love, concern and respect for her father, whom she wished to be close to and support.

Her active involvement in the diplomatic life is perhaps a little surprising in view of her frequent criticisms of diplomacy and diplomats. Commenting on this generally in reference to her father's decision to retire from his London post in 1819 – a decision that both she and her mother much welcomed – she described the diplomatic life as '*détestable*' and '*une des moins agréables à suivre* [one of the least agreeable to follow]'.[7] She observed shrewdly that if an ambassador succeeded, albeit on the basis of ambiguous instructions from his government, in successfully concluding a difficult and complicated negotiation, the minister would get the credit for it, whereas if the negotiation failed the ambassador would be blamed and disowned by the minister. It did not, however, prevent Adèle from throwing herself energetically into the life of the small French embassy in

Turin in February 1815 and, in effect, acting as chargé d'affaires when her father was absent, pursuing the dramatic developments relating to Napoleon's escape from Elba.

She tells how, in view of the shortage of secretaries and attachés in the embassy (there were obviously staff cuts in the diplomatic service in those days also), she was entrusted with maintaining the correspondence with the French ambassadors in Naples and Madrid and with the army commander in Marseilles. She says modestly:

> *Cela se bornait à expédier le bulletin des nouvelles qui nous parvenaient, en distinguant celles qui étaient officielles des simples bruits dont nous étions inondés.*

> [My duties were confined to sending a summary of the news that came in to us, distinguishing official news from the common rumours with which we were inundated.][8]

Although Adèle makes it all sound very basic and simple, it was in fact quite a skilled task for a non-professional diplomat, and it is no surprise that in some quarters 'la malveillance s'est saisie de cette puérile circonstance pour établir que je faisais l'ambassade [spiteful gossip seized on this puerile circumstance to claim that I usurped the duties of ambassador]'.[9] I suspect, however, that these carping remarks did not actually displease her and that she rather enjoyed and was proud of being able to step in to help her father at such a critical time in the history of her country. It is also worth adding that her more general criticisms of the diplomatic life referred to above related to an earlier time when her mother was ill; both she and her mother had noticed that her father was getting tired and forgetful and, in Adèle's view, no longer capable of carrying out his ambassadorial functions as fully as before. I am sure she enjoyed the social and other privileges of being a proxy ambassadress in London, just as Mme de Staël enjoyed the entrée to high society that being married to an ambassador gave her in Paris. She clearly relished the access it gave her to the court and other high circles, and it was only concern for her father that made her welcome his decision to retire and return to France.

The subject on which Fanny and Adèle perhaps differed most was that of romance and marriage. Adèle deliberately contracted a loveless marriage at the age of 17 with an older, but very rich, man of a lower social class in order to secure a good financial settlement for her parents. There was no nonsense about it. She knew what she wanted and where her duty lay; she made up her mind in only 24 hours; she even bargained toughly with her future husband to hold him to the marriage settlement figure originally mentioned to her father, and she made it quite clear that he could expect no love or affection from her.

Whether the marriage was consummated or not is not absolutely clear from her memoirs – Adèle is generally very discreet about her private life. A letter from her father of 12 June 1778 to his father (the patriarch of the family) reporting on the marriage, which was preceded by the words 'Consummatum est' and claimed to have information that *'la nuit n'a fait que confirmer les bonnes espérances* [the night has only served to confirm our good expectations]', suggests that it was.[10] However, unlike Fanny, she remained childless – another major difference between them – and she and her husband generally lived apart in the grand houses he provided, although from time to time she joined him, especially in his native Savoie, in order to perform her duties as hostess at the head of his table. Her parents also sometimes stayed with them and seem to have got on reasonably well with General de Boigne. As previously noted, Adèle described the marriage as a stormy one, and there is some evidence that he was unfaithful to her and sometimes even maltreated her physically – possibly because she did not respond to him sexually in a way he still hoped for – but, despite some severe criticisms of his character and behaviour, she wrote kindly about him when he died in 1830, speaking well of his generosity to good causes in Chambéry, where he effectively retired for the last period of his life and was revered as a generous local benefactor (there is a fine statue of him in the middle of Chambéry, supported by four stone Indian elephants).

After his death Adèle devoted herself to her long-standing friendship with Chancellor Pasquier, who was much more her intellectual, social and political equal; an intimate relationship developed between them, which lasted to the end of their long lives. We do not know whether they ever married. They took houses close to each other, but never lived together; however, as described in Chapter Two, they became an item – almost a national institution – in their declining years and nearly fled from France together in 1848 when Adèle's great friends King Louis-Philippe and Queen Marie-Amélie were driven from the throne and went into exile in England. Pasquier was the real romance of Adèle's life, but, true to her initial comments on her marriage to de Boigne, she tells us very little about the details of her relationship with him.

Fanny's experience was totally different. It is difficult to imagine her marrying for money, unless her father had put irresistible pressure on her. Her approach to love and marriage was also much more romantic, but at the same time somewhat nervous and ambivalent. When she was only 16 and resuming her childhood journal, she wrote:

> I am going to tell you something concerning myself, which, if I have not chanced to mention it before will I believe a little surprise you – it is, that I scarce wish for anything so truly, really and greatly, as to be *in love* – upon my word I am serious – and very *gravely* and *sedately*, assure you it is a real and *true* wish. I cannot help thinking it is a great happiness to have a strong and particular attachment to some *one* person, independent of duty, interest, relationship or pleasure: but I carry not my wish so far as for a *mutual tendresse*.[11]

The last words of this otherwise very romantic declaration signify the stressful dilemma that girls of Fanny's background and social class faced. On the one hand, however much they believed they had found true love, they knew that once they married they would be giving away most of their legal rights and independence for the foreseeable future. On the other hand, if they failed to find a husband at a relatively early age, they risked, unless they had independent financial means, being condemned to a life of dependency and ending up as a lonely old maid. Victorian literature is full of such cases. Adèle's earlier observations on the frantic English '*chasse à mari*' are relevant to this. It must be remembered also that at this tender age – although it was the same age at which Adèle had negotiated her mercenary marriage – Fanny had had very little experience of relationships outside the family, and her yearning for love and romance was probably tempered by fear that she might not be able to find anyone to reciprocate it. This sort of apprehension perhaps lay behind her later words in a letter of 19 September 1793 to her friend Georgiana Waddington, only two months after her marriage, when she confessed: 'I had never made any vow against Marriage, but I had long – long been firmly persuaded it was – *for me* – a state of too much hazard, and too little purpose.' She also once wrote in her diary: 'I had rather a thousand times die an old maid than be married except from affection.'[12] She was, however, deliriously happy with her eventual marriage to d'Arblay and in no doubt that, after much soul-searching and hesitation, she had made the right decision, not least because 'My dearest father, whose fears and draw backs have been my sole subject of regret, begins now to see I have not judged rashly or with romance, in seeing my own road to my own felicity.'[13]

It had taken Fanny until the age of 41 to find her man. She had suffered several disappointments and one narrow escape on the way to him. The latter occurred when she was 23 and was introduced at the house of the Thrales to a Mr Barlow, who immediately took a great fancy to her. She described him as 'short but rather handsome, he is a very well bred, good tempered and sensible young man, and he is highly spoken of, both for Disposition and morals'. Unfortunately, despite being very well read, 'his language is stiff and uncommon, and seems laboured, if not affected – he has a great desire to please, but no elegance of manners; neither, though he may be very worthy, is he at all agreeable'.[14] This sounds like just the sort of respectable, safe, worthy, but rather boring suitor that responsible parents would recommend to their daughter, but for Fanny there was obviously not a single spark of romance.

Unfortunately Mr Barlow thought the reverse about Fanny and sent her a letter containing 'a passionate Declaration of Attachment, hinting at hopes of a *return*, and so forth'. Fanny was quite sure that she could not reciprocate his sentiments and, in spite of pressure from many members of her family, with the eventual consent of her father, who had initially commended Mr Barlow, she sent him a letter exhorting him to transfer his affections elsewhere. This did not quite do the trick and she had to suffer a further excruciating interview with him before he finally gave up. She was so relieved that she wrote in her journal: 'Though I was really sorry for the unfortunate and misplaced attachment which this young man professes for me, yet I could almost have *Jumped* for joy when he was gone, to think that the affair was thus finally over.'[15]

Sadly, the boot was on the other foot on the two subsequent occasions when Fanny was ready to accept an offer of marriage. The first came at the end of 1784 when, again at the house of Mrs Thrale, she was introduced to a Mr George Owen Cambridge, an eligible and attractive young clergyman, to whom she took an instant liking. She described him as 'sensible, rational, and highly cultivated; very modest in all he asserts, and attentive and pleasing in his behaviour, and he is wholly free from the coxcombical airs, either of impertinence or negligence and *non-chalence*, that all the young men I meet [...] are tainted with'.[16] Alas, despite several further encounters in which her admiration for him grew and she believed he returned her feelings and was a serious suitor, he backed off and failed to propose to her. Initially, she took it very badly and described his conduct in a letter to Susanna in January 1785 as 'such deceit and treachery'.[17] But she reconciled herself to it, at least outwardly, and in later years, as Archdeacon of Middlesex, he became a good friend to Fanny and her son during the latter's troubles and her own widowhood.

The second occasion was more traumatic for Fanny since it happened during her period at court, when she was particularly lonely, unhappy, vulnerable and physically ill. She was, in effect, led on by Colonel Stephen Digby, vice-chamberlain to the queen, who lent her a copy of an anonymous but suggestive novel, entitled *Original Love Letters, between a Lady of Quality and a Person of Inferior Station*, and started to call on her regularly in her private apartment at Windsor. Digby's wife had died of cancer the previous year, leaving him with four children, and he was suffering severe pain from gout. This no doubt evoked Fanny's sympathy as well as her liking and admiration for him. His frequent visits to her sparked rumours that he was courting her, and Fanny truly believed that '*His heart was surely mine*', and that this would lead to her escape from court – 'a conclusion of my long confinement – incessant labours, – and perpetual indignities'.[18] Her shock and disappointment were therefore all the greater when, without warning, she learned one day that he was to be married to a maid of honour to the queen, Charlotte Gunning, who apparently had a dowry of £10,000 to offer to him. Fanny gained some comfort from the fact that several of her colleagues, even including the fierce Mrs Schwellenberg, spoke badly of Charlotte Gunning, but she was extremely upset by Digby's unexpected behaviour. Given the views she had expressed on marriage, it would not have been surprising had this episode put her off marrying for life, and it is gratifying that once she had escaped from court she found lasting love and romance with Alexandre d'Arblay.

Whereas their approach to and experiences of love and marriage were quite different, the common thread that bound Fanny and Adèle together was their writing. They were both natural writers but came to it at different times and in quite different ways. As soon as Fanny had taught herself to write, she scribbled incessantly, putting to paper poems, stories and anything else to emerge from her acute observation and imagination. After the auto-da-fé of her early manuscripts in a bonfire on her 15th birthday, she soon resumed her private journal – initially addressed to 'Nobody' – and gradually over the next 10 years supplemented it with letters to her sister Susanna, her father, the Locks, other members of the family and friends, and to Daddy Crisp. It was full of irreverent and playful observations, often poking fun at herself as well as others, and increasingly contained memorable sketches of celebrated visitors to her father's and the Thrales' households, such as Dr Johnson, David Garrick and Sir Joshua Reynolds.

At the age of 25 she completed her first, and probably best, novel, *Evelina*, and was planning others, so that by the time she went on to write about her experiences at court, her association with the Juniper Hall set, marriage to d'Arblay and life in Paris under Napoleon, she was already a successful and established professional author – eventually with four novels and eight (though not very successful) plays to her credit. Her journals and letters were initially not intended for other eyes, but as she grew older she became anxious that they should be preserved and must have realized that one day they might become public property. Indeed, at the end of her life she arranged them with great care and finally consigned them to the editor, her niece, with full permission to publish what might be judged desirable to make them intelligible, provided that, whatever might be omitted, nothing should be altered or added. It is consistent with this approach that, as time went on, she also varied the form of her journal by writing memorable self-standing set pieces or fragments, such as the court years, the description of her mastectomy in Paris, her Waterloo journal and the humorously suspenseful story of her near drowning in a cave at Ilfracombe in 1817. The description of her operation, written quite soon after the event, must stand unique in its horror among autobiographical accounts in English literature. In her final widowed years she devoted most of her time to editing and publishing her father's memoirs, with the mixed results referred to earlier in this chapter.

Adèle had none of this literary practice or background and she always took pains to make it clear that she was not a professional writer or historian. Although she did write two novels, which were published posthumously – *La Maréchale d'Aubemer* and *Une passion dans le grand monde* – they are mainly notorious for their complete obscurity. Compared with the professional novelist, Fanny, she was a literary amateur. In this respect she resembled Mrs Fanny Trollope, who also only began her successful career as a travel writer and novelist in her mid fifties (in the case of the latter in order to earn enough money to keep her large family).

Adèle began by jotting down her recollections of the court of Louis XVI at Versailles and was persuaded by a friend that, unless she continued with this, they would be forgotten – and so she just kept going. In a few years she found that she had a substantial book on her hands. She was endearingly modest about it. In the introduction to the first part (concerning her childhood) she declared that *Mémoires* was too solemn a title for it and that the term *Souvenirs* had been abused by other authors. She therefore followed the recommendation of her nephew and gave it the delightfully unassuming title of *Récits d'une tante* (*An Aunt's Tales*). She also declared forthrightly:

> *je ne sais pas écrire; à mon âge je n'apprendrai pas le métier et, si je voulais essayer de rédiger des phrases, je perdrais le seul mérite auquel ces pages puissent aspirer, celui d'être écrites sans aucune espèce de prétention.*

> [I do not know how to write and I am not going to learn the business at my age. If I wanted to redraft the sentences, I should lose the only merit to which these pages aspire, that of being written without any manner of pretension.][19]

She went on to enlarge on this, claiming that she had not consulted any documents, that there were probably many errors of dates, places and facts, but that 'on peut prétendre à une parfaite sincérité; on est vrai quand on dit ce qu'on croit [I can claim complete sincerity, and you speak the truth when you say what you believe]'. This is not an infallible guide to veracity, but in Adèle's case she generally deserves the benefit of the doubt.

This disarming modesty finds expression throughout her memoirs. She denied in particular that she was seeking to write history:

> *Je n'écris pas l'histoire, mais seulement ce que je sais avec quelques détails certains. Lorsque les affaires publiques seront à ma connaissance spéciale, je les dirai avec la même exactitude que les anecdotes de société.*

[I am not writing history, but only what I know with a few certain details. When public affairs come under my special knowledge, I will relate them with the same exactitude as I do my society anecdotes.][20]

Above all, she aimed to tell the truth as she saw it, even about herself, and not to be influenced by personal prejudice. Writing about Turin and the Hundred Days, and the condemnation and execution for treason of Charles La Bédoyère, who had deserted the king and gone over to Napoleon, she felt rather ashamed of her personal delight in his fate – she felt that he got what he deserved – but hastened to declare:

Je me suis promis de dire la vérité sur tout le monde; je la cherche aussi en moi. Il faut qu'on sache jusqu'où la passion de l'esprit peut dénaturer le cœur.

[I have promised to tell the truth about everyone; I seek it also in myself. It is necessary that people should know how far partisan passion can destroy natural good feeling.][21]

For all her disclaimers, however, Adèle was a born writer and storyteller, and it is difficult not to have great faith in the honesty and reliability of her reports. If she occasionally got it wrong, it was probably because, like Herodotus, she believed and accurately reported what she was told, rather than because she fabricated or exaggerated anything herself. The quality of her principal sources was generally high, as was the quality of her prose. She may not have been a successful novelist, but many of her set-piece writings, such as the account of the July 1830 Revolution, the assassination of the Duc de Berry, the picture of mounted Cossacks bivouacking in the parks of Paris, the roadside death of the Duc d'Orléans, the adventures of the Duchesse de Berry and the cholera epidemic in Paris of 1832, are brilliant reportage and as vivid and compelling as anything Fanny ever wrote in her letters or journals, except perhaps for her encounters with the 'mad' King George III at Windsor and at Kew, and the description of her operation in 1811. In more modern times, Adèle would have made an outstanding war correspondent.

An important difference between the substance of their writings is the strong political dimension that runs throughout Adèle's memoirs. Again, she denies any pretension to being a professional politician or political commentator. In her account of the first restoration of Louis XVIII in 1814, she went so far as to admit that '*j'ai toujours aimé à faire de la politique* en amateur [I have always liked playing politics *as an amateur*]',[22] and she again confessed, when referring to her support for her father at the embassy in Turin in 1815, '*la politique m'amuse; j'en fais volontiers* en amateur *pour occuper mon loisir* [politics amuses me; I gladly take an *amateur* part in it, to occupy my spare time]'.[23] The truth, however, is that she was a politician down to her fingertips and absolutely steeped in, and fascinated by, the politics of her day. Moreover, she not only observed and recorded, but also, not least through her astonishingly wide range of contacts, played a significant personal part in influencing important individuals and political events. This was sometimes through her salon, which attracted many of the leading politicians in Paris, particularly those on the opposition side during Napoleon's time, and sometimes through her direct personal involvement, such as during the July 1830 Revolution, when she was here, there and everywhere in the streets during the critical phases, just like the Duke of Wellington at Waterloo. One of the most apposite comments made on her was by her admirer the poet, novelist and literary critic Sainte-Beuve, who said: '*si elle fût née homme, la comtesse de Boigne eût été ministre* [if the Comtesse de Boigne had been born a man, she would have been a minister]'.[24]

By contrast, except where her life was directly affected, such as in Brussels during the Waterloo campaign in 1815, Fanny showed little interest in politics – in England or on the Continent – despite her years at court when she must have had frequent contact with political figures. Indeed, her friendship with the French politicians in the Juniper Hall colony, and especially with Mme de Staël, became a source of nervousness and embarrassment to her; she was inhibited by her fear of contagion from the exile 'constitutionalists'. One of the few passages in her journals dealing directly at any length with political developments was her detailed and allegedly verbatim account of the trial of Warren Hastings in Westminster Hall in 1788, which she attended after she had been given a ticket by Queen Charlotte, and perhaps also because friends of her father, such as Edmond Burke and Richard Brinsley Sheridan, were playing a prominent part in the prosecution. Her own sympathies were with the defendant, but more for emotional than for political reasons. She wrote of Hastings: 'I was much affected by the sight of that dreadful harrass which was written on his countenance; – had I looked at him without restraint, it could not have been without Tears.'[25] Some literary critics have seen in her novels, particularly in *Cecilia*, an underlying critique of the English class structure and inequality of wealth and income, and especially the behaviour of the nouveaux riches, but Fanny was simply not a political animal in the same way as Adèle. Given their backgrounds and the quite different occupations of their fathers – the one a musicologist, the other a diplomat and politician – this is hardly surprising.

Something that did characterize them both was their sheer toughness and energy. If you survived childhood in the late eighteenth and early nineteenth centuries and were brought up in a prosperous home, you stood a good chance of living to a reasonable age. Genes were also in Fanny and Adèle's favour – Dr Burney lived to the age of 88, and Adèle's father to 87. But it is remarkable that both our authors lived on well into their eighties and remained active until near the end of their lives. In Fanny's case it was perhaps the more remarkable, as she did not appear to have a robust constitution and was, as a younger woman, often ill for one reason or another. Her journals refer to insomnia, headaches, colds and fevers, 'languor so prodigious, with so great a failure of strength and spirit',[26] and 'frequent pains in my side which forced me 3 or 4 times in a Game [of cards] to creep to my own Room for Hartshorn and for rest'.[27] Her five years at court severely tested both her physical and mental stamina, but she quickly recovered and her ability to survive the mastectomy operation in September 1811 in Paris was little short of miraculous – even if, as is possible, she was not actually suffering from cancer.

She not only survived all these illnesses but endured hardships and hazards that would have felled lesser mortals. As we have already noted, travelling itself in Fanny's era, especially by sea, was always a risky and often very unpleasant experience. Although Thomas Cook started organizing popular tours to the Continent in the 1850s, and although British tourists had begun journeying across the Channel in increasing numbers again after the end of the Napoleonic wars, for most people such travel was a hazardous undertaking. According to Mullen and Munson in *The Smell of the Continent*:

> In the early decades of the nineteenth century, crossing the Channel was the most difficult, unpleasant and sometimes dangerous part of a European trip. In the years immediately after Waterloo, travellers going by the shortest

route (Dover–Calais) faced a number of hurdles. The trip from London to Dover by coach could take anything from twelve to twenty-four hours. On arrival they would have to find a ship to take them and would then have to negotiate getting out to the ship, after which they would wait for the outgoing tide. If lucky the passage might take only six hours. Having arrived, travellers, such as the artists Haydon and Wilkie, then had to get ashore. After this they had to cope with Customs and passport officials and then they faced a forty-eight hour trip to Paris. Travel was not for the faint-hearted.[28]

Fanny got her first taste of what was in store for her in future Channel crossings in what was intended to be a simple pleasure cruise with friends from Teignmouth in September 1775 to see the English fleet at Torbay. A short time after they set off, the sea became unexpectedly rough and the wind blew strongly against them. They began to fear for their lives and only just managed to get back to Brixham harbour. Fanny wrote that 'when we landed, I was so very giddy, that I could hardly stand – and was obliged to go into the first House for a Glass of Water: but I am only amazed that I was not dreadfully seasick'.[29] Thereafter, almost every account in her journals of a Channel crossing by herself or her husband amounted to an unpleasant and often dangerous experience, sometimes lasting several days, with the ship often returning to its port of departure because of a storm or adverse winds or arriving at an unscheduled destination. When, for example, d'Arblay sought to cross to France from Gravesend in November 1801, the sea was so 'rough and perilous' that 'the Captain was forced to hoist a flag of distress' and 'my poor Mr d'Arblay's provision basket [was] flung down and its contents demolished – his Bottle of wine broke by another toss, and violent fall – and he was nearly famished'.[30] Fanny suffered a similar experience returning from Dunkirk in 1812. The voyage lasted two days and nights. She was 'so exhausted by the unremitting sufferings I had endured, that I was literally and utterly unable to rise from my hammock'.[31] But rise and survive she did, and in due course returned to the Continent and, after the Battle of Waterloo, undertook alone a six-day journey through unfamiliar and potentially hostile territory in Belgium and Germany on a mission to find her wounded husband which can only be described as heroic.

Adèle's experiences were very similar. As Chapter Two related, at an early age she survived a dangerous horseback crossing over the snow-covered Saint

Gotthard pass with her parents. She also suffered regular periods of illness – in her case frequently migraine – and, like Fanny, faced the rigours of sea journeys and Channel crossings. Her personal courage was outstanding, not least during the July 1830 Revolution when, while Paris was ablaze with rioting and shooting, she strode imperturbably among the barricades, observing meticulously what was happening and even insisting on going to her bank to withdraw some money when the demonstrations were at their height.

She fared no better than Fanny at sea. In February 1818 she sailed from Dover to Calais, and it nearly turned out to be her last voyage. '*Par le coupable incurie du capitaine* [By the culpable negligence of the captain]',[32] the ship ran aground on a sandbank between two rocks and was very nearly wrecked against one of them. The ship was full of passengers, but there was only one small boat, which would only take seven persons, to ferry them to the nearest shore and safety. As daughter of the French ambassador in London, Adèle was as a matter of protocol offered a place in the first boatload, but she declined it in favour of a mother with five children, and so had to wait anxiously for another 40 minutes until the boat returned to take off another load. In the meantime the ship's position grew more perilous, as it was in immediate danger of crashing against one of the rocks.

The story eventually ended happily. With help from the shore, and a change in the tide, the captain finally managed to get his vessel into Calais harbour, but it was a close-run thing. Somewhat to her embarrassment, Adèle was thanked by the captain for the example she had set, '*qui, assurait-il, avait tout sauvé* [which, he assured her, had saved everything]'. Adèle's concluding comment was typical of her self-effacing modesty: '*J'ai remarqué que les grands dangers trouvent toujours du sang-froid, et les grandes affaires du secret. Les cris et les caquets sont pour les petites circonstances* [I remarked that great dangers always bring out coolness, and great affairs discretion. Shouts and cackles are only for little events]'.[33] To cap it all, after this frightening experience, and although she had left London unwell, she arrived in Paris '*très bien portante* [in top-class form]'.[34] The coolness and character that she displayed on this occasion was typical of the toughness that allowed both her and Fanny to survive on so many testing occasions.

It is a shame that, so far as we know, although there were many opportunities in both London and Paris to do so, Fanny and Adèle never met. Despite their differences, they had much in common and would have had much to talk about. They both had an interest in music, literature, the arts and the theatre, and a similar sense of irony and humour; they knew each other's capital cities very well and shared many common friends and acquaintances, not least among the Juniper Hall set. They would surely also have talked about Fanny's dear Alexandre d'Arblay. There is no record of Adèle having met him, but she must have heard something about him from Mme de Staël, with whom he had worked hard on transcribing her book at Juniper. The subject of their respective fathers, and their love and respect for them and the influence they had had on their lives, would also have come up sometime, and Adèle might even have heard of Dr Burney, whose reputation as a music scholar spread beyond English shores to the Continent.

Royalty would have provided material for a whole evening's conversation. Fanny had little acquaintance with French royalty, except at a distance, but Adèle could not only entertain Fanny with stories of Versailles and her close friendships with the Bourbons and King Louis-Philippe and Queen Amélie, but she could also talk, with personal knowledge, about George III and Queen Charlotte, the Prince Regent and Queen Caroline, and other British royals. At the same time, having heard at Brighton the Prince Regent's poignant description of meeting his old, blind and confined father, she would have been fascinated by Fanny's stories of the onset of the king's illness at Windsor and Kew and of life behind the scenes at the English court.

At some stage the names of Napoleon and Wellington would surely also have been mentioned. Both would have agreed on the disastrous nature of the progression into tyranny of the former and the desirability of his removal – although Adèle might have been a little touchy about excessive criticism of him, since, after all, despite his faults, he was still a great Frenchman – and Fanny would have seen the duke in a much more heroic light than the rather disparaging picture that Adèle, frustrated with the allied occupation of Paris, painted of him parading his Italian opera singer mistress in Paris society and perched up a ladder in the Louvre, taking down pictures that Napoleon had looted. If such a conversation had ever existed, what a bonus it would have been to have their respective descriptions of each other and their records of it. Alas, we cannot recreate it and can only speculate, but I suspect that they would have got on very well together.

EPILOGUE

Neither Fanny nor Adèle can rank among the first historiographers of their time. Their chronicles, especially Fanny's, are too selective and personal to allow us to base on them overall judgements about the historical periods they cover. But few diarists or memoirists have left us a more entertaining and vivid true-to-life picture of so many events and people in such a momentous period of European history. Moreover, the fact that they both lived in each other's country for a number of years, had a number of friends in common and knew both Paris and London well gives an added dimension of interest to their writings.

In Fanny's case, starting from a very early age, she carried into her journals and letters the consummate literary skills, not least her gift for personal portraiture, that won her success with *Evelina* and later novels. With her prodigious memory and powers of observation, she captured on paper everything and everybody around her, and committed it either initially to her diary privately, addressed to 'Nobody', later in letters to family and friends or in carefully crafted set pieces. In Adèle's case, her transition to being an author came at a much later stage in life; once started, however, she proved to be a natural and indefatigable narrator, writing with the frankness, modesty and patent honesty and good sense that make her memoirs so readable and credible.

Adèle gives us a more coherent chronological overview of the most significant events of her time, starting with the Revolution, passing through the ascendancy of Napoleon, followed by Waterloo and the Bourbon restoration, and progressing through the July 1830 Revolution, which put Louis-Philippe on the throne, to his fall in 1848 and the establishment of the Second Empire. Few of the essential events of this time are overlooked, and much of the narrative is informed and made more real by Adèle's personal involvement, often at a very high level, in many of the events she describes. We are with her, for example, when the revolutionaries stormed the Palace of Versailles in 1789 and she along with her mother and father only just escaped with their lives; in the embassy at Turin, when the news of Napoleon's escape from Elba reached them; in the turbulent streets of Paris, with the women sitting calmly under their parasols by the barricades, during the July Revolution. She gives us a special feel and flavour of these events, often in a manner that does not emerge from other memoirs or histories – as, for example, her revelation that the death of Napoleon on St Helena in May 1821 caused hardly a stir on the streets of Paris at the time and could not even sell the evening newspapers.

Moreover, this narrative of the key historical developments is entertainingly coloured and spiced with wonderful secondary anecdotes, not all of which are strictly relevant to her main story, but which are always interesting, illuminating and sometimes very amusing. They include the amazing story of the near miss at Genoa when Napoleon, escaping by sea from Elba, was nearly targeted by the Congreve rockets, the gory details of the assassination of the Duc de Berry at the Paris opera, while the show still went on, and the dying Talleyrand, that supreme diplomat, negotiating with the Pope to his last breath to regain admittance into the Catholic Church – just in case. Adèle denied that she was writing history and disclaimed any serious interest in politics, but she has provided us with a treasure trove of detailed information with which to amplify and colour the researches of more professional writers of history and politics.

Fanny's journals are different. Adèle only began to write her memoirs in her fifties after she had been persuaded by a young friend that it was her duty to posterity to do so. Writing was not until that time her *métier*, and she constantly disclaimed any pretensions to being an author, but she applied herself to it and became extremely good at it. Fanny was a born writer and wrote because of a compulsion to do so, right from the time when she could first read and write. She initially composed her diary privately and for herself only, but with her success as a novelist she realized that her compositions would inevitably one day become public, and she began to shape and craft them accordingly and eventually began to supplement them with brilliant set pieces. Although the main historical events of the day necessarily loom in the background, and indeed crucially shaped periods of her life (such as her enforced stay in Paris from 1802 to 1812), she is less concerned than Adèle with grand politics or history and more with conveying graphically and immediately to the reader her own specific experiences and impressions of the places she visited, the people she met, the events she witnessed, and her personal emotions and reactions to these. There is far less analysis and judgement in her writing.

Thus it is that she provides us with the unique portraits of David Garrick stealing the stage, both on it at Drury Lane and in company at the Burney household, of Sir Joshua Reynolds, sadly sinking into decline as his sight and hearing worsened, of the ambitious Mrs Thrale and her circle at Streatham, dominated by the shambling short-sighted presence of Dr Johnson, and of 'mad' King George III, chasing her through the gardens at Kew. Unlike Adèle, who was generally reticent about her private life and tells us little, for example, about the deep friendship with Chancellor Pasquier – her devoted companion in her later years – Fanny, sometimes in a very vulnerable way, is bursting to tell about her views on love and marriage, her failed romances and, finally, her blissful marriage to the upright and gentlemanly Alexandre d'Arblay. Most of the great events that form the background to their writings are well documented and analysed by historians elsewhere, but both Fanny and Adèle, as well as entertaining us, have invaluably helped our understanding of those events by filling in many of the gaps, adding the human touch and bringing the history to colourful life.

For a final comment on these two tough, courageous, talented and eminently likeable women, I would single out, for Adèle, her formidable intellect, her constant hyperactivity, whether in politics or society, her sound and balanced judgement and a compassionate heart which generally enabled her to see and seek the best in others. This last quality is perhaps best epitomized in her own words, when she wrote in the introduction to her memoirs:

En recherchant le passé, j'ai trouvé qu'il y avait toujours du bien à dire des plus mauvaises gens et du mal des meilleurs; j'ai tâché de ne pas faire la part d'après mes affections; je conviens que cela est difficile: si je n'y ai pas réussi, je puis assurer en avoir eu l'intention.

[As I have looked into the past, I have found that there is always good to be said of the worst people and something bad to be said of the best. I have tried not to be led by any personal predilections, although I agree that this is difficult, and if I have not succeeded, I can at any rate assure you of my best intentions.][1]

As for Fanny, who was vulnerable at times, loved to be loved, feared that she would not be, but remained modest about the praise that her literary brilliance attracted, I can find nothing better than the comments by Macaulay in the Edinburgh Review of January 1843, quoted at the beginning of Dobson's great 1904 edition of her diary and letters:

If she recorded with minute diligence all the compliments, delicate and coarse, which she heard wherever she turned, she recorded them for the eyes of two or three persons, who had loved her in obscurity, and to whom her fame gave the purest and most exquisite delight. Nothing can be more unjust than to confound these outpourings of a kind heart, sure of perfect sympathy, with the egotism of a blue-stocking, who prates to all who come near her about her own novel or her volumes of sonnets.

NOTES

INTRODUCTION

1 Lawday, p. 4.

CHAPTER ONE

1 Harman, p. 6.
2 Hemlow, p. 9.
3 Harman, p. 37.
4 Dobson, *Madame d'Arblay*, vol. 1, p. 460.
5 Ibid., p. 240.
6 Ibid., vol. 2, p. 142.
7 Hemlow, p. 11.
8 Sabor and Troide, p. xiii.
9 Dobson, *Madame d'Arblay*, vol. 1, p. 12.
10 Sabor and Troide, p. 1.
11 Ibid., pp. 1–2.
12 Ibid., p. xvii.
13 Dobson, *Fanny Burney*, p. 33.
14 Sabor and Troide, p. 31.
15 Boswell, vol. 2, p. 9.
16 Burney, *Evelina*, p. vii.
17 Sabor and Troide, pp. 86–7.
18 Harman, pp. 105–6.
19 Chisholm, *Fanny Burney*, p. 58; and note 34 on p. 298.
20 Boswell, vol. 2, p. 305.
21 Sabor and Troide, pp. 163–4.
22 Chisholm, *Fanny Burney*, p. 126.
23 Sabor and Troide, p. 204.
24 Boswell, vol. 2, p. 326.
25 Ibid., p. 428.
26 Sabor and Troide, p. 205.

27 Piozzi, p. xxx.
28 This and the further quotation in this paragraph are taken from Fanny's letter to Susanna of December 1785, cited in Sabor and Troide, pp. 211 ff.
29 Sabor and Troide, p. 234.
30 There is some uncertainty whether to spell the name 'Lock' or 'Locke'. Although Fanny and members of the family varied in their spelling, both William and Frederica wrote it without an 'e'; the memorial tablet to them and other members of the family in Mickleham church also uses the shorter form. I have followed this throughout the present book, except when directly quoting Fanny.
31 Hill, p. 56.
32 Ibid., p. 37.
33 Ibid.
34 Ibid., p. 52.
35 Kelly, p. 40.
36 Sabor and Troide, p. 355.
37 Ibid., p. 359.
38 Ibid., p. 374.
39 Ibid., p. 399.
40 Ibid., pp. 427–8.
41 Ibid., pp. 418–20.
42 Ibid., p. 431.
43 Ibid., pp. 431–44.
44 Ibid., p. 477.
45 Ibid., pp. 478–9.
46 Ibid., p. 481.
47 Ibid., p. 484.
48 Ibid., pp. 488 ff.
49 Fanny's account of her Ilfracombe adventure, and the following quotations in this chapter, is contained in her Journal entry 'Adventurr at Ilfracombe', cited in Sabor and Troide, pp. 510–31.
50 Dobson, p. 197, note 1.
51 Ibid., p. 197.
52 Sabor and Troide, pp. 537–42.
53 Harman, p. 372.
54 Chisholm, p. 285.

CHAPTER TWO

1   Berchet, vol. 1, p. 25.
2   Ibid., p. 32.
3   Ibid., p. 31.
4   Ibid., p. 32.
5   Ibid., p. 11.
6   Ibid.
7   Ibid., p. vi.
8   Ibid., p. 81.
9   Ibid., p. 33.
10 Ibid., p. 84.
11 Ibid., p. 87.
12 Ibid., p. 91.

13 Ibid., p. 92.
14 Ibid., p. 123.
15 Ibid., p. 152.
16 Ibid., p. 154.
17 Ibid.
18 These details and those in the following paragraph are taken from Boyé, pp. 86 and 150.
19 Berchet, vol. 1, p. 155.
20 Ibid., p. 160.
21 Ibid., p. 155.
22 Ibid., p. 157.
23 Ibid., p. 238.
24 Ibid., p. 213.
25 Ibid.
26 Ibid., p. 230.
27 Ibid., p. 232.
28 Ibid., p. 264.
29 Ibid., p. 301.
30 Ibid., p. 306.
31 Ibid., p. 315.
32 Ibid.
33 Ibid., p. 316.
34 Ibid., p. 379.
35 Ibid., pp. 436–7.
36 A. Trollope, pp. 360–1.
37 Berchet, p. 474.
38 Ibid., p. 507.
39 Ibid., p. 547.
40 Ibid., p. 569.
41 Ibid., pp. 649–50.
42 Wagener, pp. 182 ff.
43 Berchet, vol. 2, p. 127.
44 Ibid., p. 68.
45 Ibid., p. 69.
46 Ibid., p. 253.
47 Ibid.
48 Ibid., p. 271.
49 Ibid., p. 288.
50 Ibid., p. 289.
51 Ibid., p. 311.
52 Ibid., p. 321.
53 Muhlstein, vol. 2, p. 213.
54 Wagener, p. 10.
55 Ibid., p. 270.
56 Ibid., p. 396.
57 Berchet, vol. 2, p. 448.
58 Ibid., p. 425.
59 Ibid., pp. 370–1.
60 Ibid., p. 369.
61 Lawday, p. 211.
62 Wagener, p. 423.

CHAPTER THREE

1   Balcombe Abell, Lucia Elizabeth, *To Befriend an Emperor: Betsy Balcombe's Memoirs of Napoleon on St Helena* (Ravenhall Books, 2005), *passim*.
2   Berchet, vol. 1, p. 92.
3   Ibid.
4   Ibid., p. 93.
5   Ibid., p. 94.
6   Ibid.
7   Ibid., pp. 447–8.
8   Sabor and Troide, p. 418.
9   Ibid., p. 419.
10 Ibid., p. 420.
11 Ibid.
12 Ibid.
13 Ibid., p. 445.
14 Ibid.
15 Ibid., p. 446.
16 Ibid.
17 Ibid.
18 Ibid., p. 447.
19 Ibid., p. 483.
20 Ibid., p. 484.
21 Ibid., p. 494.
22 Berchet, vol. 1, p. 266
23 Ibid., p. 267.
24 Ibid., p. 269.
25 Ibid.
26 Ibid.
27 Ibid., vol. 2, p. 188
28 Fumaroli, p. 332.
29 Berchet, vol. 1, pp. 281–2.
30 Ibid., p. 306.
31 Ibid., pp. 306–7.
32 Ibid., p. 302.
33 Ibid., p. 329.
34 Ibid., pp. 465–6.
35 Ibid., p. 328
36 Ibid., pp. 466–7.
37 This and the following quotations in this paragraph are taken from Fumaroli, pp. 459–70.
38 Unwin, p. 3.

CHAPTER FOUR

1   M. Morgan, p. 122.
2   Sabor and Troide, p. 452.
3   Ibid.
4   Ibid., p. 453.
5   Ibid.

6 Ibid., pp. 455–6.
7 Ibid., p. 459.
8 Ibid., p. 460.
9 Ibid., pp. 480–1.
10 Chisholm, *Fanny Burney*, pp. 248–9.
11 M. Morgan, p. 119.
12 Glover, p. 226.
13 Sabor and Troide, p. 482.
14 Ibid., p. 483.
15 Berchet, vol. 1, p. 381.
16 Ibid., pp. 507–8.
17 Fumaroli, p. 456.
18 Berchet, vol. 1, p. 508.
19 Unwin, p. 13.
20 Uffindell, p. xxiv.
21 Berchet, vol. 1, p. 522.
22 Ibid., p. 523.
23 Roberts, pp. 207–8.
24 Ibid., p. 208.
25 Berchet, vol. 1, p. 600.
26 Ibid., p. 333.
27 Ibid., p. 530.
28 Ibid., p. 152.
29 Ibid., p. 184.
30 Ibid., p. 531.
31 Ibid., pp. 500–1.
32 Ibid., p. 501.
33 Ibid., pp. 503–4.
34 Ibid., p. 504.
35 Ibid., p. 505.
36 Ibid., p. 694.
37 Ibid.
38 Unwin, p. 176.

CHAPTER FIVE

1 Sabor and Troide, p. 132.
2 Ibid., p. 233.
3 Ibid., p. 234.
4 Ibid., p. 239.
5 Ibid., p. 253.
6 Ibid., pp. 240 ff.
7 Ibid., p. 242.
8 Ibid., p. 230.
9 Berchet, vol. 1, p. 375.
10 Ibid., p. 592–3.
11 Ibid., p. 376.
12 Ibid., p. 378.

13 Ibid., p. 379.
14 Sabor and Troide, p. 245.
15 Ibid., pp. 245–6.
16 Ibid., p. 247.
17 Ibid., p. 272.
18 Ibid., p. 274.
19 Ibid., p. 275.
20 Ibid., p. 278.
21 Ibid., pp. 293–4.
22 Ibid., p. 279.
23 This and the following quotations regarding the incident in Kew gardens are from taken from Sabor and Troide, pp. 280–5.
24 Berchet, vol. 1, p. 677.
25 Ibid., p. 679.
26 Ibid., p. 680.
27 Sabor and Troide, p. 301.
28 Ibid., p. 308.
29 Ibid., p. 310.
30 Ibid., p. 331.
31 Ibid., p. 380.
32 Ibid., p. 381.
33 Ibid., pp. 544–5.
34 Ibid., p. 564.
35 Berchet, vol. 1, p. 551.
36 Ibid., p. 552.
37 Ibid., p. 553.
38 Ibid., p. 557.
39 Ibid., p. 559.
40 This and the further quotations regarding Queen Caroline are taken from Berchet, vol. 2, pp. 57–8.
41 Berchet, vol. 1, p. 37.
42 Ibid., p. 81.
43 Ibid., p. 47.
44 Ibid., p. 83.
45 Ibid., p. 67.
46 Ibid., p. 68.
47 Ibid., p. 367.
48 Ibid.
49 Ibid., p. 368.
50 Ibid., p. 374.
51 Ibid., vol. 2, p. 127.
52 Ibid.
53 Ibid.
54 F. Trollope, p. 322.
55 Berchet, vol. 2, p. 29.
56 Ibid., p. 30.
57 Ibid., p. 323.
58 Ibid., p. 349.

CHAPTER SIX

1   Sabor and Troide, p. 16
2   This and the remaining quotations in this paragraph are taken from Sabor and Troide, pp. 42–4.
3   Boswell, vol. 2, p. 50.
4   Sabor and Troide, p. 73.
5   Ibid., pp. 73–4.
6   Ibid., p. 74.
7   Ibid.
8   Ibid., p. 200.
9   Ibid., p. 228.
10   Ibid.
11   Ibid., pp. 192–3.
12   Ibid., p. 251.
13   Berchet, vol. 2, p. 164.
14   Sabor and Troide, p. 34.
15   Ibid., pp. 109–10.
16   Ibid., p. 132.
17   Ibid., p. 144.
18   Ibid., p. 344.
19   Ibid., p. 344, note 2.
20   Piozzi, p. vii.
21   Ibid., p. x.
22   Sabor and Troide, p. 71.
23   Ibid.
24   Ibid., p. 72.
25   Ibid., pp. 72–3.
26   Boswell, vol. 2, p. 375.
27   Sabor and Troide, p. 92.
28   Ibid., p. 95.
29   Ibid., p. 124.
30   Piozzi, pp. 9–10.
31   Ibid., p. 159.
32   Sabor and Troide, p. 202.
33   Ibid., p. 205.
34   Ibid., p. 207.
35   Boswell, vol. 1, p. 287.
36   Chisholm, *Dr Johnson*, p. 241.
37   Sabor and Troide, p. 357.
38   Ibid., pp. 356–58.
39   Dobson, *Fanny Burney*, p. 180.
40   Sabor and Troide, p. 358.
41   Ibid., p. 360.
42   Ibid., p. 415–8.
43   Ibid., p. 417.
44   This and the following quotations in this paragraph are taken from Sabor and Troide, p. 418.
45   Sabor and Troide, p. 418.
46   Ibid., pp. 467–8.
47   Berchet, vol. 1, p. 242.
48   Ibid., pp. 242–3.

49 The quotations in this paragraph are taken from Berchet, vol. 1, p. 243.
50 Ibid., pp. 244–5.
51 Ibid., p. 249.
52 Ibid., pp. 253–4.
53 Ibid, p. 709.
54 Ibid., p. 707.
55 Wagener, p. 170.
56 Berchet, pp. 221–2.
57 Ibid., p. 234.
58 Ibid., p. 497.
59 Ibid., p. 499.
60 Ibid., pp. 499–500.
61 Wagener, p. 170.

CHAPTER SEVEN

1 Chisholm, *Fanny Burney*, pp. 165–6.
2 Boswell, vol. 2, p. 326.
3 Piozzi, p. 37.
4 Ibid., p. 41.
5 Burney, *Evelina*, p. 61.
6 The quotations in this and the following paragraph are taken from Fanny's letter, cited in Sabor and Troide, pp. 336–9.
7 Sabor and Troide, p. 469.
8 Berchet, vol. 1, p. 204.
9 Ibid., p. 315.
10 Ibid., p. 316.
11 This and further quotations regarding the trial are taken from Fanny's letter to Susanna of February 1788, cited in Sabor and Troide, pp. 256–67.
12 Sabor and Troide, p. 414.
13 Ibid., p. 412.
14 Ibid.
15 Chisholm, p. 203.
16 Sabor and Troide, p. 413.
17 F. Trollope, p. 56.
18 Ibid., p. 77.
19 Ibid.
20 Ibid., pp. 148–9.
21 Berchet, vol. 1, p. 547.
22 Ibid.
23 Ibid., pp. 547–8.
24 Ibid., p. 548.
25 Ibid., p. 584.
26 This and further quotations regarding atmospheric conditions in London are taken from Berchet, vol. 1, pp. 549–50.
27 Berchet, vol. 1, p. 549.
28 Ibid., p. 563.
29 This and further quotations regarding marriage and social habits among young women are taken from Berchet, vol. 1, pp. 563–9.

30 This and further quotations in this paragraph are taken from Berchet, vol. 1, p. 569.

31 Berchet, vol. 1, p. 379.

32 Ibid., vol. 2, p. 352.

33 Ibid., p. 355.

34 This as well as further quotations on waltzing are taken from Berchet, vol. 1, p. 566.

35 Berchet, vol. 2, p. 167.

36 Ibid., p. 653.

37 Ibid., p. 659.

38 Ibid., p. 627.

39 Ibid., p. 686.

CHAPTER EIGHT

1 Sabor and Troide, p. 207.

2 Ibid., p. 209.

3 Ibid., p. 475.

4 Ibid., p. 538.

5 Ibid., p. 540.

6 Ibid.

7 Ibid., p. 542.

8 Chisholm, *Fanny Burney*, pp. 279–80.

9 Fanny's letter to Hetty is cited at Sabor and Troide, pp. 431–43; this account and the quotations in this section are taken from the same source.

10 The account of Castlereagh's suicide and encounter with the dog is found in Berchet, vol. 1, pp. 586–90; this and the following quotations are taken from the same source.

11 The account of the assassination of the Duc de Berry is found in Berchet, vol. 2, pp. 34–43; this and the following quotations are taken from the same souce.

12 Berchet, vol. 2, p. 159.

13 Ibid., p. 564.

14 The account of the death of the Duc d'Orléans is found in Berchet, vol. 2 pp. 564–606; this and the following quotations are taken from the same source.

15 Sabor and Troide, p. 356.

16 Ibid., p. 359.

17 The 'fragment' entitled *Mort de Monsieur de Talleyrand en 1838* is found at Berchet, vol. 2, pp. 509–32.

18 Berchet, vol. 2, p. 510.

19 Ibid., p. 524.

20 Ibid., p. 525.

21 Ibid., p. 528.

22 Ibid.

23 Ibid.

24 Ibid., p. 530.

25 Ibid., p. 529.

26 Marquise de La Tour du Pin, p. 338.

27 Chisholm, *Fanny Burney*, p. 253.

28 Berchet, vol. 2, p. 84.

CHAPTER NINE

1   Wagener, p. 137.
2   Sabor and Troide, p. 76.
3   Ibid., p. 79.
4   Ibid., p. 343.
5   Ibid., p. 366.
6   Chisholm, *Fanny Burney*, p. 273.
7   Berchet, vol. 1, p. 723.
8   Ibid., p. 463–4.
9   Ibid., p. 464.
10 Wagener, pp. 77–8.
11 Sabor and Troide, p. 2.
12 Ibid., p. 369.
13 Ibid., p. 360.
14 Ibid., p. 45.
15 Ibid., p. 54.
16 Ibid., p. 194.
17 Ibid., p. 209.
18 Ibid., p. 292.
19 Berchet, vol. 1, p. 11.
20 Ibid., p. 301–2.
21 Ibid., p. 484.
22 Ibid., p. 332.
23 Ibid., p. 464.
24 Wagener, p. 10.
25 Sabor and Troide, p. 261.
26 Ibid., p. 304.
27 Ibid., p. 308.
28 Mullen and Munson, pp. 148–9.
29 Sabor and Troide, pp. 18–9.
30 Ibid., pp. 403–5.
31 Ibid., pp. 459–60.
32 Berchet, vol. 1, p. 684.
33 Ibid., p. 686.
34 Ibid.

EPILOGUE

1   Berchet, vol. 1, p. 11.

SELECT BIBLIOGRAPHY

Bainbridge, Beryl, *According to Queeney* (Little, Brown and Co., 2001)

Berchet, Jean-Claude, *Mémoires de la Comtesse de Boigne*, 2 vols (Mercure de France, 1999)

Boswell, James, *The Life of Samuel Johnson LLD*, 2 vols (Everyman's Library, 1951)

Boyé, Jérôme, et al., *L'Extraordinaire Aventure de Benoît de Boigne aux Indes* [a special volume published to mark the exhibition mounted at the Musée Savoisien at Chambéry from 14 April to 4 September 1996]

Britton, J., *The Original Picture of London* (Longman, Rees, Orme, Brown and Green, 1826)

Burney, Frances, *Camilla* (Oxford World's Classics, 2009)

———, *Cecilia* (Oxford World's Classics, 2008)

———, *Evelina* (Oxford World's Classics, 1991)

Carpenter et Lebrun, *Histoire de France* (Editions du Seuil, 1990)

Chisholm, Kate, *Dr Johnson in the Company of Women* (Chatto and Windus, 2011)

———, *Fanny Burney: Her Life* (Chatto and Windus, 1998)

Dallas, Gregor, *1815: The Road to Waterloo* (Pimlico, 1996)

Dickens, Charles, *Barnaby Rudge* (Penguin Classics, 1986)

Dobson, Austin, *Diary and Letters of Madame d'Arblay (1778–1840) as Edited by Her Niece, Charlotte*, 6 vols (MacMillan and Co., 1904)

———, *Fanny Burney* (MacMillan and Co., 1903)

Elliott, Grace Dalrymple, *During the Reign of Terror: Journal of My Life During the French Revolution* (Richard Bentley, London 1859)

Fayet, Aurélien, and Michelle Fayet, *L'Histoire de France* (Eyrolles, 2009)

Fumaroli, Marc, *Chateaubriand, Vie de Napoléon* (Editions de Fallois, 1999)

Glover, Michael, *Wellington as Military Commander* (Sphere Books, 1973)

Harman, Claire, *Fanny Burney: A Biography* (Flamingo, 2001)

Harsanyi, Doina Pasca, *Lettres de la Duchesse de la Rochefoucauld* (Mercure de France, 2001)

Hemlow, Joyce, *The History of Fanny Burney* (Oxford, Clarendon Press, 2009)

Herodotus, *The Histories* (Penguin Classics, 1972)

Hibbert, Christopher, *George III: A Personal History* (Viking, 1998)

Hill, Constance, *Juniper Hall* (John Lane, The Bodley Head, 1904)

Keller-Noëllet, Jacques, *Note sur Sainte-Beuve et Madame de Boigne* (private note to author)

Kelly, Linda, *Juniper Hall* (Faber and Faber, 2009)

La Tour du Pin, marquise de [Henriette-Lucie Dillon], *Journal d'une femme de cinquante ans, 1778–1815* (Editions Berger-Levrault, 1954)

Lawday, David, *Napoleon's Master: A life of Prince Talleyrand* (Pimlico, 2007)

Longford, Elizabeth, *Wellington: Pillar of State* (Weidenfeld and Nicolson, 1972)

Malraux, André, *Vie de Napoléon par lui-même* (Editions Gallimard, 1930)

Moorehead, Caroline, *Dancing to the Precipice: Lucie de La Tour du Pin and the French Revolution* (Chatto and Windus, 2009)

Morgan, Kenneth, *The Oxford History of Britain* (Oxford University Press, 2010)

Morgan, Matthew, *Wellington's Victories* (Michael O'Mara Books Ltd, 2004)

Muhlstein, Anka, *Memoirs of the Comtesse de Boigne*, 2 vols (Helen Marx Books, 2003)

Mullen, Richard, and James Munson, *The Smell of the Continent* (Pan Books, 1988)

Nicoullaud, Charles, *Memoirs of the Comtesse de Boigne*, 3 vols (William Heinemann, 1907)

Ormesson, Jean d', *Une autre histoire de la littérature française* (Nil Editions, 1997)

Piozzi, Hesther Lynch, *Anecdotes of Samuel Johnson* (Cambridge University Press, 1932)

Proust, Marcel, *Figaro* (edition of 20 March, 1907)

Roberts, Andrew, *Napoleon and Wellington* (Weidenfeld and Nicholson, 2001)

Sabor, Peter, and Lars E. Troide, *Frances Burney, Journals and Letters* (Penguin Books, 2001)

Schama, Simon, *Citizens: A Chronicle of the French Revolution* (Penguin Books, 1989)

Sermoneta, the Duchess of, *The Locks of Norbury* (John Murray, 1940)

Thompson, Neville, *Wellington after Waterloo* (Routledge and Kegan Paul, 1986)

Trevelyan, George Macaulay, *English Social History: Chaucer to Queen Victoria* (Longmans, 1961)

——, *British History in the Nineteenth century and After, 1782–1919* (Penguin Books, 1968)

Trollope, Anthony, *He Knew He Was Right* (Oxford University Press, 1978)

Trollope, Frances, *Paris and the Parisians* (Alan Sutton Publishing Ltd, 1985)

Uffindell, Andrew, *Great Generals of the Napoleonic Wars and Their Battles 1805–1815* (Spellmount, 2007)

Unwin, Brian, *Terrible Exile: The Last Days of Napoleon on St Helena* (I.B.Tauris, 2010)

Wagener, Françoise, *La Comtesse de Boigne* (Flammarion, 1997)

INDEX